THE WAY TO FREEDOM

The Way to Freedom

LETTERS, LECTURES AND NOTES
1935–1939

FROM THE
COLLECTED WORKS OF

Dietrich Bonhoeffer

VOLUME II

EDITED AND INTRODUCED BY
EDWIN H. ROBERTSON

TRANSLATED BY
EDWIN H. ROBERTSON
AND JOHN BOWDEN

COLLINS
ST JAMES'S PLACE, LONDON
1966

Contents

Introduction   *page* 11

I   THE TRAINING OF THE CONFESSING CHURCH   27

    1. The First Year at Finkenwalde   29

    2. The Nature of the True Church   42

    3. The Beginning of the Fateful Year 1937   129

II THE YEARS OF DECISION   145

    1. The Attempt to Destroy the Confessing Church 147

    2. The Second American Visit   203

Appendix I: Circular Letters from the Finkenwalde
             Seminary to the Brethren   259

Appendix II: An Imaginary Conversation   265

Index   283

Acknowledgements

I should like to thank the many people who have helped in the preparation of this second volume. I express my debt fully to P. H. Newby and Terence Tiller for their help in constructing the appendix, 'An Imaginary Conversation', on page 265. John Bowden has once again been invaluable in preparing the sections I selected from the *Gesammelte Schriften* in a good English translation. Although his assignment was merely to provide a first draft, many of the passages are entirely his own work. He has also been kind enough to work through the proofs in my absence. Eberhard Bethge has generously placed himself at my disposal for consultation, as has Ronald Gregor Smith of Glasgow, whose wife made several valuable suggestions in translation. Like *No Rusty Swords*, this second volume has also been seen carefully through the press by Caroline Scott and proof-read by Lesley Walmsley. To both these charming helpers I am much indebted. As publishers, Collins have been most understanding of my many delays due to travel and other work. I am particularly grateful to Mrs Collins for agreeing to extend the work to three volumes and for publishing separately *Christology* which would have upset the balance of this volume and which is now in a handy form for theological students, to whom it is specially addressed.

E. H. ROBERTSON

INTRODUCTION

Introduction

The title of this second volume of selections from Bonhoeffer's Collected Works is derived from one of the most important of his poems – 'Stations on the way to Freedom' – which first appeared among his *Letters and Papers from Prison*[1] and was for some reason printed in English as prose, and published in the prose section of the book. It is of course poetry, and shows the steps Bonhoeffer himself trod to achieve that freedom of the spirit which enabled him to write such liberating letters at the last. The period covered by this volume of his papers illustrates very clearly the four stations.

The first is '*Discipline*':

If you set out to seek freedom, you must learn before all things
Mastery over sense and soul, lest your wayward desirings,
Lest your undisciplined members lead you now this way, now that way.
Chaste be your mind and your body, and subject to you and obedient,
Serving solely to seek their appointed goal and objective.
None learns the secret of freedom save only by way of control.[2]

The very first paper included in this second volume deals with the necessary first step: *discipline*. In outlining his plan for a Protestant community, Bonhoeffer writes:

'The brethren of the community live together with a strict liturgical ordering of their day.'[3] This much he had learned from his visits to Kelham and Mirfield. He adds, 'They are bound together by brotherly admonition and discipline and by open confession'.

[1] *Letters and Papers from Prison*, Fontana, pp. 161–2.
[2] *Ethics*, Fontana p. 15.
[3] page 31.

Those who were members of that first community tell of Bonhoeffer's insistence upon discipline. He was not trying to create a 'catholic' monastic order, and took care to show that what he was doing represented the best traditions of German Protestantism. This meant *self*-discipline and *mutual* discipline, not the obedience that a monk gives to his superior. In his little book, *Life Together*, which reflects the emphasis on discipline of this period, he writes quite firmly, 'It is not a good thing for one person to be the confessor for all the others,' and later, 'Confession as a routine duty is spiritual death.'[1] Within the best tradition of Luther's call for the freedom of a Christian man, he sought to preserve the discipline which alone enabled a man to be free. At the heart of his seminary was to be a community of disciplined men who could take up leadership in the church struggle. His men tell of more than spiritual discipline. There were the almost Spartan conditions at Finkenwalde and then the exercise in the early morning. Bonhoeffer believed in a body kept fit for action. A Christian was a man in training. In his *Cost of Discipleship*, he describes the path of discipleship in a way that leaves no doubt that he believes in discipline as the first step on the road to freedom:

'The way is unutterably hard, and at every moment we are in danger of straying from it. If we regard this way as one we follow in obedience to an external command, if we are afraid of ourselves all the time, it is indeed an impossible way. But if we behold Jesus Christ going on before step by step, we shall not go astray. But if we worry about the dangers that beset us, if we gaze at the road instead of at him who goes before, we are already straying from the path. For he is himself the way, the narrow way and the strait gate.'[2]

In the very interesting paper on 'Daily Meditation', included in this volume, reveals the temper of his mind with the answer to the question, *Why do I meditate?*, with the words:

[1] *Life Together*, SCM Press, p. 110.
[2] *The Cost of Discipleship*, SCM Press, 1959 edn., p. 170.

'Because I need a firm discipline of prayer. We are fond of praying as our fancy takes us, for a short time, for a long time, or even not at all. That is wilfulness. Prayer is not a free offering to God, but the bounden duty that he requires. We are not free to carry on as we wish. Prayer is the day's first service to God. God claims our time for this service.'[1] To support his argument on this occasion, he quotes what had become his favourite psalm since he heard the men at Mirfield pray it through: Psalm 119.

The problem of discipline had for long occupied Bonhoeffer's thoughts. He had seen his contemporaries attracted to the discipline of the Hitler Youth, and in a brilliant analysis of the different generations in his paper attacking the 'leadership principle', he showed how disciplined were the men who had taken part in the First World War and how confused were those of the next generation – his own – who inherited the problems without the hard discipline.[2] He worked on this as he saw his own generation fall for the attractions of National Socialism. Their call for discipline had to be matched by an equal discipline in the Confessing Church. He saw that the purpose of the discipline, not the discipline itself, was wrong. And so 'mastery over sense and soul' became part of his programme for the march to freedom. He was totally committed to the thesis that, *'None learns the secret of freedom save only by way of control'*.

The second station was that of *Action*:

Do and dare what is right, not swayed by the whim of the moment.
Bravely take hold of the real, not dallying now with what might be.
Not in the flight of ideas but only in action is freedom.
Make up your mind and come out into the tempest of living.
God's command is enough and your faith in him to sustain you.
Then at last freedom will welcome your spirit amid great rejoicing.[3]

There is no better example of Bonhoeffer's belief in action than a decision he took at the end of the period covered by this volume. Once he knew that war was inevitable, he decided, against the

[1] page 57 f.   [2] *No Rusty Swords*, pp. 190 ff.   [3] *Ethics*, p. 15.

advice of many, to return to Germany from the safety of America. The imaginary conversation recorded in an appendix to this volume is reconstructed from the papers of Bonhoeffer and of Richard Niebuhr. It shows faithfully the arguments used by Bonhoeffer in favour of taking this difficult decision. High among his reasons is that when a man knows enough of the facts to take a decision he should take it and act rather than remain in indecision. He believed in coming 'out into the tempest of living'.[1] Quite early in this volume we find Bonhoeffer at odds with the church because it had done nothing about the 'resurrection feast'. The Evangelical Church had refrained from comment and thus left many devout Christians in confusion. They felt something was wrong and might have refrained from the pagan feast; but they feared not only the punishment of the state, but also the reproach of the church. Was the church behind them in their protest? The church, even the Confessing Church, kept silent. The brethren wrote: 'There should have been a clear statement on the subject of this day, making a firm distinction between the Christian resurrection hope and this popular-idealistic idea of resurrection'.[2]

The letter addressed to the Council of Brethren of the Old Prussian Union[3] leaves no doubt about his insistence upon action once the facts are known. He sees this action as a liberating thing. No man can be free while he is caught in the web of indecision.

Much of the interest in the letters and papers by Bonhoeffer in the earlier part of this volume springs from these decisions of his, which at times appear to be precipitate. They are always the result of much careful thought, even the simplest of them. The papers which I have selected illustrate this, and if at times they seem to concern themselves with slight matters it is because this period of the church struggle was very much a matter of small decisions. The Nazi appeal to young men was very strong and it could not be answered by high-sounding declarations from the pulpit. The church was not being attacked, it was being seduced, and the form of seduction appealed to

[1] page 13. [2] page 36. [3] *ibid.*

the highest rather than the lowest. Many of the present leaders in the church today, who are venerated for their resistance to Nazism, were in the earlier days partial supporters of many things the Nazis advocated – discipline, pride in Germany, the need to complete the work of Martin Luther, the moral reform of Europe, etc., etc. The man who in the early days opposed everything the Nazis did was either very perceptive, beyond his peers, or he had lost all hope for humanity. The Confessing Church did not have a clear black and white issue to fight. It could not ally itself with every opponent of Hitler. We can see something of this in the horror with which many good people received Bonhoeffer's apparently fanatical statement that whoever cut himself off from the Confessing Church cut himself off from the Church of Christ. Some, like Helmuth Goll-witzer, saw that he was right, but we can sympathize with those who felt that he was being fanatical.[1]

There are many tiresome arguments in the early papers in this volume and at times it is difficult to see the wood for the trees. This reflects the atmosphere of the period, which was not simply a matter of heroics – whether you were brave enough to die in a concentration camp – but a matter of day-to-day decisions. Hence Bonhoeffer's constant insistence upon the importance of the Barmen Declaration as a guide to true doctrine, and the Dahlem Declaration as a guide to true church order. This comes up constantly and sometimes tire-somely in his complaints. The papers reproduced here are no more exciting at first reading than life was in those days. Most ministers were concerned most of the time with problems of day-to-day pastoral work and administration, as they are still. Bonhoeffer knew this and many of his papers deal with the need to pray or keep in fellowship with the brethren. He was not always fighting the Ger-man Christians! He was, however, always fighting against indeci-sion, the second obstacle on the way to freedom. *'Not in the flight of ideas but only in action is freedom.'*

[1] pp. 97 ff.

The third station was that of *Suffering*:

See what a transformation! These hands so active and powerful
Now are tied, and alone and fainting, you see where your work ends.
Yet you are confident still, and gladly commit what is rightful
Into a stronger hand, and say that you are contented.
You were free for a moment of bliss, then you yielded your freedom
Into the hand of God, that he might perfect it in glory.[1]

The first volume of Bonhoeffer's papers[2] revealed a man successful in almost everything he attempted. Academically, he won honour after honour. Ecumenically, he was accepted quite young into the councils of the church leaders. Pastorally, he was successful with his young men from the Technical College – children, we should perhaps call them – and this confirmation class in Wedding is our one glance of him dealing with young people.[3] In every way he achieved honours. He travelled and was liked. In Germany, Spain, America, England and in the committees of the ecumenical movement, he was obviously a coming man. He raised his voice as one of the first against the Nazis and the German Christians. Even Karl Barth approved of him! '*These hands so active and powerful*' fitted him well. This second volume opens at Finkenwalde, which is both the scene of his greatest achievements and the scene of his first real failures. It is with the closing of Finkenwalde that Bonhoeffer begins to learn the meaning of Suffering as a station on the way to freedom.

In February 1937 he failed to convince Henriod and others at Geneva that the Confessing Church must be represented at ecumenical gatherings, and that if it could not contribute its share to the German delegation, there should be no German delegation. Bonhoeffer knew that the German Christians could dominate the German delegation by seeing to it that the others did not receive permission to leave the country, but he failed to convince the bureaucrats and had to watch the ecumenical movement accept the other side.[4] He was not yet 'tied, and alone and fainting', but he could

[1] *Ethics*, p. 15. [2] *No Rusty Swords*, pp. 27 ff. [3] *ibid*, pp. 140–52. [4] page 136.

begin to see what it could mean. The time had not yet come to 'commit what is rightful into a stronger hand'. He fought on, and once again won his way. He does not, however, triumph over his enemies. About this time comes the Judas Sermon.[1] His attitude to those who are in process of rendering him, as they think, harmless – his seminary closed and his permission to preach withdrawn – is that of the church to Judas: 'O poor Judas, what is it that thou hast done?' He takes refuge in the Christ 'who hung upon the cross for all our sins'. Within a few months, Martin Niemöller was arrested, and later Finkenwalde was closed with the subsequent arrest of twenty-seven of its former students. It was a year when the Confessing Church was to know its first big defeat. In this same year, the conference on Faith and Order met in Oxford without a German delegation. This was the year in which Bonhoeffer first saw the real weakness of the Confessing Church and began to consider active participation in the political resistance.

In 1938, he learnt the power of National Socialism, saw his political enemy move from strength to strength, and with it the German Christians. 1938 was the year of Munich, the annexations of the Sudetenland and of Austria. Despite powerful opposition it looked as though Hitler would get his way and that even a war would not be disastrous for his ambitions. Bonhoeffer had to contemplate the possibility of defeat. His careful defence of his article on 'Church Union' shows that he is prepared to risk much. He will not consider the Confessing Church to be a movement within the church. He sees it as *the church*. As such, it can suffer defeat and its leaders can be destroyed, its enemies triumph. But if it is the Church of Jesus Christ, *it* cannot be destroyed. The suffering of the members of the church leads them to place their responsible charge in stronger hands. The church has always known how to suffer and its enthusiasm can never depend upon its success. Thus a man's freedom is at stake again. No man is free so long as his freedom depends upon his

[1] pp. 137 ff.

success in a world where failure is possible. Bonhoeffer has an important section in his study of American religion called 'Protestantism without Reformation', already printed in the first volume of his papers.[1] This paper really belongs to the period of the present volume but it was included in the first volume to help assess the influence of America on Bonhoeffer's thinking. The second visit in 1939 was in fact responsible for it, and the section on 'Freedom' bears clear marks of the situation in Germany at that time. There he maintains that the essential freedom of the church is not a gift of the world or the state, but a gift of God. The whole argument which is summed up in the words, 'The freedom of the church is not where it has possibilities, but only where the Gospel really and in its own power makes room for itself on earth, even and precisely when no such possibilities are offered to it',[2] applies as much to the freedom of a man as to that of the church. The same dangers are evident in a false sense of freedom. One could equally say of man what Bonhoeffer says of the church, that 'where thanks for institutional freedom must be rendered by the sacrifice of freedom of preaching' man is in chains, even if he believes himself to be free. That same study of American religion also deals with the right to flee, and points out that flight is permissible to preserve true freedom, while apostasy is not. The voluntary acceptance of exile as well as martyrdom itself, are both forms of suffering that lead to freedom.

Thus in three steps, Bonhoeffer has taken the Christian man a long way on the road to freedom. Of discipline he has said, *'None learns the secret of freedom save only by way of control.'* Of action he says, *'Not in the flight of ideas but only in action is freedom.'* Now he adds, *'You were free for a moment of bliss, then you yielded your freedom into the hand of God.'* This third step is much the same as George Matheson's *'Make me a captive, Lord, And then I shall be free.'* Writing of the last of the Beatitudes, Bonhoeffer pointed out that Christ was blessing those who suffered, not only for confessing the name of Christ, but for

---

[1] *No Rusty Swords*, pp. 92 ff.   [2] *ibid*, p. 104.

righteousness: 'The world will be offended at them, and so the disciples will be persecuted for righteousness' sake. Not recognition but rejection is the reward they get from the world for their message and works. It is important that Jesus gives his blessing not merely to suffering incurred directly for the confession of his name, but to suffering in any just cause.' Suffering rates highly in the Bible, from the Suffering Servant of Isaiah to the cross. Bonhoeffer recognizes this in all his work and nowhere more clearly than in his famous treatment of the Sermon on the Mount in *The Cost of Discipleship*.[1] At the end of his chapter on the Beatitudes, he concludes: 'Having reached the end of the Beatitudes, we naturally ask if there is any place on this earth for the community which they describe. Clearly, there is one place, and only one, and that is where the poorest and the meekest, the most sorely tried of all men is to be found – on the cross at Golgotha.'[2] Thus suffering in this sense of helplessness is recognized as a station on the way to freedom.

The fourth and last step is *Death*:

Come now, highest of feasts on the way to freedom eternal,
Death, strike off the fetters, break down the walls that oppress us,
Our bedazzled soul and our ephemeral body,
That we may see at last the sight which here was not vouchsafed us.[3]

Before quoting the concluding two lines that sum up this remarkable poem, it is most important to say that what Bonhoeffer is talking about here is no attitude to death that compares with the Greek idea of a bird flying from the cage of the body at death. What he says about death concerns our attitude to death here and now. No man can be free until he has accepted death as a part, a liberating part, of life. You cannot live until you know with all your being that you are going to die. All evasion of this fact is sheer make-believe. Freedom requires the acceptance of death. The life that develops through the years looks to death as to a fulfilment, not as a tragic denial of life. This is the only alternative to Albert Camus's philosophy

[1] SCM Press, full text in the 1959 edition. [2] *op. cit.*, p. 103. [3] *Ethics*, p. 15.

19

of the absurd. Unless death has liberating powers and comes as a meaningful step in the whole process, then it is tragic and absurd. For Bonhoeffer, death is a clarifying of vision, '*that we may see at last the sight which here was not vouchsafed us*'. The link of death with freedom is never more clearly defined than in Bonhoeffer's discussion of 'Suicide' in his papers published posthumously as *Ethics*.[1] He distinguishes man from the beast in his opening paragraph: 'Man, unlike the beasts, does not carry his life as a compulsion which he cannot throw off. He is free either to accept his life or to destroy it. Unlike the beasts man can put himself to death of his own free will. An animal is one with the life of his body, but man can distinguish himself from the life of his body. The freedom in which man possesses his bodily life requires him to accept this life freely, and at the same time it directs his attention to what lies beyond this bodily life and compels him to regard the life of his body as a gift that is to be preserved and a sacrifice that is to be offered. Only because a man is free to choose death can he lay down the life of his body for some higher good. Without freedom to sacrifice one's life in death, there can be no freedom towards God, there can be no human life.'[2] Bonhoeffer does not condemn suicide, but shows its relation to sacrifice. He does of course distinguish the noble laying down of one's life from suicide for purely personal reasons of fear or dishonour or love. He talks of 'the liberty and the right to death', but only in the sense of sacrifice for a cause. The right to death is seen, not 'as the destruction of life' but as surrendering life for a good which is higher than the value of the bodily life. There is a real understanding for the suicide in Bonhoeffer's writing. 'Suicide,' he writes, 'is a man's attempt to give a final human meaning to a life which has become humanly meaningless. The involuntary sense of horror which seizes us when we are faced with the fact of a suicide is not to be attributed to the iniquity of such a deed but to the terrible loneliness and freedom in which this deed is performed, a deed in

[1] *Ethics*, pp. 166–72.   [2] *op. cit.*, p. 166.

20

which the positive attitude to life is reflected only in the destruction of life.'[1] Suicide is of course the disastrous failure and the lurid illustration of the freedom of death. For the martyr as well as for the man who will die rather than betray his cause, death is the end only in the sense that it eventually became the Bonhoeffer himself: 'This is the end; but for me the beginning' – the *highest of feasts on the way to freedom eternal*'.

The last quotation in this volume is about death, a subject which became inevitable as more and more of the brethren fell in battle. In it, Bonhoeffer distinguishes between the two kinds of death: *the death which comes to us from outside*, 'the fearful foe which (cf. p. 254) comes to us when it will . . . the man with the scythe, under whose stroke the blossoms fall'; and *the death in us* which has much to do with love towards Christ and towards men, we die 'when we love Christ and the brethren from the bottom of our hearts, for love is total surrender to what a man loves'. It is this second sense of death which features in the poem. This is the station on the way to freedom. This is the highest of feasts and a man may pray that the death which comes from without shall coincide with the death from within. A man may pray to be ready for death, his own death. Then a man's death may be a 'consummation of love'. Bonhoeffer concludes this part of the letter with a sentence which prepares the way for the last stanza of the poem: 'Our death is really only the way to the perfect love of God.'[2]

And so to sum up:

Freedom we sought you long in discipline, action, suffering.
Now as we die we see you and know you at last, face to face.[3]

The period of Bonhoeffer's life covered by the years 1935 to 1939 will be described in our history books as 'The Drift to War', but in the life of this man as 'The Way to Freedom'.

So much for the title of this volume. The appendix which contains 'An Imaginary Conversation' also needs a word of explanation and acknowledgement and this will be found on pp. 265 ff.

[1] *op. cit.*, p. 167–8.   [2] page 255.   [3] *Ethics*, p. 15.

The second part of this volume, which I have called 'The Years of Decision', is inevitably dominated by the rapidly moving political events that put the Confessing Church in danger of extinction, and by the personal problems of Bonhoeffer himself as he decides to go to the U.S.A. and then later decides to return. In that part, the theological material is at a minimum, although what there is is of supreme importance. The earlier part, 'The Training of the Confessing Church', shows much more clearly the theological shifts in Bonhoeffer's thought. His most important paper for this is the one on 'The Question of the Boundaries of the Church and Church Union'. The article caused great scandal, both because of Bonhoeffer's shattering statement, reported as 'he who cuts himself off from the Confessing Church cuts himself off from the Church of Jesus Christ', and because of his treatment of the Reformed Church as one with whom Lutherans might unite in a common cause amounting to Church Union.[1]

In order to give this controversy in depth, I have included a paper by Helmuth Gollwitzer.[2] While I am aware that these volumes are a collection of the writings of Dietrich Bonhoeffer, it becomes increasingly obvious that he cannot be heard alone as though speaking in a wilderness. He was no John the Baptist! The controversy over the boundaries of the church is the most important controversy of this period, because it raises the question as to whether the Barmen Declaration, with its sequel at Dahlem, is to be taken seriously as a Confession of the church. Helmuth Gollwitzer's paper shows the seriousness of the issue and clears up the meaning of Bonhoeffer's much-discussed article. Gollwitzer points out that Bonhoeffer was misunderstood because the whole of his article had not been read. This is a defect which was to occur often later. Bonhoeffer writes very carefully, building up the basis of his case before putting his own contribution. Thus many readers omit the earlier sections and get down to the controversial, of which there is nearly always plenty!

[1] page 93 ff. [2] page 97 ff.

This has had disastrous results in the case of the papers and the letters written in prison. They have been ransacked for controversial points without due consideration given to what the earlier letters say. Some have said that the last letters represent a rupture in Bonhoeffer's thought and that they are the result of pressures upon him rather than of his earlier theological development. This is an arguable point of view. I do not agree with it; but it is possible that letters written by a man as honest as Bonhoeffer can reveal an unrelated change in attitude. What is not possible is that the earlier part of a paper should represent a different point of view from that of its conclusion. Bonhoeffer was far too well-trained a thinker for that. Gollwitzer points out that much of the criticism of Bonhoeffer for his article on 'The Boundaries of the Church' was beside the point because the critics had not read or had forgotten what he said in the earlier part of the article. The earlier parts are in fact the basis for the statements made in the third part. I have quoted above the form of the scandalous statement as it was bandied around the critical circles of Germany. That was how it was remembered. Gollwitzer rightly points out that the statement was rather different and that in the light of the earlier part every word of the statement was important. Bonhoeffer was really expounding what no good Lutheran could possibly object to: *extra ecclesiam nulla salus*. The actual statement by Bonhoeffer, after he had shown that the Confessing Church was the church of the confessions, was 'Whoever *knowingly* cuts himself off from the Confessing Church in Germany cuts himself off from salvation'. This was not Bonhoeffer's invention, but the logical conclusion of accepting 'Barmen' as the 'Confession' which gave the Confessing Church its basis. If Bonhoeffer's position is not taken, then Barmen has not really been accepted. Gollwitzer is also clear in showing that Bonhoeffer does not intend his sentence to be taken legalistically. Once again the earlier part of the article makes that clear. It is important to follow Gollwitzer here or we shall have an impression of a fanatical Bonhoeffer rather than the Lutheran which

23

he remained to the end, with a horror of 'enthusiasm'. When he says that the Confessing Church is the 'one true Church of Jesus Christ', he does not mean that only he and his supporters are the true church; but he does mean that their confession is that of the true church. The Confessing Church thus raises the claim that in itself the voice of the true church has come to be spoken. Gollwitzer has equally clarified and defended the statement Bonhoeffer makes about the Augsburg Confession, that with the Synod of Barmen the letter of the Augsburg Confession has been 'abandoned in a decisive way'. It is no wonder that this was found to be most objectionable by many Lutherans. Gollwitzer again clarifies and supports by pointing out that Bonhoeffer is not talking about the theological statements in the Augsburg Confession, but about one particular article which condemns the Reformed eucharistic practice. The real issue refers to the inclusion of the Reformed Churches in the Confessing Church. Gollwitzer shares Bonhoeffer's joy that the Lutheran Churches have been brought to 'an audible, pertinent confession of their faith and that in this they joined with (cf. p. 106) the confessing remnant of the other denominations'. His parody of the Jews' complaint against Jesus is telling and shows Bonhoeffer's mind: 'It is not seemly that you should hold a synod with the Reformed Church and join in a confession with it!' (based upon the words of John 5. 10). Both men would follow the response of our Lord on this occasion of healing on the Sabbath day, which was to ignore the rebuke and speak to the man who was healed: 'See, you are well! Sin no more, that nothing worse befall you' (John 5. 14).[1]

The controversy, which concerned the status of the Confessing Church as the church and not just a movement within the church, and the matter of union with Reformed Churches in Germany, continued for many years. It troubled many who were not German Christians and separated Bonhoeffer from many who would have liked to support him. It was a crucial controversy and on its outcome

[1] page 106.

depended the future of the church in Germany. When Bonhoeffer returned to Germany after the short visit to America he found it still alive. He and Karl Barth were the clearest in seeing that on this matter there could be no compromise. There were to be no 'neutrals' in the battle that was now joined between the children of light and the children of darkness.

E. H. ROBERTSON

Yeovil, 1966

PART ONE

The Training of the Confessing Church

1935   *June* – Work commences at Finkenwalde.
         November – First five circular letters.

1936   *February* – Fourth Synod of the Confessing Church at
         Bad Oeynhausen – protest from Finkenwalde.
         February-March – tour of Denmark and Sweden with
         his students.
         August – Olympic Games in Berlin.
         20th-26th August – Universal Council for Life and Work
         meets at Chamby with two German delegations.

1937   *April* – Reunion of Foundation Year at Finkenwalde.
         – Bonhoeffer on Church Discipline.
         September – Finkenwalde closed by order of Himmler.
         – Publication of *The Cost of Discipleship*.
         14th March – Sermon on Judas preached at Finkenwalde.

1. *The First Year at Finkenwalde*

Shortly after the move to Finkenwalde[1] Bonhoeffer wrote a brief letter to Martin Niemöller to thank him and his church at Berlin-Dahlem for the generous help they had given to the new seminary. Then he proceeded to work on a paper which would set out quite clearly what the purpose of a community house would be within the general structure of the Confessing Church. The paper was completed by 6th September, and addressed to the Council of the Church of the Old Prussian Union (i.e. the Union of 1817) at Berlin-Dahlem.

Finkenwalde, near Stettin, 6th September, 1935

TO THE COUNCIL OF THE CHURCH OF THE OLD PRUSSIAN UNION
BERLIN–DAHLEM

SUBJECT: THE ESTABLISHMENT OF A COMMUNITY OF BRETHREN
AT THE FINKENWALDE SEMINARY

   I. Basic considerations.
   II. Practical tasks.
   III. Concrete requests.

   I. With a number of young men whose names are listed below, I have formed the plan, which has already been in my mind for several years, of setting up a Protestant community in which we shall attempt to lead a common Christian life as pastors, for the space of a few years.

The following considerations and experiences have led us to this decision:

   1. The pastor, and particularly the young pastor, suffers from

[1] *No Rusty Swords*, p. 297.

29

being by himself. The burden of preaching is particularly heavy today for the solitary pastor who is not a prophet, but just a servant of the church. He needs brotherly help and fellowship not only to show him what he is to preach, but also to show him how to preach it. The years of the church struggle have therefore seen the formation of associations of pastors wherever the responsibilities of the office were taken seriously. These first beginnings of fraternal community require more definite organisation. The new task is seen to be not only theological working parties and occasional services together, but a well ordered, well regulated common life. Preaching which has its roots in practical work, as well as in the life and experience of the community, will be more relevant, and less likely to run the risk of either being intimidated or bogged down.

2. The nature of the Christian life is again being questioned by the younger generation of theologians. They can no longer be met with slogans like 'Fanaticism' or 'Unlutheran Attitude'. This is regarded as simply dodging the issue. But neither can the answer to their questions be in abstract terms; it can only be given through a concrete, down-to-earth life together, and a common regard for the commandments. The vague feeling that all is not well in the life of the pastorate will only be satisfied by the practical attempt at a common training in obedience to the commandments. The damage done to the credibility of our preaching by our life and by our uncertainty as to what Christian life compels us to think again and to embark upon new practical ventures.

3. There is a need for a group of completely free, trained pastors to preach the Word of God for decision and for discerning the spirits, in the present church struggle and in others to come, and to be immediately ready to serve as preachers at the outbreak of any new emergency. They must be ready to be where their service is needed whatever the external circumstances, even renouncing all the privileges of clergy, financial or otherwise. They will find their home and all the fellowship they need for their service in the community from

which they come and to which they return continually. The aim is not the seclusion of a monastery, but a place of the deepest inward concentration for service outside.

4. The pastor who exercises his office alone is in constant need of a spiritual haven in which he can strengthen himself for his office in a strict Christian way of life, of prayer, meditation, study or Scripture and brotherly discussion. Such places of refuge should be created and from them the question of replacement could easily be settled by the community. Lay people too must be offered such places of refuge.

5. In full knowledge that every young pastor today is needed to serve in the parishes, and despite the difficulty of asking for anyone temporarily to stand aside from this service, it is nevertheless our view, tried by conscience, that the service of a number of young preachers in this work, which goes beyond that of an individual parish, is indispensable. In each individual case, the decision must be made with the full agreement of the Council of Brethren.

As a result of what has been said, the following plan and pattern has suggested itself to us:

The brethren of the community live together with a strict liturgical ordering of their day. They are guided through the day not by cultic forms, but by the word of the Bible and by prayer. They are bound together by brotherly admonition and discipline and by open confession. A common theological and ecclesiastical consideration of preaching and the Word of God in the Bible will keep them down-to-earth and practical. Renouncing everything except the simple necessities, they take upon themselves to lead a common life. The director of the community will assign to each brother his particular work. Here the position is envisaged as being like that of a house of deaconesses. The brethren, living in this ordered community and being supported by it, put themselves at the service of the church, to follow any call that may come to them. The brethren agree to work for a lengthy period of time in the community, but are free to depart at any time. The community itself decides upon admission. Its size is not to be too large.

II. The practical tasks of the community will take roughly the following form:

The Finkenwalde seminary needs a staff of brethren to preserve the inner continuity of the community once it has been established. It is impossible for the director himself to create and maintain a community with changes at such frequent intervals. The community once started will only be able to carry on through brotherhood. Alongside the work with the new arrivals, contact must be maintained with brethren who have left the seminary, by regular circular letters, reports, sermon meditations and reunions. In this way the director of the seminary will not be overburdened by the work of the community.

In addition to this, the seminary will gradually become a natural centre for the associations of pastors, and for the ordinands and students of Pomerania. Our service to the ministers of the church in Pomerania has already begun in reunions and it will be furthered with vigour. Our work with the students of Greifswald is particularly important to us; it began with a missionary week conducted by our seminary there in June, and with a brief conference here at the beginning of August. In cooperation with, but at the same time as a supplement to, the work of the professors, who as teachers of the church have to play the chief part in this work, the community will keep the rising generation informed about church decisions and prevent the drifting back to the consistory court, by regular work among the young theologians of Greifswald. The members of the community will be particularly suited to this because of the nearness of their age and yet their greater experience. Finally, they are to try to help in the advancement of a fraternity of students in Greifswald, which has had so promising a beginning. We are also already in contact with the ordinands and will have a retreat with them at the beginning of October.

Members of the community are further to be appointed to work for a longer or shorter period in places where the church is hard pressed, and are also to deputise in their parishes for younger ministers who need theological companionship or who want to work for examinations and for this reason wish to be accepted in the community for a while.

Negotiations for the care of the Confessing Church in the parishes of Finkenwalde and Podejuch are already in hand with the Pomeranian Council of Brethren and Superintendent Wick of Podejuch.

A detailed plan has already been drawn up of the theological work which the brethren are to do.

III. We would ask the Council of the Church of the Old Prussian Union to recognise our plan in principle and to permit the brethren of the community (about six in number) to have rooms in the seminary without charge; there are a great many of them. I am limiting myself to one and a half rooms. Modest funds are also available from private means for the maintenance of the brethren and we also hope to find a regular post for one of the brethren through the Pomeranian Council of Brethren in Podejuch and Finkenwalde, etc.

The list of names of the men who wished to be accepted for the community was added. G.S. II pp. 448–52

This was a startlingly new kind of community for Protestant Germany, but it is clear how much Bonhoeffer had learnt from Mirfield and Kelham. By the end of October, the seminary at Finkenwalde was able to send out a greeting which showed how clearly it understood its purpose.

A GREETING FROM THE FINKENWALDE SEMINARY

When we made our new home here at Finkenwalde in June, we did not know where to begin. The great house stood empty except for a few poor pieces of furniture, and the rooms had been neglected. So we asked the parishes and pastors of the Confessing Church to help

C

us. Our request was heard to a degree which surpassed all our expectations. We are grateful for everything that has been given to us over the weeks and months, and also for the good wishes which make us conscious of our fellowship in faith and intercession. Our letters of thanks have run to more than a hundred. We had hardly made our request when many, often quite considerable, gifts of money came to us from parishes and individual members of the Confessing Church. And much, much more has been given to us in other ways, furniture of all kinds and so many books that we now have quite a respectable library. . . . And our food too has been well taken care of. At Harvest Thanksgiving we received a large basket of pears and a ten mark piece from an unknown donor, 'for the Harvest roast'. One Sunday a member of the Confessing Church in Frankfurt am Oder paid us a visit and brought a large suitcase full of household utensils. . . .

We would like to give a brief impression of our house for the sake of those friends who are unable to visit us:

First of all the three large common rooms on the ground floor had to be put in order: the lecture room, the refectory and the common room proper. – The tables were given by the Confessing Church from Stolp, the chairs by the Confessing Church from Köslin. On the walls hang Dürer's two great Apostle pictures. A simple but beautiful chandelier gives light in the evening. And there are curtains at the windows already – which is not yet the case in most of the other rooms. The refectory is at the same time the chapel, in which we have the devotions that begin and end the day. The third of the large rooms is the one we have fitted out the best. Two grand pianos are its crowning glory. They belong to two of our brethren. Comfortable leather armchairs and other chairs, which of course have also been given to us, make this room the favourite. It is here that we have our regular evening discussions and here too that we spend our hours together on Sunday, singing, reading aloud, making music and providing our own entertainment. . . .

In expressing our gratitude for all this, we would at the same time like to say something about why we are here together and what our work is. The special character of a seminary of the Confessing Church derives from the difficult situation in which we have been placed by the church struggle. The Bible forms the focal point of our work. It has once again become for us the starting point and the centre of our theological work and of all our Christian action. We have learnt here to read the Bible once again prayerfully. That is the significance of our morning and evening devotions in which we hear the word of the Bible continuously. After we have read a psalm together, each of the brethren in turn reads one passage from the Old Testament and one from the New, interspersed with verses from hymns and leading up to a free prayer and the Our Father said together. In the daily period for meditation we consider a fairly short biblical text appointed for the whole week. In the morning we listen to lectures . . . which end with a discussion. Half an hour's singing of chorales ends the morning's work. . . . It is the Lord's Supper, however, that has been the chief means of bringing us together. Confession and brotherly talk together have become our necessary and most important preparation for this.

Not only is the seminary of service in preparing for practical work; but even here we have already started some practical work which will be developed still further in the future. Every Sunday the members of the Confessing Church in Finkenwalde have been gathering in our little chapel. Our chapel used to be the gymnasium when the house was a school. Herr Gross the sculptor from Oranienburg helped us to make it into a chapel. . . . But more than anything else, our house is increasingly becoming a meeting place for the ordinands and young pastors of Pomerania. We have already had several retreats here. All our ministers coming from parish work should be given a quiet time for reflection here among us. If the seminary is to fulfil these purposes, there must be a small staff of brethren here for prolonged periods, not changing every six months but carrying on the work continuously and preserving a continuity between the courses. Some brethren have therefore decided to stay here for a longer period. A community of brethren is incorporated in the seminary. The brethren of the community will lead a common Christian life and will be at all times ready for the service of the church. Scholarly work should be done, and there should be a number of young pastors here at the disposal of the church who can take over wherever the need arises. . . .

Once again, let us say thank you to all those who have been so generous with their gifts. We greet you!   G.S. II pp. 453–5

It would not have been surprising if in those early months the seminary had become so involved in its own domestic problems as to forget the church struggle. But this was not so. Already on the 9th November, Bonhoeffer was moved to protest against the celebration of the 'resurrection of the dead' with pagan rites. The following was not written by Bonhoeffer, but his mind is behind it.

THE FINKENWALDE SEMINARY TO THE COUNCIL OF BRETHREN OF THE OLD PRUSSIAN UNION

10th November, 1935

On 9th November the German people witnessed a 'resurrection feast' for those who fell in Munich in the year 1923.

We note that this was a state celebration with explicitly cultic forms and deliberately using biblical terminology. By an express decree from the Minister of the Interior, the Christian churches have been ordered to take part in this celebration by the use of banners. Here the Evangelical Church has been led astray into a manifest violation of its confession. There should have been a clear statement on the subject of this day, making a firm distinction between the Christian resurrection hope and this popular-idealistic idea of resurrection. The least that might have been done would have been to give visible expression to the church's position by refraining from displaying any flags. The state seems to have sensed this: on the radio broadcast, those who could not accept this 'devotion' (*sic!*) were several times asked to refrain from it.

We know that many pastors have been distressed at not having been given any guidance on this serious occasion. They have been left alone in their difficult decision. They must now be under the impression that they will also remain unprotected if penal consequences ensue from their decision to stand by the confession. We know that investigations into the matter have already been begun by the police in Pomerania. And the parishes are in severe danger of having their faith damaged because they have not been shown clearly that this 'positive Christianity' of the state has nothing to do with the message of Jesus Christ.

1. We would ask the church government most urgently to be mindful of its office of guardian in view of the pseudo-Christian state cults which are increasing, and to make a clear pronouncement on the subject without delay, in pursuance of the Dahlem declaration of March of this year.

2. We would ask the church government to make a regulation about the use of flags, so that the occasions on which flags are to be flown on churches are carefully considered. We would ask the church government to take up a position *post eventum* concerning 9th November of this year for the sake of pastors and their parishes. *There were 26 signatories to this document.*   G.S. II pp. 456–7

At the same time, the community began to send circulars about Finkenwalde to those who had been students there. The first five cover the period up to February 1936. These circular letters are intended to keep the old students aware of what is going on at the seminary and what the community is thinking. The first has a postscript by Bonhoeffer: all are from the community, written by Albrecht Schönherr. Together they give a good picture of the activities at Finkenwalde and show that it was not dominated by Bonhoeffer, although of course he was the director. His many activities meant frequent absences from the seminary, but his absence did not mean the silence of the community. Bonhoeffer had already shown his dislike of the 'leadership principle' in church and state and he was true to his convictions in the leadership of Finkenwalde, which was a community of brethren leading a common life.

Selections from the first five circular letters, with their dates and signatures, addressed in the first instance to those who had been at Finkenwalde, are to be found in Appendix I (pp. 259–64).

They are more than circular letters to former students, but clear criticisms of the failure of the Confessing Church to use the organisation it had set up. Finkenwalde was a necessary stimulant to the Confessing Church in those areas from which its students were drawn, and it continued to remind the 'emergency' church government of its duty! One of the stiffest criticisms came after the meeting of the Fourth Synod of the Confessing Church, which was held at Bad Oeynhausen, 17th–22nd February, 1936. It was written on behalf of the seminary to Superintendent Albertz, who was the secretary responsible for the training of the ministry.

MEMORANDUM TO SUPERINTENDENT ALBERTZ

Finkenwalde, 28th February, 1936

1. The Confessing Church has made no progress beyond the decisions taken at Barmen[1] and at Dahlem[2] for almost a year. That is ominous. For despite Barmen (pure doctrine) and Dahlem (pure government), serious errors are still widespread in the Confessing Church. For this reason, even within the Confessing Church its claim to be the true Church of Christ in Germany is not being taken seriously or is being disputed. Many practical consequences arise from this, and they have led to increasing confusion. The state has taken advantage of this confusion by appointing church committees, seeking to give the impression that in the struggle between church and non-church

[1] The First Synod of the Confessing Church held at Barmen, 29th–31st May, 1934.

[2] The Second Synod of the Confessing Church held at Dahlem, 19th–20th October, 1934.

38

only personal issues are at stake. Large numbers in our church have fallen victim to this deceit. The word for which we have waited in vain is a ruling on the question of church recognition and should have formed the basis of church discipline.

2. We expected a clear word of this kind from the Oeynhausen Synod. But nothing has been said that in practice goes beyond Dahlem, indeed in some places it must be regarded as going back on Dahlem. If the readiness to cooperate in a new order is expressed, then one can only ask: What is the order we are waiting for after Dahlem? The concept of emergency law carries no indication of limited validity or of temporary character; the term merely states something about the circumstances of its origin.

3. We expected some *directive* for those who believe they can reconcile membership of the Confessing Church with working alongside the committees in some way. Nothing has been said even about that, let alone about the question of church communion with such brethren. A statement of this nature has been made only by the Reformed churches–but the Synod has not expressly taken it over as its own. Here in our opinion the only possible conclusion has been drawn from the Dahlem emergency law, namely a prohibition on brethren who have in any way taken part in the work of the committees.

4. Instead of this, we read in the practical part of the resolutions of the Synod, 'On Church Government': 'It pertains to the office of the organs of church government appointed by the Confessing Church that they test the measures of the church committees by the confession and give brotherly counsel to churches and pastors on what their attitude is to be to them.' We cannot see that our church government has 'the office' of considering in any way or suggesting to its pastors and congregations ordinances of another 'church government' which has neither calling nor truth.

In this way it surrenders its Confessing status, for the committees designated by the resolution of the Synod are, whether they wish it or not, fixed in their character as church government.

5. It is our conviction that not 'brotherly counsel' but a firm, binding statement of real guidance belongs to the *office* of the Confessing Church. In practice, the Synod leaves the decision for or against the committees to each individual. If the Confessing Church has already been shown that it should itself exercise the government of the church by emergency law through Barmen, Dahlem and even through the theological declaration (A) of the Oeynhausen Synod, then it is hard to see why the Synod should suggest that each individual find his own way. In view of the confusion, which is almost destroying the Confessing Church, this is not only a renunciation of leadership, but a way of acting which is in the highest degree unbrotherly and uncharitable. According to the theological declaration (A), any compromise with the committee means the destruction of the church. This destruction is the fault both of the pastor who obeys the committees in any point whatsoever and of a church government which gives no clear directives to the pastors and congregations in its charge. Should it not pertain to the office of the church government to act resolutely to avoid the destruction of the church?

6. We – and as we have discovered, other brethren too – doubt whether our churches and clergy have really been helped by the statement of the Oeynhausen Synod. The assertion of the unity of the Confessing Church is indeed cheering, but it has been bought at too dear a price and furthermore leads men astray into trusting in the 'arm of the flesh' rather than in God's promise alone. According to the Synod of Oeynhausen a man has a home in the Confessing Church even if he cooperates with the committees or pays attention to them, although the Councils of Brethren have hitherto urgently advised against this. How do we younger clergy stand towards those who allow themselves to be tested or set in office by the committees? Is it only a matter of conscience or the Word of God that separates us from them?

As this writing deals with a basic matter of principle we believe

THE FIRST YEAR AT FINKENWALDE

that it might be sent to other brethren of the Confessing Church
also.   G.S. II pp. 467-9

Among those who signed it on behalf of the seminary were:
  Wolfgang Büsing
  Christoph Harhausen
  Gerhard Lohmann
  Alexander v. d. Marwitz
  Albrecht Schönherr

*The foundations of Finkenwalde had really been laid and its voice could
not be ignored in Germany. Bonhoeffer's next task was to see that its
influence extended beyond the boundaries of the Third Reich. This he did
through the ecumenical movement.*

2. The Nature of the True Church

Bonhoeffer's reputation in the ecumenical movement meant that the activities of Finkenwalde were watched with more than a curious eye by many churchmen outside Germany. And an interest in Finkenwalde meant an interest in the Confessing Church. Bonhoeffer cultivated this, because he soon saw its importance. His time in England had confirmed this. In 1936, he angled for an invitation which would enable him to take some of his students out of Germany: an invitation from the Swedish Ecumenical Centre, to visit Sweden and Denmark. Such a team could make clear to a wide circle of church people abroad the issues of the German church struggle. Bonhoeffer picked his men and went, from the 29th February to the 10th March. They had extraordinary opportunities in university and church to build up a real support for Finkenwalde and for the Confessing Church, which would stand them in good stead in the years ahead. Bonhoeffer spoke frequently about the church, and a paper which he prepared before leaving on 'The Visible Church' probably gives some idea of the contents of many of his talks to Swedish and Danish congregations.

THE VISIBLE CHURCH IN THE NEW TESTAMENT

The present situation in theology and in the church poses the following question: Does the Church of the Word of God have a place in the world, and if so, what is the nature of this place? It is basically the question raised by the whole theological discussion with the state.

There are two dangers:

a A docetic eschatology, derived from idealism; the very claim that the church has a place in the world is called in question; the

42

church is regarded as being by nature an incorporeal concept, which can lay no claim to such a place;

b A secular ecclesiology, derived from materialism, associated with a magical attitude to the sacrament.

Both these dangers are very acute in our case, in Protestantism. The former danger arises from the theology of Barth, understood wrongly; the latter from the theology of Dibelius, understood correctly. The problem for Protestants, in their discussion with the state concerning orders of nature, etc., is this question of place, keeping clear of both dangers. It is a question of finding the right way. We have such difficulty in answering all concrete questions because we have no clear view of the preliminary question, of the place the church has itself to claim by virtue of the Word of God. Is the place of the church merely the mathematical point of the Word of God, which flashes out here and there? Is it the *punctum mathematicum* of justification? Is everything all right so long as the church is left this place? Experience over recent years has taught us that the church reacts more acutely, over and above our theological consciousness, at certain limits of its body, limits of which it had earlier been unconscious. It has felt that a line must be drawn where beforehand the dogmatic view was that there were no limits at all. The church has felt itself to be a wider place, a wider body, than had formerly seemed to be the case. This is the explanation of the theological problems of the theological faculties, the academic world and the parishes. The church struggle has been carried on by pastors and parishes, not by university theologians. The reason for this is that it has been the pastors and the parishes, not the faculties, who have realised the question of the place of the church. Theology and the question of the church stem from the empirical experiences of the church in her encounters. The church suffers blows and recognises that the body of the church is pursuing its way in the world. The question is, how is the place of the church to be marked out in a recognisable way from the other spheres surrounding it? Is the relationship between church and state that they stand side by side (Rome)? Is the former set above the latter (Geneva)? Is the one in the other (the theology of Rothe)? Is the state above and the church under it (false Lutheran Orthodoxy of the 18th century)? This is where the New Testament comes into play. The New Testament deals with four themes:

    I. The place of proclamation and of confession.

    II. The place of office, of officers and of gifts.

    III. The place of the Christian commandments (new life, discipleship).

    IV. The limits of the place of the church.

    a Towards the sphere of the state

    b Towards the *leges naturae*

    c Towards the sphere of the kingdom of God

The presupposition is that the church is a church of the Word. The question is that of the place occupied by this church in all these relationships. Therefore a visible church.

I. *The Founding of the Church*

The church of the New Testament as the fulfilment of God's promises is created by the sending of the Holy Spirit; it is the historical reality of the Holy Spirit, and thus prohibits any docetism. The church is the end and the fulfilment of God's revelation in the history of his people. It has a beginning in history, just as the coming of the Spirit also has a beginning in history: Whitsuntide. It is not wrong to speak of a church of the Old Testament. The church of the Old Testament, like the church of the community of Jesus with his disciples, is a church of the promise, because the Holy Spirit was not yet given. It is really a church. The church of the New Testament lives in the joy of fulfilment, and waits only for the return of Christ. The church of the Old Testament waits for the coming of the promise. Both churches are one in this: There is one and the same church, one God who has called it, and one faith in the one Word. Therefore the ancient church is a church of the Spirit, but in promise, not in the fulness of the Son of God who has entered time, and the Spirit who has entered the community. The church of the New Testament is the church of the Spirit who has come.

II. *Acts 2*

a A gathering of men has come together. The Spirit comes upon the assembled gathering. They are all one in 'having the same mind', waiting for the Spirit because of Jesus' promise (Acts 1). First the gathering, then the Spirit comes. The gathering is not already the church. It only becomes the church through the Spirit. But the Spirit comes on those who are already gathered together. Man can do nothing for his salvation, but he can go to the church; the promise of the Spirit is given to the individual only in so far as he is a member of the community, gathered together. Now the entirely new thing happens: the Spirit comes.

b The coming of the Spirit and the founding of the church is a visible event, and not an incorporeal concept. The Spirit makes a place for himself in the world by coming with visible signs. The community is immediately placed visibly before everyone else; it is given up to their judgement. The founding of the church is no hidden thing, 'done in a corner'; it is a visible designation of all those who have been called. The Spirit exposes his community to the world. It immediately becomes 'the city on the hill, which cannot be hid'.

c The Spirit comes in the Word, not in stuttering and stammering, but in words that can be understood by all. That is the meaning of the miracle of tongues: it is a language understood by all. It is the unitive Word. It is a Word which makes man responsible. The Spirit says the one word that everyone understands.

d By becoming visible, the church is immediately subjected to the judgement of the world. The visible phenomenon of the Spirit is thus nothing unequivocal in the world. Where the Spirit is, the world sees drunkenness and folly. But it is precisely the world's mockery that will again and again be the sign that the church is on the right road; it is a clearer sign than the world's applause. Where the church retreats into invisibility, it despises the reality of the Spirit.

e Peter's speech: The testimony to Christ awakened through the Spirit. Clear, significant language. Not in the unconsciousness of drunkenness, but in clear, responsible words, Peter bears witness through the Spirit of Christ. Through the Spirit Peter embraces the promises of Israel. What happens here at Whitsuntide is fulfilment, which is given to the people of Israel. What happens in Christ is the fulfilment of the promise given to David. The church of the New Testament understands itself from the first moment of its existence to be indissolubly bound up with the church of the promise, for there is only the one God. A church which dissolved this unity would no longer be the church of the Holy Spirit, for the Spirit binds the church to Israel and to the Old Testament. Where the '*filioque*' is abandoned, the link with the people of Israel is abandoned too.

f Peter's testimony forces the listeners to ask, 'What shall we do?' (Acts 2. 37). The question means that through the fact of the risen Christ who is borne witness to and now proclaims himself in power, the listener is clearly shown that his whole existence is confronted with something new. This proclamation of facts is experienced by the listeners as God's judgement over their previous life and thought. They have heard of the grace to which Peter bears witness, but they know that this grace does not belong to them. It is at first only proclaimed grace. That is the judgement, to hear of grace and to know of it, and yet to know that it does not belong to you. This tension leads straight to the question '*What shall we do?*' What shall we do for this grace to belong to us, so that it does not become judgement? The response of the listeners is not, That was a good sermon; the problem of the Old Testament promise is solved; with the proclamation of grace all is in order and we can go on living as we have been doing.

They know that where grace is proclaimed man is called to ask *'What shall I do?'*, because otherwise grace becomes a judgement on him. A proclamation of grace which does not put this question is delirium. Grace must always be seized.

It is precisely grace freely promised which provokes the question 'What shall we do?' And Peter's answer is not 'Everything has been done,' but, 'Repent and be baptised – and you shall receive the gift of the Holy Spirit', i.e. the grace of the presence of God. Is Peter a synergist? No, he proclaims the full, free grace of God which calls men to action, to repentance, to new life. 'Repent', in other words, 'Let yourselves be called to the church'. Through grace, on the strength of the call of God, take the step to the community of those who have been visited with grace, the community which has been called out of darkness. This community is no longer subject to the *exousiai tou skotous*. These are concrete, historical orders in this world, from which men are called into the Church.

III. *Acts 2. 42–7. The New Community*

a The coming of the Spirit is a new creation, simply because it leads the community into fellowship with Christ. *Kaine ktisis* (2 Cor. 5. 17, Gal. 6. 15), the second creation after the old, corrupt creation, is man in the community, the community itself (Eph. 2. 15). Part of the world is made afresh after the image of God (Col. 3. 10). Thus no new religion has been founded; a part of the world has been made anew. That is the founding of the church. The event of Whitsuntide thus does not consist primarily in a new religiousness, but in the proclamation of a new creative act of God. And that means that the whole of life is requisitioned. It is not for a moment a matter of putting the religious before the profane, but of putting God's act before both religious and profane. Here is the essential difference between the church and a 'religious fellowship'. A 'religious fellowship' is concerned to put the religious above the profane, to divide life into the religious and the profane; it is concerned with an ordering of value and status. A religious fellowship has its end in itself in the 'religious' as the highest – one might go on to say 'God-given' – value. The church, as a part of the world and of mankind created afresh by God's Spirit, demands total obedience to the Spirit which creates anew both the religious and the profane. Because the church is concerned with God, the Holy Spirit, and his Word, it is therefore not specially concerned with religion, but with *obedience* to the Word, with the *work* of the Father, i.e. with the completion of the new creation in the Spirit. It is not the religious question or religious concern of any form which constitutes the church – from a human point of view – but obedience to the Word of the new creation of grace. In other words, the church is constituted not by religious formulae, by dogma, but by the practical doing of what is commanded. The pure teaching of the Gospel is not a religious concern, but a desire to execute the will of God for a new creation. In the church, the Holy Spirit and obedience take the place of 'the religious'. The second creation of God by Christ in the Holy Spirit is as little a 'religious matter' as was the first creation. It is a reality of God. The total claim of the church, which is not content with the priority of the 'religious', is grounded in the claim of the Holy Spirit to be creator in the church. Where the Word and the Action of God are torn apart to the extent that they are in the Orthodox churches, the church must become a religious institution and there is no longer any protection against the pietistic, total dissolution of the concept of the church in which piety constitutes the church – and the action of God is identified with human, pious work.

b In Acts 2. 42 ff., 4. 32 ff., we can already find the first beginnings and the hints of the direction in which this new creation is to take shape. The place of preaching and the confession, the teaching of the Apostles, breaking of bread, prayer, the place of officers and of gifts, signs and wonders, the place of the Christian commandments, of discipleship and community of goods, and the limits of this place,

48

towards the people in Acts 2. 47 and towards the kingdom of God in the mission.

c Acts 2. 42. 'They remained steadfastly in the Apostles' doctrine.' Each word is significant. The testimony of the Apostles following Peter's sermon is called *didache*. In contrast to any form of religious speaking, instruction, the imparting of past events, is meant here. That something has happened is testified, is taught – and also that something is to happen (Acts 2. 38 f.). The content of what is to be said is therefore fixed, it needs only to be handed on. *Didache* is the work of mediation between firm facts and an audience – mediation understood in a purely formal way, and nothing else. *Didache* has of itself no 'religious' character. Now it is only meaningful to impart something that is not already known. The imparting of something already known is senseless. Thus it seems to be a feature of the concept of *didache* that it makes itself superfluous. *Didache* is only sought as long as its subject is unknown. But this is contradicted in a very strange way in our text by the word 'steadfastly'. . . . There must therefore be something in this *didache* which distinguishes it from any other, so that it does not make itself superfluous. The steadfastness is essential and necessary. Why? Is there a sense of duty, that the assembly must be kept up? Is it responsibility for the others? i.e. has this 'steadfastly' an ethical basis? Or is it the feeling of being at home in some church or assembly, a mere emotional love of liturgy? i.e. has this 'steadfastly' an emotional basis? All this, as we can see today, would not have the power to build a community. There is rather a practical necessity in the linking of this *didache* with steadfastness. It lies in the fact that this testimony, precisely as *didache*, is a work of God, of the Holy Spirit himself. The Holy Spirit himself speaks in this *didache*. He himself is the fact of this *didache*. And because the church is the church of the Holy Spirit, it builds itself up daily through this *didache*. The Holy Spirit exists in the *didache*. The guarantee of this lies in the third thing that is mentioned, namely that it is the teaching of the Apostles. The Apostles are the witnesses of

D

the facts, chosen by the triune God, not as onlookers, but as those of whom God has made use in a special way, as his instruments. They are the witnesses whom the Holy Spirit has chosen and to whom he has made himself known. They are the foundation on which the church is built up, with Jesus Christ the chief corner-stone (Eph. 2. 20). They are the living link of the Holy Spirit with the teaching – and each further sermon must be able to be called apostolic preaching on this foundation if it is to be the *didache* to which the community devotes itself steadfastly, i.e. *didache* which has the promise of the Holy Spirit.

The second special feature of this *didache* is that it does not leave the listener as an individual, like any other simple imparting of facts, such as a lecture. Each one does not take up his things and go home – this *didache* creates *koinonia*. The listeners do not remain a public. This is the way the close sentence construction must be understood. Even here no ethical norms, no emotional elements go to form the community – even here a practical compulsion must be sought. It will again be found in the fact that it pleased the Holy Spirit to promise himself not to the individual but to the gathering. It is the visible gathering which receives the Spirit and which is brought to *koinonia* through the Spirit. The liturgical gathering is the origin of the *koinonia* and is similarly its goal. Brotherly fellowship grows only with the hearing of the Word, and all brotherly life in turn stands in the service of proclaiming the Word. It is not without significance that *koinonia* is mentioned in between the teaching of the Apostles and the breaking of the bread. That is in fact the place of Christian brotherliness. Founded on and made possible by the preaching, fulfilled by and directed towards the breaking of the bread, in the community of the body of the Lord. Fellowship in the Lord's supper is the goal of brotherly fellowship and is its fulfilment. *Koinonia* is the waiting to share in the eternal Lord's supper that Christ will drink with us new in his Father's kingdom. Fellowship stands between Word and sacrament, between the earthly feast and the eternal feast.

It is from here that it receives its orientation on eternity. From this fellowship there grows a fellowship of prayer, of thanksgiving and of intercession. And in this prayer is contained a confession of God, who has given himself in Word, in brotherliness and in sacrament.

G.S. III pp. 325-34

These are little more than notes, but they indicate the way Bonhoeffer's mind was developing as a result of the church struggle, and give some indication of what he would be telling the congregations of Denmark and Sweden about the visible church.

A detailed account of the tour appeared in 'Junge Kirche', May 1936, pp. 420-6. The following is a short news piece giving essential details only:

REPORT OF THE STUDY-TOUR OF THE FINKENWALDE (POMERANIA) SEMINARY OF THE CONFESSING CHURCH IN DENMARK AND SWEDEN

The evangelical seminary at Finkenwalde, consisting of twenty-four young clergy, the Inspector of Studies, Pastor Wilhelm Rott, and the Director of Studies, Pastor Lic. Dietrich Bonhoeffer, made a study-tour of Denmark and Sweden from 29th February to 10th March, 1936. This followed an official invitation by the 'Svenska Ekumeniska Nämden' (the Swedish 'Ecumenical Council') which was issued by the Private Secretary to Archbishop Dr. Erling Eidem with the approval of the latter. As the Swedish hosts most generously covered all costs in Sweden, the financing of this tour presented no difficulties.

The chief destinations of the study-tour were Copenhagen, Lund, Uppsala, Sigtuna and Stockholm.

The seminary was greeted most warmly everywhere by representatives of church authorities and organisations, and was made as thoroughly conversant as possible with the church situation in each particular place. On the German side, a number of lectures were given to invited audiences on fundamental questions of theology and the church.

The German students were also invited by Archbishop Eidem to an official reception in the archiepiscopal palace at Uppsala. The Archbishop showed his interest in the German visit by entertaining three of the young theologians as guests at his home.[1] The seminary also held a memorial service in the presence of his widow at the grave of Archbishop Söderblom, who lies buried in the cathedral at Uppsala. Members of the Royal Family sent their good wishes to the seminary. Prince Oscar Bernadotte, the brother of the present king, met the German theologians at an evening reception given by the KFUM (YMCA), while a second brother of the king, Prince Eugene, gave the guests a tour through the private art gallery in his castle. The daily press quite understandably paid considerable attention to the German visit, publishing pictures and full reports on the progress of the tour almost every day.

Both in Copenhagen and in Stockholm, the German theological students maintained close connections with the German pastors and congregations there. Contact was also made with the German Embassy in Stockholm.

By and large, the whole tour can be regarded as having been completely satisfactory. Not only did it provide the men with a wealth of valuable stimuli for the work of their own church; it also gave their Swedish hosts a real glimpse of the problems of the German church and renewed and strengthened the bonds of friendship between the churches of both countries. G.S. II p. 470-1

This was very much a formal report and it came into the hands of Bishop Heckel who was responsible for the foreign affairs of the church. He was obviously worried about this visit and anxious most of all that Sweden should not take sides in the church struggle by supporting the Confessing Church. His report to the Minister for Religious Affairs in Berlin shows definite anxiety.

[1] The longer report in *Junge Kirche* adds here of the Archbishop: 'He assured them that the Swedish Church remembered in constant prayer the struggling and suffering sister churches in Germany, and would continue so to pray for them.'

OFFICIAL REPORT FROM BISHOP HECKEL TO THE MINISTER
FOR RELIGIOUS AFFAIRS

As is known to the National and Prussian Ministry for Religious
Affairs, the church department for foreign affairs pointed out at the
time that this tour, which was only made known at the last minute,
was to be treated with the utmost suspicion so far as church politics
were concerned. The foreign department also informed the German
Embassy in Stockholm to the same effect. The chairman of the
national church committee, in collaboration with the department for
foreign affairs, has taken steps to make the position of the study-tour
to Sweden clear.

The Archbishop of Sweden has been asked personally for information about the character of the tour, and particularly whether by
its invitation the Church of Sweden had intended to take up a one-
sided position on church politics within Germany.

It transpired first of all that the seminary had not been invited by
Swedish officials, but had itself asked the secretary of the Swedish
Ecumenical Council whether it would be welcome and whether it
could be given hospitality. This question was answered in the
affirmative. I may observe confidentially that in several personal
letters the Archbishop of Sweden has explained that this action did
not in any way mean that either the Swedish Church or its Ecumenical Council was intentionally making a stand in church politics.
The matter had been regarded from the Swedish side merely as one
of personal friendship. The Archbishop has added that from the
start, when the plan of the tour appeared, he had emphatically
declared that he did not want to be involved in the German church
struggle and that his person was not to be exploited to this end, but
that he did not want to grudge the young men a recreational tour to
Sweden. He also wished the Swedish Ecumenical Council to help in
defraying the costs of the tour with a gift, but it was not to be officially behind the project. In order to have permission to travel

abroad, the Finkenwalde theologians had on their side asked for a direct invitation from Sweden. This request was granted (in fact, as has been said, the Finkenwalde people invited themselves). The Archbishop then, however, consistently and firmly insisted that the matter was not to be treated in an official way. He noticed later with some uneasiness that this invitation from the Swedish Ecumenical Council, which was only issued to make the students' tour possible at all, was afterwards emphasised as official in the students' reports. The Swedish Church had not intended any interference in church politics whatsoever.

The chairman of the National Church Committee then took the opportunity pursuant to this correspondence to give the Archbishop of Sweden a detailed picture of the actual situation in the German Church at the moment.

It would appear from this course of events that the responsibility for the way in which the tour of the Finkenwalde seminary in Sweden under the leadership of Lic. Bonhoeffer, already known to you, has been publicly brought into church politics lies not with the Church of Sweden, but with the German participants.

I am sending a copy of this memo to the National Church Committee for information. G.S. II pp. 473–4

Shortly after the return from Sweden, a greeting was sent out from Finkenwalde to let friends of the seminary know that despite all the crises they were still alive and active. It provides a good picture of the seminary when two sets of students had been through a term at the centre and a third batch was due to arrive.

A GREETING FROM FINKENWALDE

23rd March, 1936

As you have heard nothing from us for so long, the thought may have occurred to one or two of you that the existence of our seminary has become uncertain. To this, however, we can say with great joy and thankfulness that despite an atmosphere of crisis we have been able to work through a second semester by and large in peace and quietness, and are now facing a third semester here in Finkenwalde. So we greet once again all the friends and helpers of our seminary.

We would like to give you a brief report of past work. Eighteen new brethren arrived on the 1st of November, five from Pomerania, seven from Brandenburg, two from Westphalia, two from the Rhineland, one from Oldenburg and one from Saxony. All the brethren came from serving in parishes of the Confessing Church where each had already some pastoral experience of his own, so that they shared a common experience. The daily routine and the plan of work were on the whole the same as those for the previous semester. . . .

The course of the semester did not pass without its anxieties. In the first weeks of December we believed our stay here at Finkenwalde endangered by the decree of 2nd December, issued by the National Minister for Religious Affairs; we even had to contemplate the closing of the seminary. But we may say with joyful and thankful feelings that we have once again been freed from this deep anxiety.

We remember with special joy the multitude of our visitors. Almost every Sunday we had with us some of the brethren who are at present on military service. Every four weeks we had a meeting here of the pastors of the Confessing Church from the Stettin district.

On the second Sunday in Advent we had our own parish here for Advent music, and finally on 16th February about 120 members of the Confessing Church from Stettin paid us a visit. As well as this our seminary provided hospitality with increasing frequency for our brethren in office who were travelling through, so our house is in process of becoming a centre of church life in the region. Towards the end of the semester we made a study-tour of Sweden as guests of the Swedish Church, on their invitation. This tour was particularly fortifying for us because it made us realise how we are united in faith with our Christian brethren outside Germany. In the coming semester, probably in June, we will have the pleasure of having Archbishop Eidem, by whom we were received, as a guest at the seminary.[1]

For the next semester, which will begin on 15th April, we are being sent twenty-four new brethren by the Council of the Confessing Church of the Old Prussian Union, and this will present us with a new work and at the same time with new difficulties. As you know, money for training the pastors of the Confessing Church must be provided exclusively by the parishes of the Confessing Church. To guarantee that our work continues smoothly, we would now once again come to you with the very great request to help us as much as you can. Because of the considerable increase in the number of brethren – with the brethren of the house, the director and the inspector, we will then number thirty – we find ourselves in great need of money, provisions and furniture. And quite naturally we still lack important books and works for our library. Up till now we have not been able to take up an offer of the Erlangen edition of Luther from a second-hand bookshop (150 RM). . . .

With the beginning of the new semester a whole year will have passed. We have experienced many signs of love and of readiness for sacrifice. But the most important thing of all is the intercession of all those who help us and contribute to our work. To that we would call you with all our hearts.   G.S. II pp. 476–7

The circular letters from Finkenwalde continued. The eighth, sent on 22nd May, was written by Eberhard Bethge and gave disturbing news of the struggle, which was now in earnest, as the following short extract shows.

BETHGE TO THE BRETHREN: As you can see from the enclosed, the seminary is active. We found last Sunday's visit to Seelow and to Frankfurt/Oder most important. We heard on Saturday that Br.

[1] The Archbishop's proposed visit did not in fact take place.

Brandenburg had also been arrested and we decided to go straight away to visit Br. Preuss to help him. We were glad to find him in good heart and already being helped by Br. Johannes Müller, who had come over from Friedland. We could not get an entry into the prison at Frankfurt, but we were allowed to send in a card of greetings. On the next day, both prisoners were to be allowed visitors for the first time. Frau Pecina will be given priority. Do not cease to think of her each day. On the previous week Br. Bonhoeffer spoke to a crowd of 5–600 people and preached. . . G.S. II p. 478

The enclosure was a paper on daily meditations, which had been written by Eberhard Bethge under the general supervision of Bonhoeffer.

INTRODUCTION TO DAILY MEDITATION

1. *Why do I meditate?*

Because I am a Christian and because therefore every day on which I do not penetrate more deeply into the knowledge of the Word of God in Holy Scripture is wasted. I can only go on with certainty on the firm foundation of the Word of God. And as a Christian I learn to know Holy Scripture only by hearing sermons and by meditating prayerfully.

Because I am a preacher of the Word. I cannot expound Scripture unless I let it speak to me every day. I will misuse the Word in my office if I do not keep meditating on it in prayer. If the Word is often empty to me in the daily office, if I no longer experience it, that should be an unmistakable sign that for a long time I have stopped letting it speak to me. I offend in my office if each day I do not look for the Word that my Lord would say to me on that day. Acts 6. 4 lays particularly the office of prayer on those who preach the Word. The pastor must pray more than others and he has more to pray.

Because I need a firm discipline of prayer. We are fond of praying as our fancy takes us, for a short time, for a long time, or even not at all. That is wilfulness. Prayer is not a free offering to God, but the bounden duty that he requires. We are not free to carry on as we wish. Prayer is the day's first service to God. God claims our time for this service (Ps. 119. 147 f., 164). God needed time before he came to us in Christ for our salvation. He needs time to come into my heart for my salvation.

Because I need help against the unseemly haste and disquiet that also endangers my work as pastor. Truly devoted service each day comes only from the peace of the Word of God.

II. *What do I expect from meditation?*

In any case, we want to rise from meditation different from what we were when we sat down to it. We want to meet Christ in his Word. We go to the text curious to hear what he wants to let us know and to give us through his Word. Meet him first in the day, before you meet other people. Every morning lay upon him everything that occupies you, concerns you and troubles you, before fresh burdens are laid on you. Ask yourself what is still preventing you from following him completely, and let him be Lord over it before new hindrances come your way.

His fellowship, his help and his direction for the day through his Word, that is the aim. In this way you will begin the day strengthened afresh in faith.

III. *How do I meditate?*

There is both free and biblical meditation. We advise biblical meditation for the shaping of our prayers and at the same time for the disciplining of our thoughts. Finally, we prefer biblical meditation because it makes us conscious of our fellowship with others who are meditating on the same text.

The Word of Scripture should never stop sounding in your ears and working in you all day long, just like the words of someone you love. And just as you do not analyse the words of someone you love, but accept them as they are said to you, accept the Word of Scripture and ponder it in your heart, as Mary did. That is all. That is meditation. Do not look for new thoughts and connections in the text, as you would if you were preaching! Do not ask 'How shall I pass this on?' but, 'What does it say to me?' Then ponder this Word long in your heart until it has gone right into you and taken possession of you.

It is not important to get through the whole of the proposed text each day. We will often stay hanging on one saying all day long. Leave incomprehensible passages quietly on one side and do not rush off into philology. There is no place here for the Greek New Testament; use the familiar Luther text.

If your thoughts stray, while meditating, to people near to you or those about whom you are concerned, then keep them there. That is the right place for intercession. In that case do not pray in general terms, but make a quite particular prayer for the people commended to you. Let the Word of Scripture tell you what you are to ask for. To help us, we may also write down quietly the names of the people of whom we want to think every day. Intercession too demands your time, if it is to be serious. But at the appointed time take care that intercession does not in its turn become an escape from the most important thing, asking for the salvation of your own soul.

We begin meditation with a prayer for the Holy Spirit. Then we ask for composure of mind for ourselves and for all those whom we know to be meditating as well. Then we turn to the text. At the end of the meditation we will be in a position to say a prayer of thanksgiving with a full heart.

What about the text, and how long should it be? It has proved useful to meditate for a whole week on a text of approximately 10 to 15 verses. It is not good to meditate on a different text each day, as our receptiveness is not always the same and the texts are usually far too long. Whatever happens, do not take the text on which you are to preach next Sunday. That belongs to sermon preparation. It is a great help for a brotherhood to know that it is gathered round the same text all week long.

The time for meditation is in the morning, before work begins. Half an hour is the minimum time demanded by a proper meditation. Obvious prerequisites are complete external quietness and the intention of allowing oneself to be distracted by nothing, however important.

One activity of Christian brotherhood, unfortunately practised very rarely, but quite possible, is occasional meditation in twos or more. There is a narrow path here between false pious loquacity and speculative theological discussion.

IV. *How do we overcome the difficulties of meditation?*

Anyone who takes on the daily practice of meditation at all seriously will soon find himself in considerable difficulty. Meditation and prayer must be practised long and seriously. The first thing to remember is not to get impatient with yourself. Do not cramp yourself in despair at the wandering of your thoughts. Just sit down each day and wait patiently. If your thoughts keep running away, do not attempt to restrict them. It is no bother to let them run on to their destination; then, however, take up the place or the person to whom they have strayed into your prayers. In this way you will find yourself back at the text, and the minutes of such digressions will not be wasted and will not trouble you.

There are a great many helps which each will seek for his own special difficulties: Read the same saying again and again, write down your thoughts, from time to time learn the verse off by heart (in fact one will be able to have any text that has really been meditated upon off by heart anyway). We will also soon learn the danger of escaping from meditation to biblical scholarship or something else. Behind all the needs and difficulties there really lies our great need of prayer; many of us have remained all too long without any help and instruction.

In the face of this, there is nothing for it but to begin again, faithfully and patiently, the very first practices of prayer and meditation. We will be helped on further by the fact that others are also meditating, that all the time the holy church everywhere, in heaven and on earth, is praying together. This is a comfort in the weakness of prayer. If at any time we really do not know what we are to pray, and are in utter despair about it, we still know that the Holy Spirit is taking our part with sighs that cannot be expressed.

We may never give up this daily concern with Scripture, and must begin it straightaway, if we have not already done so. For it is there that we have eternal life. G.S. II pp. 478–82

It is possible to trace the progress of this extraordinary seminary at Finkenwalde through the circular letters which continued to appear. The articles, such as that just quoted on 'Meditation', which often accompanied the letters were of various kinds and they tell quite clearly the way the brethren were reacting to the world outside, and sometimes give news of that world. The tenth circular takes up the story in July 1936.

TENTH CIRCULAR LETTER

22nd July, 1936

BONHOEFFER TO THE BRETHREN: Let me begin by thanking you most sincerely for all your letters and reports. It is becoming increasingly clear that these letters have a great practical value for us over and above the great personal joy which they give to all of us here. In this way, at fairly regular intervals, we keep getting quite a comprehensive picture of the state of the Confessing Church, of its ups and downs, its needs and its hopes. Some have to take the first wearisome and often sacrificial steps towards the building of a Confessing Church. Other brethren are able to work in firm, well-tried

Confessing communities. One sows, the other waters. But it is one work everywhere, and each one knows of the other and thinks of him. This is a great help and a great joy. Most of our brethren from the province of Saxony have a hard job to do. Brother Beckmann reports in great detail about his first 'geographical' clashes, as does Br. Dell.

I preached the day before yesterday with Br. Vibrans, as I had to go to Magdeburg for a wedding. It is very good for people like us at Finkenwalde to get to know the field from actual experience. Twelve people in the best congregations, still less in others. There is no spiritual life worth mentioning in these parishes. And then the utter solitude. God grant all brethren in this situation the power of patience and waiting, and at the same time the joy of the missionary. We think of the brethren particularly every evening here in our devotions. It is a great strength and joy to us here that we have brethren who can and must occupy what is from a human point of view such a solitary post. And yet we should not forget Matt. 10. 13 f. completely. I have advised Br. Vibrans in a while to write a letter to his whole congregation telling them that this is possibly the last offer of the Gospel to them and that there are other communities whose hunger for the Word cannot be satisfied because there are too few workers.

Br. Schönherr's work in Greifswald is very different, but no less difficult. It is a hard fight, in which the whole of the faculty is against him, but it is harder still for the small band of students who take it upon themselves to make a break with a faculty whose members once enjoyed a high reputation. They are like outlaws today, simply because they stand firmly behind the Council of Brethren, and one hears that the German Christians are never left so completely alone as they are. It is a great and splendid task for Albrecht, but unfortunately the fronts seem to be hardening a little, so that the possibility of a hearing can no longer be guaranteed. Here in fact the Confessing Church is being torn apart in the name of the Confessing

Church – circumstances which really cannot be tolerated for long. Everything is in urgent need of clarification. I have been to Greifswald several times, to help Albrecht. We had a retreat for the students here in Emmaus with all sorts of impromptu lectures, on behalf of the faculty. On this occasion we also had Professor Wolf-Halle for a lecture with the students. Unfortunately the situation at Greifswald is symptomatic of the state of affairs throughout the province. Indeed it often seems that the laity are more clear about things than the theologians.

The Rhineland brethren Koch and Rose, and Krüger, Lohmann, Maechler, Harhausen, Grunow, Schlagowsky, to take a sample, are engaged in quite different work. They can hardly keep pace with the demands made on them. Br. Grunow has erected an emergency church in his parish. Br. Harhausen also preaches in an emergency church. One cheering sign is the readiness to give to the collections in many of these parishes. Several of these brethren are right in the middle of examinations. This demands a very disciplined ordering of the day and considerable powers of application. Br. Koch delights those of us at Finkenwalde, and probably not only us, with occasional short greetings, for which we are most grateful. He has a hard battle behind him. The Confessing pastor in his parish made peace with the German Christians on his own initiative. Br. Koch succeeded in withdrawing the agreement. We keep hearing from some brethren no more than that they have had so much to do that they never got round to writing. A pastor should really never seem to have too much to do. But easier said. . . . Nevertheless, we are not giving up hope of gradually hearing regularly from everyone once again. The collection of letters is already quite a respectable volume. It is becoming a unique document. When brethren come to visit us, they always get hold of it to read first of all, and find it a great delight. Br. Krüger has been ordained, and Br. Preuss and Br. Keusch a fortnight ago. Br. Preuss is in Arnswalde/N.M. with Superintendent Gramlow; Br. Keusch is in Schönfeld, Kalau.

Rumour has it that something happened at this ordination which I don't quite understand: each of the ordinands stated before the congregation the basis of his ordination; one, the Lutheran Confessional writings; another, the Bible; and a third, the Confessional writings which are accepted in the Union. Unfortunately there has been no confirmation of this report as yet. But the solution of the Confessional question does not yet seem possible in this form.

Now and then, in addition to letters, we are delighted by the visit of one of our former brethren. When I got back from a journey the day before yesterday, to my great astonishment and delight I came across three brethren all at once, who had met one another here by chance. They were Br. Harhausen, Br. v. d. Marwitz and Br. Grunow, who was taking back his car! It has now served us faithfully for nine months and displays many marks of its honourable service. All those of us who have enjoyed the advantages of the car thank Br. Grunow once again from the bottom of our hearts. He has done the seminary a really great service in this way. There is great joy here whenever a former brother comes to us, and someone said that he had never found things as good here in Finkenwalde as when he came on a visit. It is also splendid that a firm group of brethren has grown up in Berlin, meeting regularly and providing mutual help. On a recent trip to Berlin Br. Rott saw all the brethren there. Br. Krüger is in Jacobi's office, composing circular letters and grappling with the committees. Br. Zenke, up till now also in Berlin, is on a visit to Saxony to see the brethren there now that his work is finished. Br. Kanitz and Br. Schrader are in the same district and meet frequently, to their delight. At the end of this week a group of four is going for a people's mission with Br. Berg. There are further plans afoot in this direction.

And now a few words about us. We are united in our position as a church, as our statement along with those of the other seminaries has shown you. This is a special cause for thanks. Work on the Holy Scriptures and completely practical questions and decisions are this time more in the foreground than before. It has again been a wonderful semester, but it is already coming to an end with great speed, in a way different from all previous courses. This strikes the elder brethren, who come to visit us, too. For my part, I can only say that I am very grateful for each of the previous courses and for this one too. Working through the summer is quite exacting and at the moment we are all somewhat in need of fresh air and sea breezes. So in a week's time we are going to the Baltic for three days, so as to be able to work steadily for the remainder of the semester. We finish at the end of August. On this occasion, just a word about the brethren taking examinations. There are probably twelve of them. Would you come here for a retreat from Saturday, 29th August to noon on Monday, 31st August? I will gladly put myself at your disposal. Unfortunately it is impossible to make this later or longer, as Frau Struwe has to travel without fail and business here must be kept to a minimum. Nor do I yet know where I myself will be then. We have therefore arranged to put up four brethren at a time for a couple of weeks with people friendly to us so that they can work. If anyone is interested in doing this, will he please write to me as soon as possible so that we can make the necessary arrangements. (The whole business is becoming uncertain once again. It is possible that I shall have to travel on official business at this time. You will get further news when you write.)

You will be surprised that I am writing the letter this time. But the community has gone off. Fritz Onnasch has very sensibly gone to the Riesengebirge for a fortnight. As steward he has really deserved this holiday. The garden would astonish all the brethren of the first course, and this time the work has had not only its moral, but also its not inconsiderable economic, significance. Br. K. F. Müller has been in Stettin since his mother was taken seriously ill, but is coming back to the house any time, as his mother is on the road to recovery. Eberhard Bethge has been called most urgently to Helbra for a six-week *locum tenens*, with the express instruction that he is to be

E

released again after that. Most of you will know about Helbra from the circular letters. Conditions there are most unusual. It is hard to tell whether there is a real revival. Be this as it may, during the last three years a congregation has grown up out of an unchurched parish. It stands firmly by the Confessing Church, attendance at services has increased enormously, and great sacrifices have already been made for our cause. Now the pastor, to whom they cling with perhaps an excess of devotion, is to be removed by the Provincial Church Committee. So he is banned from the church, in which a professional stand-in from the German Christians preaches to thirty people, whereas last Sunday about four hundred people went to hear the father of our Br. Vibrans, who was preaching about five miles from Helbra. In the absence of Br. Seeler, Eberhard now has to look after and to guide the extremely excited congregation. It is a very responsible business; the danger of an explosion is so tremendous. We should remember faithfully both him and the congregation.

We have been given very great joy by a letter from Br. Brandenburg and Br. Pecina. We are also filled with gratitude that two brethren managed to visit Br. Brandenburg. His health is not too bad. He just needs fresh air. They still very much hope to be released before August. We should let no day go by without remembering them in our prayers (the letter is enclosed[1]). It is remarkable the weight that any words coming from such a position carry. Do write to both brethren, even if you do not know them.

My dear brethren, we all feel that things are again moving that concern our church. We do not know where they will lead. The Lutheran Council is my greatest worry. We are on the verge of the proclamation of a Lutheran National Church. Then we will have the Confessing Church that many people crave. And the incomprehensible thing will be that we will not be able to go in on it. Then the distress and anxiety tearing our consciences will become enormous. The night is getting darker than ever. We will ask 'Watchman,

[1] See page 67.

what of the night?' And it may be that the watchman will answer
'Morning comes, and also the night. If you will inquire, inquire;
come back again' (Isa. 21. 11 f.). Will we then endure? Or will the
Lord help us by scattering the clouds himself? Will HE open the eyes
of men to what they are doing? We may not cease to pray for this.
Now we must pray much more. May God not put us to too hard a
test. May God build a wall around us so that we remain together.
Let no one think that he can still stand alone at such a time.   We all
stand together through the prayer which we are able to offer for one
another. Even if everything gets still darker and still more unforesee-
able, it will only be a short time before everything becomes quite
clear. All the more, then, should we be faithful in our daily service,
should we be sober, placing our hope completely on grace. The
deeper we have to go in now, the quicker we shall come out again.
Let us keep to our daily meditation on the Word, to intercession and
to the study of the Scriptures. Let us be firm in brotherly service, in
which each strengthens the other. Let no one be ashamed if temptation presses on him too sorely. But help one another on the way. If
only we made ourselves say every day that we were not troubled
about anything, that we would be free from ourselves. God be with
you all, dear brethren, who are alone in a parish at this time. We
others think of you first. And to the rest of you, sincere greetings in
the fellowship of our faith and our hope. 'And I will walk at liberty,
for I seek thy commandments' (Ps. 119. 45).   G.S. II pp. 489–96

*This circular letter had three enclosures attached to it: a letter from prison by
Br. Brandenburg to Bonhoeffer, an appeal for help on a more regular basis,
and an article for use in furthering the appeal. The seminary was obviously
facing hard financial times.*

LETTER FROM BR. BRANDENBURG IN PRISON IN FRANKFURT/ODER

We get a great deal of post from outside every day, with constant
thoughts and intercessions. But we always find most especially

helpful and comforting a letter from you or from the seminary brethren. So our gaze goes continually back to Finkenwalde as to a spiritual
home. How glad I am and thankful to the Lord even in this place
that he has sent us Finkenwalde. I do not mean to be praising in a
human way, you will understand. And so I am looking forward very
much to next semester, as I hope to be with you then. My thoughts
and prayers are with you for the mission. That something of this
sort is possible in a seminary! It seems to me to be a reason for incessant
thanks. But I will keep quiet about it, as it irks me to have to sit here
so quietly and inactively. But I shouldn't complain even about that,
for I have been allowed to learn here that God's ways and his mercies
are wonderful. Even when he sets all our plans and our ambitions at
naught and takes us in the opposite direction from that in which we
have been struggling ardently. So we may sit quietly here and hope,
and it has become clear throughout the house that we stand for the
Lord Jesus. We need not worry about the future if only we hold
firmly to him and to him alone, no, if we allow ourselves to be held
by him; then he stands even by us with his power, whether we recognise him by word, deed, or by the stillness. I know that I am particularly close to you through my morning meditation on Hebrews, and
there is no other fellowship that draws men closer together than that of
the Word. Through Heb. 13. 13-14 I have fully comprehended for
the first time what Good Friday means. His shame that is our shame.
What can still keep us – in this time of all times – from going out
to him from the camp and bearing his shame? And that means to be
sneered at, to be humiliated, to be beaten and to be driven outside all
human regard as he was, in other words to be driven out of the
fellowship of faith by the deluded and treacherous guardians and
shepherds as he was, i.e. to be driven out of the society of the state or
of the people as he was by Herod and Pilate, i.e. to be destined for
death as he was through his fugitive disciples and the weeping women.
For here we have no abiding place. That means to be driven out of
this world, but it means to be accepted by God.

So much that one considered indispensable and so much that one loved above all else falls away from one. It is all so void and meaningless and comfortless in the face of the end. But the Lord Christ! That is life, that is blessedness, for that is the forgiveness of sins. One knows it as a good theologian, but in a situation like this one experiences it.

You see, we have much cause for thanks. That should make us – I know – only more humble, more obedient, more faithful and more zealous in our office. No other aim and no other thought but the one, to proclaim his grace and the fellowship of the one holy church that is his body . . . And now sincere greetings to you, dear Br. Bonhoeffer, and all the brethren. We think of you all and of your work every day. The grace of Our Lord Jesus Christ be with us all.

LETTER OF APPEAL TO SUPPORTERS OF FINKENWALDE

You heard last month of the threat to the existence of our house and at the same time of our work. We are now appealing to the friends of our house and asking them for a regular contribution towards our work. A number of people have already taken it upon themselves to help us each month with a gift; some of you have already heard our appeal, so that we can really only say, thank you. But you will understand our view that proper thanking demands proper asking, so that the old givers do not become weary and new givers are brought in. We now have a great request to make of you, though I am sure that it will seem very small to those of you who know the value and the task of Finkenwalde: could each one of you show yourselves ready to help us monthly with a fixed gift? I am thinking in terms of 1 or 2 RM, though of course more will not be refused. It would mean a great deal to us if we received 50 or 60 RM a month.

As well as this request, which is the most important thing for us, some suggestions. Have you told your Confessing congregation about

Finkenwalde? Could your congregation or even individual members of it join the circle of friends with a regular gift? And your Women's Guild – I am thinking particularly of those of you in the country – will certainly be glad to collect all kinds of produce for Finkenwalde. Recently the Women's Guild at Stemnitz sent us two hundred and twenty-five eggs as a thank offering for their tenth anniversary, and another Women's Guild sent us sausages, bacon, eggs, butter and flour. When we asked them not to forget us in the future and to take our seminary into their sphere of help, the president wrote back to us, 'It is really wonderful that our women now have some definite work which they can do with all their hearts.'

And now we appeal to you, put yourselves in the forefront. We are sure that hands which pray for Finkenwalde will also be opened to give. Help us to enlarge our circle of friends.

ARTICLE EXPLAINING THE PURPOSES OF THE SEMINARY

The Finkenwalde seminary is one of the five seminaries of the Confessing Church in the Old Prussian Union. It was founded in April 1935. As most of the older seminaries have fallen into the hands of the German Christians, the Confessing Church had itself to see to the regular education of its young theologians. Alongside the old seminaries of Elberfeld and Naumburg am Queiss, which were brought into the Confessing Church by their directors, during the church struggle, seminaries have sprung up in Bielefeld, Finkenwalde and Blöstau in East Prussia.

The task of the seminary is to bring together for six months young theologians who, after the conclusion of their studies and the passing of their first examination, have been doing parish work as curates in the Confessing Church for a year or more. Here they are to think through and work through the basic questions of Holy Scripture, practical work and true evangelical teaching with the cooperation of the director of the seminary. The young brethren will thus engage in a common Christian life of daily devotions together, quiet times for prayer, and mutual service. In accordance with the situation of the Confessing Church, their life will be one of extreme simplicity, focused only on the great office which the brethren are to undertake shortly afterwards with their ordination. But over and above the seminary work proper, a seminary of the Confessing Church is increasingly finding itself being given the important task of taking a practical part in the service of the church in the region. Only recently our seminary arranged a six-day popular mission in a Pomeranian church district, alongside other regular outside work which is done by a small group of brethren, some ordained, who are remaining at the seminary for a longer period and who keep themselves free for any urgent church service.

The theological faculties *of the state* at the moment foster almost without exception either the German Christian heresy or indecision. Thus the rising theological generation is in great danger of no longer coming into contact with a theology decisively based on the Confession. At the moment, the seminaries of the Confessing Church are almost the only places in which the Confessing Church can in complete independence train people to have an attitude towards doctrine and life that is firmly governed by the Confession.

Hitherto the Confessing Church has been bearing the great burden of the seminaries all alone. But it must be our aim that the free forces of the Confessing congregations find themselves more and more ready to understand the seminaries as their own responsibility and contribute towards them, so that the seminaries can continue their work on the basis of free gifts. We are now concerned to build up our seminary entirely on the freewill offerings of a large group of members of congregations. We will be grateful for any help.

G.S. II pp. 496–500

That was in July. The following month, August 1936, was a month of great opportunity for the 'Advocates Abroad' of the Confessing Church.

The Olympic Games, held that year in Berlin, attracted many foreign visitors to Nazi Germany. If it gave to Hitler not only much needed foreign currency, but also an opportunity for propaganda to assure the democracies that he was doing a good job and that the rumours about him were wildly exaggerated, it also gave to the Confessing Church a chance to explain its position and to moderate the Nazi propaganda! Daily addresses were given in a central church in Berlin by leaders of the Confessing Church on aspects of the church struggle. Bonhoeffer was one of those chosen to speak. His notes on this enterprise are worth following chronologically. The following are taken from letters to Eberhard Bethge:

21st July: I have been invited to the Olympic service on the 1st August, in the Olympic village. Lecture at 5. I would like best of all to say No to everything. I have been particularly annoyed that we are asked to send a photograph, because they want to make a propaganda book with our pictures. I find that laughable and unworthy and will under no circumstances send one. They are so old-fashioned!

31st July: I am lecturing for the Olympiade on Wednesday, at 5 in the afternoon, 'The Inner Life of the German Evangelical Church since the Reformation'. In half an hour! I am making a collection of hymns: Luther, Gerhardt, Zinzendorf, Gellert. It isn't easy.... Jacobi, Asmussen, Dibelius and Niemöller are speaking as well as myself. They reacted so strongly against my attempt to drop out that I must go on with it now. I must do some church history for my lecture. Yesterday it was Zinzendorf and I was very depressed at the end of it! What rottenness there is beneath all this piety. I tell you I found things there that I am almost embarrassed to repeat to you. And all this in hymns too! Yes, that's man! pious man!... We need the fresh air of the Word to keep us clean and still we cannot leap outside of ourselves. But enough of this, away with human eyes! It is disgusting! G.S. II pp. 276–7

The lecture was eventually given in St. Paul's Church and it was reported in 'Die Christliche Welt' No. 16, by Hans Schlemmer:

While the lectures given in the church of the Holy Trinity were academically satisfying, they were hardly well attended; those in St. Paul's were the opposite of this. Night after night, the enormous church was not only filled to overflowing, but parallel meetings had also to be held in another large church to cope with the mass of visitors. Dr. Bonhoeffer struck the same tone as Dr. Jacobi had done and illustrated his exposition with a number of hymns. According to him, the decline began as early as Paul Gerhardt; Pietism, the Enlightenment and the Nineteenth Century sink lower and lower. Only in the present and especially in the hymns of Heinrich Vogel (!) do we begin to rise again to the heights of the Reformation. The speaker tried to prove his thesis by means of selected hymns and was even successful because of the complete arbitrariness of his selection. He did not shrink from quoting the first half of a verse when the second half, left unquoted, made the opposite point. When we consider that here we have a pupil of Harnack, we can only deplore this treatment of history. The third speaker, Professor Iwand of Königsberg, followed much the same line.

To sum up: in Holy Trinity, valuable theology developed in a scholarly way, but a very small audience; in St. Paul's, narrow and very suspect theology, but great religious enthusiasm and vast congregations, listening with the deepest devotion. This state of affairs must cause great alarm among those concerned with the future of the Evangelical Church.   G.S. II pp. 278–9

And then Bonhoeffer's own report of what happened in St. Paul's, a letter to Eberhard Bethge:

6th August: Yesterday evening was very good. The church filled to overflowing, people sitting on the altar steps and standing all around.

73

I wish I could have preached instead of giving a lecture! Some 1500 or 2000 people and an overflow service. I was taken from one church to the other by car in grand style! In one bookshop, I saw a placard;

> After the Olympiade,
> We'll stew the Confessing Church to marmalade!
> The day the Jews are kicked out,
> The Confessing Church won't cock a snout!

Lovely poetry! An American took a photograph of it and has sent it home. So he told Niemöller.   G.S. II pp. 280–1

Scattered throughout these letters about the Olympiade, there are remarks that tell of a gathering storm. The Confessing Church was in no doubt that something drastic was about to happen as soon as the temporary freedom of the Olympiade was over. Bonhoeffer and his friends therefore used these days to consult and keep foreign visitors informed. The gathering storm also made Bonhoeffer more than usually anxious to go to Chamby for the next meeting of the Universal Council for Life and Work, which was to prepare for the World Conference on Church, Community and State to be held the following year in Oxford. The letter of the 6th August from which I have already quoted also contained references to this:

. . . if we could have met, there would have been so much else of importance to discuss which I cannot entrust to a letter – extremely important church matters. At the moment, I can only say this, we should try to remain in Switzerland beyond the time of the conference. This can be very important. I have applied for money, which must do for both of us. We may have to remain there an extra ten days. Be prepared for that and stay somewhere near the conference. Please do not speak to anyone about this!

That letter was to Eberhard Bethge, who went with Bonhoeffer to Chamby at the end of August. There were two German delegations: the official German Christian delegates with state support, and those of the Confessing

74

Church. The conflict between these two groups sharpened Bonhoeffer's attitude to the German Christians. As they face each other at this ecumenical conference, it might be well to see clearly what Bonhoeffer's attitude was to the German Christians. Earlier in the year, he had written a paper on 'Church Union', which he regarded highly enough to publish that summer.[1]

THE QUESTION OF THE BOUNDARIES OF THE CHURCH AND CHURCH UNION

The Reformation set free the question of the nature of the church from the question of who belongs to it. This was a decisive stage. Roman Catholicism and the pre-Reformation church had thought that the question of the nature of the church could be answered by a definition of its extent. The Reformation, and particularly the Lutheran concept, first says what the church is and leaves the question of its boundaries open. Its first concern is not the unveiling of the divine mystery of who belongs to the church and who does not, the question of election and rejection, it is not aimed first and foremost at judging and distinguishing men; the most important thing is that the manifest saving act of God, the present Christ, his Word and his sacrament, should be seen and adored. There are no theoretical statements about the saved and the lost, there is no verdict 'This man belongs to the church, that man does not', but simply the joyful cry of those who have been granted a share in a great, astonishing gift, 'Here is the Gospel!' 'Here are the pure sacraments!' 'Here is the church!' 'Come here!'

The bearing of this on relations with other churches, on the boundaries of the church, was a completely secondary question. The nature of the church is not determined by those who belong to it but by the Word and sacrament of Jesus Christ which, where they are effective, gather for themselves a community in accordance with the promise. It was a firm belief, grounded on the promise, that if only

[1] Delivered as a lecture 22nd April, 1936, article in *Evangelische Theologie*, June 1936.

the Word and the sacrament were administered purely, those who belonged to the church would always be there. Who those are, the Lord, who calls and assembles, knows. That was enough.

The prime concern could never be the possibility of calling these by name and enumerating them, of distinguishing them from those who did not belong or who only seemed to belong; these have already been judged. Moreover, the Last Day will bring this to light. Why then should the believer be so eager to know already today where the boundaries are, where the distinctions lie? Does he not know enough if he is permitted to know the gracious saving act of God? Why should the believer be concerned to unmask the hypocrite and the heretic? How can he desire to uncover the fearful mystery of rejection prematurely, before the joy of eternal life with Christ helps him to overcome his terror and his grief at the last judgement of God? The believer indeed knows the sort of terror concealed in this concept of 'the extent of the church', which seems so harmless. And he thanks God daily that he is still blind here, that he can still stand in intercession, that he can still keep to the church of salvation with the community of believers in all the joy of his knowledge of salvation. The believer thanks God that he has again been given his word and sacrament pure and entire, and that he knows where the church of God is. Why should he ask where it is not, if he is completely swallowed up in this joy?

So primitive Christianity and the Reformation did nothing more at this point than to cry confidently one after the other 'Here is the church!', 'The true Church of Jesus Christ!' This cry is one of humility and thankfulness. It is not boasting, but praise of God. If he has really heard and believed, who thinks of asking still whether the church might not perhaps also be found somewhere else? Who is concerned with such a question except those who do not want to hear and believe at this point? If we heard and believed that an inexhaustible vein of gold had been found which would yield enough for all men and all times, then we would hardly be interested in the

question whether perhaps some gold might possibly be found somewhere else. Maybe so, maybe not – what does it matter in view of the
fact that here there is enough and to spare? Would we not then also
give this joyful message to all those who were struggling hard to
discover other veins, would we not shout to them to come along, to
abandon all their efforts and simply run and take from where everything was to be found in the utmost abundance? We might then have
doubts about the seriousness of their search if they did not come, but
insisted on saying 'I'm looking for my own gold'. Here obstinacy is
stronger than the wish to find gold. We would have to leave them
behind with great sorrow, for who knows whether in the end they
might not go away empty? We would have to run to where the
great offer was made.

So it is with the Reformation message of the church. Here is the
true church. Might it not also be found somewhere else? But that is
not the question. God has given it to us here. Will you stand aside
and obstinately search to see whether God could not also give it to
you somewhere else? It might be so – but then it really might also
not be so. Would we risk that? Anyone who takes the risk has in fact
already lost, for he has not heard and believed that the true church is
already there. Otherwise he would no longer take the risk at such
moments. And if he has not heard, neither does he know what the
true church is, and so he does not know what he is really looking for
and will never find it. In that case the search is an end in itself and
therefore no longer a genuine search.

So the church, always beginning with the recognised truth of what
and where the church is, now proclaims to the world, 'Come here,
the church is here!' And that is the reason why it does not enter into
discussions about where else the church might be. In face of the
certainty that the church is here, everything else is uncertainty, non-
church. Of course it is non-church! Otherwise the others too would
be here, where the church is. But because they are not here, and do
not want to come here either, they must be non-church. But what is

the point of saying this? There is no point except to be able to cry all the more confidently and all the more joyfully 'God has given us once again the true church'. 'The church is here!'

The true church, therefore, can never want to determine of itself the position of those who do not belong to it. Its claim to be the church is never meant to imply that now the separation of the just from the unjust is to take place. Rather, this claim that the church is here, is itself the call to salvation, which goes out to all the world. It is the Gospel itself. It must be proclaimed in this way and in no other. Of course those who are unable to hear it as Gospel hear it as law. And understood as law it carries within itself the whole hardness of the question of the extent of the church. Those who hear the church's call to salvation as law, who know that this law applies to them, protest against it and have to regard themselves as those to whom the call does not apply. This is where the question of the extent of the church, of the boundaries, of the distinction between the elect and the rejected arises. Wherever the call to salvation is not heard, the church's claim becomes judgement, it divides those who hear it from those who do not hear it. Whereas this distinction is again and again done away with by the preaching of the Gospel, in that the salvation of the church is offered to all and promised to all, in a legalistic understanding of the church it becomes hardened. The question of the extent of the church must now consistently determine its nature. But this legalistic understanding is foreign to the nature of the church. It is not the purpose and the commission of the church to preach the Gospel on its fingers. The Old Testament prohibition of a popular census is a warning here. It is enough to know that salvation is there and that God will always create his community. The extent of the community is reserved for the knowledge of God. So our result hitherto, the question of the extent of the church, i.e. of its boundaries, derives from a legalistic understanding of the evangelical concept of the church. This question, therefore, should never be linked with that of the nature of the church; it will always appear as a foreign question, where the church's claim is understood in a legalistic way. It will always be put to the church from outside, and the church itself may and must only take up the question then, in the consciousness of that fact. The question of the extent of the church is the question of church membership. Who belongs to the church? Who no longer belongs to it? That is the question. The church reflects on its boundaries. Why? Because its call to salvation is not heard and believed, but comes up against boundaries. The church finds that men refuse its summons. It is not the church that sets the boundaries; it comes up against boundaries that are imposed upon it from the outside. Now the church experiences its call to salvation as the law which judges the world, as the boundary which cannot be passed. Now it must take account of the situation.

As it is not the church which sets exclusive boundaries, as the boundaries are drawn arbitrarily by the world, which shuts itself off from the church by not hearing and believing, the church cannot *a priori* determine where its boundaries must run. It will always simply be able to take note of and to confirm the boundaries which are drawn from outside against it at any one time. The church has no control over the way in which unbelief marks itself off from the church. For this reason the establishment of the boundaries will always be a difficult one. Because *the knowledge of the extent of the church is never theoretically at the church's disposal* but must always be ascertained at any given time, there is no theoretical standard by which church membership could be measured. If there were such a standard, the church would have misunderstood itself legalistically in its claim, as it has done in Catholicism, Orthodoxy and Pietism. This brings the element of living decision into the determination of the boundaries of the church for the Reformation concept of the church. The boundaries of the church are always decided only in the encounter between the church and unbelief; the act is a decision of the church. If it knew the answer beforehand it would have separated itself from the world and would be unfaithful to its commission to proclaim salvation. It must be its very own decision to recognise and to confirm a boundary drawn by the world as such. It must decide whether and where its call to salvation comes up against a last boundary. Therefore the question of church membership can only be answered concretely in the authoritative decision of the church. This characteristic of decision is a purely objective one. It would be both subjective and arbitrary were the church to wish to draw the boundaries beforehand and thus to complete the division of its own accord. The apparent objectivity of a theoretical knowledge of the boundaries of the church is itself a dissolution of the true objectivity which is achieved in decision.

However, the church is not left without measures by which alone it can make its decision. Even so, a consideration of them shows the utter impossibility of regarding them as clear legalistic criteria for decision. As the process of decision has gone on, the church has learnt to understand *baptism* as a determination of its boundaries. But at the same time this determination of the extent of the church presents extreme difficulties. On the one hand it is not wide enough (hence the doctrines of baptism by desire, blood baptism, etc.). On the other hand it is not narrow enough, for among those baptised there are false teachers and dead members who cannot belong to the church. Furthermore, baptism is recognised as the sacrament common to all Christian churches and its repetition on entry to another Christian church is impermissible. It is thus a unitive bond of all Christian churches and cannot therefore be the condition of church membership. True, the true church can never give up the claim that all those baptised really belong to it, but it must at the same time concede that there are those who are not in its communion. So the church knows on the one hand a relative exterior boundary, which is given in baptism, and at the same time an inner boundary which embraces only a part of those who have been baptised.

The church has learnt to determine this inner boundary by the concept of teaching and the confession. The confession of the church is constitutive of church membership. But which confession? The symbols of the ancient church? The Formula of Union of Lausanne? In that case what is the justification for the distinguishing doctrines of the individual churches?

The Lutheran confessional writings were of the view that there was confessional material common to both the Lutheran and the Roman Church. Luther reckoned as a common basis the doctrine of God, the doctrines of the Trinity and Christology, and yet it was impossible to unite on the basis of these articles because there was disagreement on the doctrine of justification by faith. If this disagreement was removed, union would be possible. Similarly, in the Lutheran attitude towards the Reformed churches it was the doctrine of the eucharist which stood in the way of church union. Should the dogmatic theologians of the confessional writings not have known that a disagreement in these articles must necessarily have resulted in a complete disagreement in any article, that a false doctrine of justification necessarily includes a false Christology, a false doctrine of the Trinity and a false doctrine of God? And vice versa, a real consensus in Christology would also include a consensus in the doctrine of justification and in fact restore church communion.

Our question now is: What does it mean if nevertheless this consequence is not drawn, if on the one hand a common confessional material is preserved and on the other hand church communion is broken over a specific article?

It means in the first place that the claim which is already raised in reference to the baptised members of other churches is now extended to the confessing members of other churches. They have the right confession, but they have fallen away from it. In reality the one confession is there even if it is understood quite falsely by the other church. In this confirmation of the confession the evangelical call to salvation is maintained: there is only one confession, here is the true confession, come here! The concern therefore is not the drawing of boundaries as such, i.e. as a law; the boundaries drawn by the other

F

churches are taken seriously, but only to make all the clearer the call to salvation: 'In truth you belong to us, here is the right confession'.

Secondly, it means that church union is always something qualitatively total. It is not to be achieved by the enumeration of all the common features which manifestly outweigh the differences; as long as there is disagreement at one point, no consensus is possible. It is a given, total unity. This unity is the *a priori* of church union. It cannot be produced by comparison; it must be given unity. But in turn, on the basis of this unity all possible differences are tolerable which must necessarily arise and to which the Lutheran confessional writings therefore pay heed. As a result of the previously given unity they are then no longer divisive differences. While the presence of this unity is expressed by complete confessional agreement, the readiness to keep theological differences in the framework of a confession from becoming divisive differences and to work towards a unitive formula of confession, i.e. the fact of the achievement of a consensus in respect of a formulated confession, is itself already an act of decision on the part of the church and never logically or theologically binding. In other words, the unity of confession of a church is an act of church decision as a decision of faith, not of theological formulation.

Thirdly, it means that the ascertaining of the point at which disagreement becomes a divisive discord is itself an act of decision on the part of the church. Why did the Reformation not develop the doctrine of God into a divisive disagreement? The decision stemmed from the fact that the church detected the enemy attack in a particular way at a particular place and therefore offered resistance at this place. A war is decided by a battle in one particular place. Where this battle is fought depends on where the enemy is. A decision must be sought here. It is therefore by no means the case that the place of decision must always remain one and the same place. It may well be that a situation which is dangerous today is no longer decisive for the course of the war tomorrow. The article which divides the churches today may no longer be divisive tomorrow. This follows from the free decision of the Reformation to bring to a head its difference with Rome in a single article and to let all other differences go. Only where the church establishes its boundaries itself, legalistically and beforehand, and thus betrays its commission to call men to salvation, does the opposition harden and remain fixed at one point. This leads to the last point.

Fourthly, it means that a clear distinction is seen between the task of dogmatics and that of the confession. The confession is not a compilation of dogmatic sentences from which all the consequences are to be drawn. Otherwise the Augsburg Confession and the Schmalkald Definition would be the worst of all confessions. For here the dogmatic inconsistency of isolating the doctrine of justification by faith is clear. And further, any difference on any point of doctrine would necessarily have to be divisive. Each theological school would have to become its own church. The mere fact that this is the case, is support enough for the view that the question of church membership should not be answered by theology alone, but by a decision of the church. The faithful rally not round theology but round the confession. Any confusion here is dangerous. Theology gives weapons to the whole army so that it is ready to fight at any time and in any place. But the fight is carried outside not by theology but by the confession. Otherwise one would fall into orthodoxy, one would become legalistic, one would know beforehand the boundary of the church and deprive oneself of the freedom of the church's decision. The confession is the church's decision about its boundaries made on the basis of theology. It is not a representation of the whole of the church's teaching, but a decision of the church taken on the basis of the whole of its teaching to join battle at a specific place. In the confession, theology is actualised by the decision of the church. In the limitation which distinguishes the confession from the whole body of teaching, there always lies at the same time the church's claim to unity of confession with the dissentients, on which these are to be thrown back. This is confirmation of the fact that the

83

church itself does not draw the boundaries, but merely recognises the boundaries drawn from outside. It also allows for the continual proclamation of the unbounded call of the church to salvation.

It thus transpires that even the presence of a confession is not suited to give a definitive outline of the extent of the church. The boundary between differences which separate schools and differences which separate churches cannot be drawn in principle. Therefore, the facts of baptism, the common confessional material in the symbols, the articles of difference can always serve only as material for the church's decision about the extent of the church at any one time. The boundaries themselves are not at the disposal of the church but must be confirmed by this decision.

As the boundary of the church is a boundary drawn from outside it can be as multiform as enmity towards the Gospel. The boundary differs, depending on whether it is drawn by the world, by an anti-Christian church or by 'another church'. Only theological doctrinairism can deny these differences. The Reformation recognised them very clearly; one need only think of the different Lutheran attitudes towards the Roman Church and towards the Greek Orthodox Church. But the distinction between an anti-Christian church and 'another church' is in its turn not clearly ascertainable by theology; it is a matter for the decision of the church. It may well be that the same false teachings can be demonstrated by theology in either case but that nevertheless one church is anti-Christian and the other is merely 'another church'. In that case all communion must be broken off with the former, while the conversation with the other church is carried on and a communion of hope is preserved. In this it becomes clear that there is another factor which governs the decision, outside false teaching. It becomes quite clear where a church declares that it recognises the confession and is responsible for no false teaching, so as to wage war on the true church all the more purposefully in this unsuspected way. Right teaching becomes false teaching the moment it is used in the struggle against the true church. To continue the figure of a war: in such an instance the officers desert with their weapons and their men and go over to the enemy camp. They have the same weapons as the army they have betrayed, but they are now directing them against their former friends.

There is a decisive difference in whether false teaching moves against the true church with a manifest intent to annihilate it or whether it stands alongside the church without a struggle. In the first instance true and false churches stand over against each other, each with the intention of being the death of the other. Here there is a life and death struggle. Here there is no communion. Here the true church recognises anti-Christ. In the other instance, the true church knows of erring churches which have no will to destroy the true church, which themselves contribute to the mystery of the brokenness of the church, with which therefore the true church stands in a common confession of guilt. Here unity can again be sought in connection with the common confessional material. This is roughly the situation in ecumenical work. We learn from it that even church union, like the boundary of the church, has different forms. From the full communion in word and sacrament which finds expression in an agreed confession, to a communion which is sought in faith on the ground of a common possession. It would be as false to reject and deny this communion *a limine* as it would be to equate it with full church union. It is on the one hand a fact of the church, on the other hand a state of emergency, a transition which must lead either to full communion or to separation. But because the church is not able to declare *a priori* where such communion or definitive separation exists it must take seriously the situation at any given time and leave it to God to make of it what pleases him, waiting on the hour of decision.

If it is clear that the question of church union can be answered only by the decision of the church, it must now be said that this decision of the church can in no case remain pending. It will accompany the church struggle step by step. True, it will always remain the 'strange work' of the church. But it must be made because otherwise the church's proper work can no longer be done. The church's decision on its boundary is in the last resort a merciful act both to its members and to those outside. It is the last, the 'strange', possibility of making the call to salvation audible.

The Confessing Synod of Barmen has repudiated the teaching of the German Christians in its decisive points as false teaching. This repudiation means that this false teaching has no place in the Church of Jesus Christ. The Confessing Synod of Dahlem took it upon itself to declare that the government of the National Church has separated itself from the Christian church by teaching and by action. It did not bring about any exclusion from the church, but stated a *fait accompli*. At the same time it formed its own church government and claimed to represent the true Church of Jesus Christ in Germany. Since then the Confessing Church has recognised that it has the responsibility of being and the commission to be the one true Church of Jesus Christ in Germany. That is a fact of church history.

What does this mean? What does it express? Everything in the Confessing Church centres on this question. To make the inevitably vain and never conclusive attempt of asking about the views of those who were responsible for this decision of the synod is no sufficient answer. If we take this statement of the Synod at all seriously we will recognise that God the Lord himself wills to be responsible for it. But in that case the statement must be received as it was issued and we must look for the will of God in it. So on the presupposition that here in all human weakness and differences of opinion, through all kinds of human moods, anxieties and hastinesses, the Word of the Lord became clear to the church when the Synod declared that the government of the National Church had cut itself off from the Church of Jesus Christ, we must ask what this statement means. Anyone who does not share this presupposition does not speak of Barmen and Dahlem as Christian Synods, and does not share the presuppositions of the Confessing Church. Things are really in a bad way if today in large circles of the Confessing Church there is wilful and undisciplined talk, more among the clergy than among the laity. We can no longer go back behind Barmen and Dahlem not because they are historical facts of our church to which we must show due reverence, but because we can no longer go back behind the Word of God.

The question then is: What did God say about his church when he spoke through Barmen and Dahlem? The government of the National Church has cut itself off from the Christian church. The Confessing Church is the true Church of Jesus Christ in Germany. What does that mean? It undoubtedly means that a definitive boundary has been recognised and confirmed between the government of the National Church and the true Church of Christ. The government of the National Church is heretical. But does that mean that the man in office who continues to offer obedience to this repudiated church government falls under the same verdict? Has each German Christian pastor cut himself off from the Church of Jesus? Furthermore: must we also regard the German Christians among members of the congregations and those parishes which accept their German Christian pastor without protest as cut off from the Christian church? Can the pastor of the Confessing Church claim the German Christian members of the congregation as members of his congregation? Is he permitted to exercise his office without distinction both to members of the Confessing Church and to German Christians? Where are the boundaries of the congregation for the pastor of the Confessing Church? Is there here a difference in principle between church government and congregation? And in addition: what is the position of the so-called neutrals? Finally: Does anyone engaged in common church work or even church government with the German Christians share in their sin of destroying the church? Does the Dahlem verdict also apply to the church committees? Does it apply to all those who obey the church committees? To sum up: must the division which has grown up between the government of the National Church and the Confessing Church now extend

87

consistently to all these others just mentioned? An answer must be given. The congregation must know to whom they may listen and to whom not. The pastor must know how he is to understand his office rightly. Pastors and congregations largely do not know this today, and they cannot know it because they have not been told.

It would certainly be the easiest solution either to draw all the above-mentioned consequences neck and crop or to stand blindly by Dahlem and to draw no consequences at all. Both these courses are equally unchurchlike according to everything that has been said hitherto. Drawing consequences is no help at all, because the Word of God demands not consequences, but obedience. But to draw no consequences at all can be wilful disobedience towards the Word. Thus each single question must be examined and a decision must be sought step by step. In this way it is possible to reach a certain degree of clarity, for example, in the case of those who hold German Christian office. In parishes in which there are only ministers of this kind the Confessing Church has taken care that the true preaching and the true ministry is preserved. It has instituted emergency ministries and in this way demonstrated that the German Christian minister is deprived of his office. Nothing of this sort has happened in the case of the neutrals. The attitude towards the congregations is of a completely different nature. The mere fact of the institution of emergency pastorates is an expression of the full claim of the Confessing Church on the congregation. The attitude of the Confessing Church towards the committees and towards the members of the committees who belong to the Confessing Church, and also to pastors who offer allegiance to the committees, is completely obscure.[1] This obscurity is pernicious. Before anything is said on the subject, however, we must look at the situation from yet another aspect.

Whereas on the one hand a continued process of separation is going on, on the other hand an extremely significant understanding

[1] cf. page 38 ff.

88

is coming about between the churches of Lutheran and Reformed confessions. Since Barmen, Lutherans and Reformed have been speaking with one voice in Synodal declarations. Schismatic differences of confession no longer make it impossible to form a Confessing Synod, though of course the Synods are without intercommunion. This is to be taken into consideration as an actual fact. Of course disputes arise on the Confessing side. But the fact is there, and it is up to God to make what he will of it.

It cannot be disputed by any means of the Confession that this fact, the recognition of 'Confessing churches of equal rights', is already a decisive breach of the Augsburg Confession. The Confessing Synods cannot be justified by the letter of the Lutheran Confession. How then are we to understand the formation of the Confessing Synods despite continual reference to this very point? How are we to understand the participation of decidedly Lutheran theologians in them? We must begin by establishing the facts, that the Confessing Synods exist, and that in view of this only two attitudes are possible: either one repudiates these Synods *a limine* in the light of the Augsburg Confession or one accepts them in wonderment and humility and allows God to make of this what pleases him. In any case, the present situation is significant and instructive enough for the question of church union. On the other hand, the inexorably consistent application of the doctrinal concept leads to division of the churches, on the other hand there is a manifest neglect of the doctrinal concept, and a church union which disregards decisive and hitherto divisive differences in doctrine has already been pioneered. If we imagined the inexorably consistent application of the doctrinal concept as it is exercised against the German Christians directed say against the Reformed Churches, it would be theoretically conceivable that the old divisive differences in eucharistic doctrine or Christology would break out again here as well. Analogously a slackening of consistency could create a common basis with the German Christians. This, in any case, is how the situation must look to confessional orthodoxy.

What is at the bottom of this absurd possibility? Is some sordid game being played here with church union?

At this point there is a further complication. The Confessing Church has found ecumenism. This meeting has up till now brought about two distinctive results. At Fanö, in 1934, in the presence of representatives of the Confessing Church the ecumenical movement declared the 'principles and methods' of the German Christian church government to be 'incompatible with the nature of the Church of Christ'. By the election of a representative of the Confessing Church to the ecumenical council it has asked for the cooperation of the Confessing Church and has been given this church's promise. The Confessing Church has not yet, however, sent official representatives to any ecumenical conference. The reason for this must be found in the presence of representatives of the government of the National Church with whom conversation even on neutral ground is no longer possible for the Confessing Church. So while conversation with other, erring 'churches' would be possible, such a possibility no longer exists for conversation between the National Church and the Confessing Church. Doubtless it would be easy to point out the false doctrines of the German Christians in many other churches. Nevertheless the Confessing Church recognises a qualitative difference.

All this must appear both incomprehensible and contradictory both to the orthodox and to those in principle without a confession. The orthodox does not understand how it can be possible to treat the clauses of the confession in a different way. He does not understand the openness of the Lutherans of the Confessing Church towards the Reformed or towards the ecumenical movement. Those without a confession, among them the great number of pastors under the sway of pietism and liberal theology, do not, on the other hand, understand the obstinacy in the application of the doctrinal concept against the German Christians.

The Confessing Church takes its confident way between the Scylla of orthodoxy and the Charybdis of confessionlessness. It bears the burden of the responsibility of being the true Church of Jesus. It proclaims 'Here is the church!' 'Come here!' In proclaiming this it comes up against both friends and enemies. Where it recognises enemies it confirms the barriers they have drawn consistently and without compromise. Where it recognises friends, it finds common ground and is ready for conversation in the hope of communion. The church will recognise friend or enemy by the Confession, but the Confession is not an ultimate, clear-cut measure. The church must decide where the enemy is standing. Because he can stand now on eucharistic doctrine, another time on the doctrine of justification, a third time on the doctrine of the church, the church has to decide. And in deciding it makes its confession. Orthodoxy confuses confession with a theological system. The confessionless confuse the church's confession with the testimony of piety. It would be very much easier if the Confessing Church could think in a clear-cut way here. But by so doing it would be unfaithful to its commission to give the call to salvation; in that, it is at the same time both open and bounded.

If it is thus clear that decisions about the boundaries of the church can only be taken in each individual instance, it is now necessary to consider briefly the concrete questions raised earlier.

1. That the German Christian ministers have cut themselves off from the church is a recognition which needed only Synodal confirmation. In Lutheran teaching it is only possible to institute an emergency pastorate if it is clearly declared that a man has forfeited his office. Otherwise this would be an impermissible encroachment on someone else's ministry, a matter against which Luther could not utter enough warnings. Hand in hand with this should have gone a direction to the congregations to abstain from all ministerial acts of a false teacher for the sake of the Word of God and the salvation of their souls, and to live and die without word or sacrament rather than go to a false teacher.

2. In this matter a distinction must be made between ministers and

members of congregations, the leaders and those who are led. It is impossible to argue the exclusion of a congregation by the mere fact of the exclusion of its minister. The Lutheran Confessional writings did not declare individual Catholics but the Pope, i.e. the church government, to be Antichrist. The Synod of Dahlem spoke in the same way. The government of the church has become heretical. But this is in no way to give up any claim on the congregations. The congregations must be helped to find the right ministers. Of course the congregation itself is also called to pass judgement on false teaching. If it does not do that, if despite warning and admonition it persists with the false teacher, here too after some time a limit must be set to patience and church membership must be regarded as dissolved, with all the consequences of the denying of ministerial functions, etc. This is the last act of mercy of the church to the congregation, the last call to communion, the 'strange work' through which the call to salvation is given. It is, however, also an obligation of the church towards the office which would otherwise be guilty daily of the dissipation of the sacrament.

3. The Confessing Church can no longer avoid a clear decision about the church committees. The statement of the Oeynhausen Synod is not enough. It is impossible to see where the Church government of the committees differs from the government of the National Church. Indubitably the church committees are more dangerous to the true church government than the government of the National Church. It has been stated by the Confessing Synod that this church government cannot be recognised, but hitherto the unequivocal prohibition against taking part in it has not been given. This makes for confusion. Where the boundaries are recognised, the practical conclusions must be drawn. In the same way as a member of the Confessing Church who joined the government of the National Church would cut himself off from the Church of Jesus, so according to the fundamental insight expressed in the Oeynhausen Synod anyone who takes part in the governmental functions of the committees

does the same thing. But from this there necessarily follows the prohibition of such participation. This and nothing else applies to those
ministers who submit to the committees. It is not good to practise on
ordinands what one is willing to drop in the case of pastors. The
longer the government of the church avoids the decision laid upon it,
the more it confuses the congregations, the more unmerciful it is
towards the pastors and the less it can give its own call.

4. The neutrals are a particular problem. First of all it must be said
that there are really no neutrals. They belong on the other side. But
they themselves want to be neutral. It is therefore impossible to
have an unequivocal attitude towards them as their own attitude is
not unequivocal, because the boundary drawn by them against the
true church is not clear. Jesus Christ spoke twice about the neutrals:
'He who is not with me is against me' (Matt. 12. 30) and 'He that is
not against us is for us' (Mark 9. 40). The neutrals cannot claim just the
second saying for themselves, neither can the church use just the
first saying against them. But it must continually be demonstrated
that the neutrals are in just this questionable situation described
by the two sayings. Of course if neutrality is elevated to the status
of a principle, it is then possible to use just the first saying. For in
that case a clear position has been taken up outside the church and
a boundary has clearly been erected against the claim of the true
church.

These brief remarks cannot have the significance of anticipating
the decision of the church. But they must serve to remind the government of the church that it must take this decision. In doing it step by
step, it will be doing the strange work so as to be able to pursue its
true work rightly. The dissolution of fellowship is the last offer of
fellowship!

Extra ecclesiam nulla salus. The question of church membership is the
question of salvation. The boundaries of the church are the boundaries of salvation. Whoever knowingly cuts himself off from the

Confessing Church in Germany cuts himself off from salvation. That is the recognition which has always forced itself upon the true church. That is its humble confession. Whoever separates the question of the Confessing Church from the question of his own salvation does not understand that the struggle of the Confessing Church is the struggle for his own salvation.

Is that not the Roman heresy of the church? In so far as Roman doctrine cannot think of salvation without the church and cannot think of the church without salvation, it is right. But in so far as the statement that there is only salvation in the church means anything but the call to the visible church, in so far then as this statement is not an existential expression of the faith of the true church but is intended as a theoretical truth about the saved and the lost, in so far as it is anything but an offer of grace, the means of salvation, it is reprehensible. For then a statement of faith is made a speculative statement. *Extra ecclesiam nulla salus* is in the strict sense a statement of faith. The believer is bound to God's saving revelation. He knows no other salvation than this in the visible church. In the light of this he is not free to look for God's salvation anywhere else than where the promise is given. He cannot in principle recognise salvation outside the church and it can therefore never become a point of doctrine for him. Salvation is recognised only in the promise. And the promise is given to the proclamation of the pure Gospel.

But what if the Gospel were now preached purely in a single congregation of the Roman Church or the National Church? Is not then the true church there also? There is no pure proclamation of the Gospel independent of the whole church. And if someone preached the Gospel as purely as the Apostle Paul and was obedient to the papacy or to the government of the National Church, he would be a false teacher and a misleader of the congregation.

But what if there are people in the other church whose piety and Christlikeness have been proved? What about the good Christians on the other side? Is it not unmerciful and un-Christian to pass judgement on them? Is it not intolerably pharisaic to put forward against them the claim of being the only true church? That is a spirit of judgement, we hear it said. There is an element of rebellion against the claim of the church in this question, and it is to be found right in the midst of the Confessing Church. It is this which tears the Confessing Church apart from within at this moment. The answer begins with the counter question:

1. Why are these Christian people with the German Christians and not with the true assembly of the faithful? Why do they not come to where the call of the true church is given? Why? Because it is not important enough to which church they belong? Because they have enough with their piety and their holiness? Is that what it means to be a good Christian?

2. How do we know who is a good Christian and who is not? Am I a judge over another's Christianity? Is this not an intolerable spirit of judgement which pretends to look into another's heart? Is not this supposed Christian love which would exclude no pious man from salvation unutterable *hybris* and the deepest hatefulness because it anticipates God's hidden judgement on the soul of the individual?

3. Who really calls the church? The Holy Ghost through his word and sacrament? Or I myself, with my verdict on good and bad Christians? That is the fearful calumny which lies in the question of these loving Christians, that they want to found and gather together and limit the church of God themselves, and in so doing destroy and deny the true church of the Word.

It must be said again and again that for the church to deny its boundaries is no work of mercy. The true church comes up against boundaries. In recognising them it does the work of love towards men by honouring the truth. *Extra ecclesiam nulla salus.* If this statement is indisputable, the other one must also be added which has its analogy in the doctrine of God. True, God is everywhere, 'but it is not his will that you should look for him everywhere'. There is a difference between the presence of God and the possibility of knowing him. As surely as the known God is our God and the unknown

God can never be our God, so surely must this distinction be preserved precisely as an expression of faith which holds by the revealed God and in so doing celebrates the uniqueness and the wonder of the revelation. So now it can also be said of the church that it is only known where the promise of God rests, in the visible church. Not there is it our church. But the believer who has become certain of his salvation in the visible church celebrates the wonder of this salvation precisely in daring to speak of a being of the church beyond the manifest church of salvation. He can never do this to negate the sole salvation through the visible church, he can never do it even for the sake of this or that pious man who stands outside, he can never do it to judge and to discover himself where the 'church beyond' is. It remains unknown, believed in by the church of salvation so as to praise all the more highly the glory of the known revelation of salvation. Woe to those who make this, the last possibility of faith of the church which lives by faith, *extra ecclesiam nulla salus*, into a presupposition for their pious speculation on the saved and the lost. This is not our task. We must rather flee from the temptation of such questions to the manifest salvation of God in the true church.

The question of the boundaries of the church can become a temptation for faith. But it should only serve to make faith more certain. It is the cause of the church to make this continually clearer and to make the congregation more certain of its salvation in any decision about its boundaries. G.S. II pp. 217–41

This paper is really a discussion on the boundaries of the church, and clearly states Bonhoeffer's attitude to the German Christians, an attitude not always shared by his colleagues in the Confessing Church. But he was forcing them to face up to the consequences of their acts at Barmen and at Dahlem. The article led to vigorous discussion, which is taken up in the following extract from an article by Helmuth Gollwitzer.

96

The vigorous discussion which resulted from Dietrich Bonhoeffer's article in the June issue of *Evangelische Theologie* indicates the urgency of the question by which the whole church is troubled today – and will be troubled still more when pressure from outside forces the individual parts of the Christian church still more closely together. Since the law for the security of the German Evangelical Church of 24th September, 1935, once again meant to do away with the whole question by a union of the disputing 'groups', the National Church committee itself has had to forego this union at one point and to draw a dividing line between the church and the German Christians of Thuringia – a division whose seriousness and legitimacy is of course disputed with notable objections by the German Christians of Thuringia. So even the committees are involved in the problems of the question which they wanted to avoid. But the very urgency of the question shows that it is necessary to clear up some of the misunderstandings over Bonhoeffer's remarks which have arisen and on the other hand to bring into the light a number of hesitations.

The basis of Bonhoeffer's article comes in its first part. What is said there really leads on further – for the confessional problem as well – and cannot be given enough consideration. Unfortunately, too little notice has been taken of it. Criticism of individual sentences of Bonhoeffer's has shown what a rare art reading correctly and understanding in context is. It seems that by the time some readers reached the third part of the article they had already forgotten the first part and no longer remembered that this last part was only to be understood within the framework mapped out by the first part. Parts were taken in isolation, and these were all the more unexpected because Bonhoeffer himself sought to safeguard his own understanding immediately after his most incriminating sentence. This sentence is Bonhoeffer's exposition of *extra ecclesiam nulla salus*: 'Whoever knowingly cuts himself off from the Confessing Church in Germany cuts himself off from salvation'.[1] The 'knowingly' should be underlined; it means in a clear decision against the confession of the Confessing Church. Bonhoeffer stresses that this is not his invention; the church has 'always' thought this way. And he is right. The question of the true church cannot be separated from the question of the soul's salvation. It is a matter of *articuli fundamentales,* of clauses of the Christian faith necessary for salvation. Otherwise the church struggle would be priests' bickering.

Bonhoeffer's sentence is not to be understood legalistically: he opens his article by saying that the question of the boundaries of the church derives from a legalistic concept of the church. The church looks not to its boundaries but to its Lord; its own boundary is hidden from it and therefore can always only encounter it. This 'allowing itself to be encountered', over which it has no control, happens precisely in the fact that it has no 'ultimate unequivocal standard to use' lying ready to hand where despite difference or in view of a difference it can no longer recognise communion of faith and preaching. Bonhoeffer's much attacked sentence cannot therefore serve as an empirical statement; it is not a clue to a statistic of participation in salvation by means of red, green, or grey cards. This becomes still clearer in the following section: it is not a speculative sentence for enumerating the saved and the lost; the sentence only has significance as address, offer, admonition, as the summons of preaching to take the object of the battle and the 'church political' decision seriously. What is meant is this: If you knowingly cut yourself off from the confession of the Confessing Church you cut yourself off from salvation (whereby the freedom of God over his gift of salvation is not restricted; as Bonhoeffer rightly says, preaching has nothing to say about this). Understood in this way, however, the sentence means no more than what Luther said in the Augsburg Confession: *reddidistis Deo sacrificium electum confessionis . . . ut, qui non crediderint, sint inexcusabiles.* Understood in any other way it

---

[1] cf pp. 93–4

would be sheer nonsense. And some people will have to ask themselves whether they did not attribute this nonsense so readily to Bonhoeffer because they did not want to take the first sentence of the Declaration of Barmen as seriously as Luther took the first sentence of the Augsburg Declaration.

Reference to this point cannot be made without the raising of doubts about the formulation of Bonhoeffer's sentence. The term 'Confessing Church' can mean the visible group of people – or the confession that gathers the congregation. Only in the second sense can it be said that the Confessing Church is 'the one true Church of Jesus Christ in Germany'. That should then mean in more accurate and more unmistakable language: Their confession is that of the true church. They must say that if their confession is to be taken as at all serious and authoritative. But in the first sense even the Confessing Church is an *ecclesia mixta*. This must be stressed less against Bonhoeffer himself than against some others who are not clear that by *ecclesia vera* is meant the church of true proclamation and not the *ecclesia proprie dicta* (the *coetus vera credentium*). The Church of Jesus Christ 'is' neither the Lutheran nor the 'Confessing' nor the Roman Catholic Church, but simply the one Christian church in which the Lord has accepted us through baptism; any Confessing Church is no more than part of the one Christian church which in confirmation of its baptism and today furthermore in repetition of its confirmation vow (the red card means that and no more!) – has assembled round the right voice of the Christian church, rejecting its false voices. Our present controversies suffer very much from the lack of clarity in these distinctions.

The very problem of the neutrals shows that the language here must be circumspect. Bonhoeffer calls it even 'a special problem'. He raises all the questions which present themselves here; but one cannot say that his answers as he gives them here are in themselves satisfactory ones; it was a good thing that he himself limited their significance with the explanation that he did not want to anticipate the decision of the church, but only to remind it of what was necessary. Probably nothing more can be said in general terms than what Bonhoeffer says right at the beginning, that the neutrals are in a 'questionable position', determined by Matt. 12. 30 and Mark 9. 40. It might even be enough for a serious address to this stratum which believes that it may remain undecided or preserve some special concern in the face of this struggle between the true and the false voices of the church. Bonhoeffer's further declaration that whoever preached the pure Gospel and still offered obedience to the Pope or to the government of the National Church was a 'false teacher and a misleader of the congregation' compels us to ask him whether he does not think that here he has a clear measure of the boundaries of the church, in obedience to the false church government. It is hard to see how he can avoid a 'legalistic' understanding of the concept of the church here.

Furthermore, obedience to a church government is a very multifarious concept; it extends from the recognition of this government as the central place of administration to subscription to episcopal leadership. Precisely with regard to the neutrals the fact that the church does not draw her boundaries but comes up against them must be taken seriously. General judgements are not in place here, serious as the general danger is in which a neutral finds himself with his preaching if by his action in the church he gives his preaching the same sort of commentary and the same sort of context as it would have if he were in the ranks of the false church government. The neutrals and similarly the so-called 'better German Christians' will have to be told that they are incurring the guilt of hypocrisy. When in the years before the World War the church of the Bavarian district was stirred up by the controversy with the moderate liberals (Geyer and Rittelmeyer) this was the charge which one of the positive spokesmen in the dispute, the church council of Nägelsbach, made, at the same time rejecting the consequence of drawing boundaries around the church: 'As long as deviation from the confession does

100

not progress from tacit reticence over the saving facts to the open rejection of them, tolerance has always been recommended, but of course only such tolerance as clearly designates as evil the evil still to be tolerated and thus firmly avoids the idea that it is completely justified.' Our verdict today must be analogous to this attitude and thus remain in the line of the judicious words with which the preface to the Formula of Concord speaks of Christians in church districts with other doctrines.

The Confessing Church has raised the claim that in itself the voice of the true church has come to be spoken. But the explanation which Bonhoeffer gives of this is impossible. The Confession of the church is not the Word of God but the church's testimony of the Word of God. It is not God, but the church which has spoken at Barmen and at Dahlem, however great the part played by God may be thought to have been. It is hard to see why that should not be enough. Anything more than that would contradict the statements of Barmen (see the first article[1] and the appeal to the congregations). As long as he takes Barmen seriously, Bonhoeffer cannot mean what must be and has been assumed from his formulation. There is no clearer and firmer barrier against any heresy than has been erected by the Barmen Declaration in its statements. It is regrettable that with his remarks Bonhoeffer has furthered an artificial misunderstanding brought about by the confessionalistic side of the common word that 'has been put into the mouth of the Synod'.

Studious people, who would make the Barmen Declaration itself heretical despite the unmistakable state of affairs, have taken that up eagerly. Against them nothing can be surrendered in the element of truth of Bonhoeffer's statements. The church may believe of the Synod of Barmen, as it believes of the Augsburg Confession, that

---

[1] 'The undisputed basis of the German Evangelical Church is the Gospel of Jesus Christ, as it is recorded in Holy Scripture and brought newly to light by the Reformation Confessions. The power which the church needs for her mission is determined and limited by this.'

here there has been an act of God precisely because at Barmen it has not, as Schlatter wrongly thinks, denied the action and the guidance of God in our lives. Anyone who can see nothing but heretical arbitrariness in this belief overlooks the fact that it is grounded not in the enthusiasm of the hour but in the fact that at Barmen the church saw itself led through God's work to God's Word. In that case he may say that it is heresy when in respect of the Augsburg Confession Luther writes under the picture of his elector this verse:

> *I suffer for the sake of God's Word,*
> *I confess it from the bottom of my heart freely . . .*
> *God gave me this special gift*
> *And to the world it seemed a miracle . . .*

or when Georg Major calls the Augsburg Confession '*doctrinae normam tunc Spiritu Sancto dictante a Melanthone perscriptam*' or when the Formula of Concord says that the doctrine of the best articles of our Christian doctrine have been brought to light in the Reformation *immensa Dei Optimi Maximi bonitate atque miseratione*, or when Lutheran dogmatic theologians call the books of the symbols *theopneustoi* and stress that in respect of their heavenly and divine material *periculosum est sine adjecta declaratione libros symbolicos humana scripta appellare*. He can dispute that it is appropriate to speak in this way in the case of Barmen and can offer proof of this, but he will not be able to reject this way of speaking *a priori* as heretical. In this he may remind himself that Karl Barth of all people has described the better knowledge of the provisional character of the church's confession and of its difference from the Word of God as an advantage of reformed thought over the Lutheran, 'God's Word and Luther's doctrine' – the same Karl Barth who is now said to have become a heretic all of a sudden.

No less zealous has been the attack on Bonhoeffer's statement that with the Synod of Barmen the letter of the Augsburg Confession has been 'abandoned in a decisive way'. If Bonhoeffer meant by this that by the common stand in the Synod of Barmen the condemnation of article ten of the Augsburg Confession was repealed and Zwinglianism has been recognised as a doctrine of equal validity, then it is impossible to agree with him. In the Confessing Church the reduction of the Lord's Supper to a fraction of church tradition as a memorial meal is, one hopes, no less prohibited than before. The Declaration of Barmen does not contradict this condemnation, but includes it. It can stand before the letter of the Augsburg Confession. But should this condemnation of article ten of the Augsburg Confession be extended so that it is used to repudiate not only Zwinglianism but also the form of the Reformed eucharistic doctrine accepted today (and some parts of Lutheranism have indeed always made this extension and even today still insist on it), then we may be clear that not only the Confession of Barmen, but the mere fact of the Church Alliance of the German Evangelical Church contradicts the letter of the Augsburg Confession thus understood. It was indeed precisely such an alliance that Philip von Hessen planned and that was meant to be prevented by this condemnation. '*Utinam illa coniunctio impediatur. Nam mori malim quam societate Cinglianae causae nostros contaminari,*' wrote Melancthon at that time. There is no choice here: Either the reformed communities in Germany today fall under the condemnation of Augsburg, in which case the Church Alliance of the German Evangelical Church is contrary to the confession, or they do not fall under it, in which case the letter of the Augsburg Confession speaks as little against this Church Alliance with its common church government disposed in accordance with the confession as against a common Synod and, if it is required not by wilfulness but by obedience, a common confession. The concept of a Confessing Church, like that of a German Evangelical Church, can then be used without in itself representing an impermissible blurring of still extant differences. These differences as little stand in the way of so striking a demonstration of community as is represented by a Church Alliance, even with so 'improperly' used a title as

'church', as they already enable full unification. Only a false interpretation of article seven of the Augsburg Confession – taken as a
unity of schools – (which in that case however would completely
burst the concept of the 'Lutheran Church' current today) can be
advanced against this possibility.

The assertion that the eucharistic doctrine of many reformed
communities and theologians today is not as schismatic as Zwinglianism is a theological verdict for which the individual himself must
first and foremost take responsibility. It does not anticipate the
church's confirmation through which alone the two churches could
again become one, but it inquires after it. Neither Barth nor Asmussen nor anyone in the present provisional government of the German
Evangelical Church has disputed Breit's sentence: 'The coming
together in practice of the Lutheran Church and the Reformed
Church in doctrine and church order can only be made binding on
the churches by a church government firmly wedded to the Confession. The consensus reached in theological conversations does not
have this binding character.' This is not of course to decry the necessity of theological conversations and the significance of agreement in
them.

But in that case what can the 'Confessing Church' still be? The
title itself today arouses a great deal of suspicion among some who
would nevertheless number themselves among its members. But is
there not an artificial complication here? The Confessing Church is
the confessing remnant of the German Evangelical Church. It was
firmly established at Barmen itself and has since then been disputed by
none of the leading people that this remnant, like the original whole,
consists of Lutheran, Reformed and United congregations, pastors
and districts and that these differences have not yet been removed by
the newly given community of confession. This is not, however, on
the other hand to deny that the good confession made at 'Barmen'
was the obedient word of the true Church of Jesus Christ and that it
must be significant both for Lutherans and Reformed if they are

meeting without arbitrariness in the union of the confession of the true Church of Christ, in other words, if a 'partial confessing union' (Barth) has been achieved which came about without being planned by them and which they could have avoided only at the risk of disobedience to Holy Scripture. Now Bonhoeffer, as far as I can see, would not want to assert more than this *de facto* unanimity in the confession demanded today by the one Church of Jesus Christ. For neither he nor anyone else worth noticing has spoken of the theological curiosity of a 'new' church 'founded' at Barmen outside which there is no salvation; they have spoken of the true, permanent Church of Christ which has 'always' held its faith to be necessary for salvation, the church in the continuity of which men have been permitted to know thankfully, indeed 'in humility and wonder', that they stand wherever pastors and congregations have, in these three years, confessed their one Lord. We can ask in return whether any of Bonhoeffer's critics really believe that anyone who knowingly cuts himself off from the confession of the Lutheran Church does not cut himself off from salvation and what a Lutheran Confessional Church would be if they did believe that.

There has come about today what amounts to a judgement on the representatives of Lutheran confessionalism: they forget that the duty of theology is in the first place not the defence of a denomination but the self-criticism of a denomination before the Word of God, and in so doing they lose the most effective possibility of defence: the powerful, positive testimony of the glory of their confession. They do not call us with power to the same confession (as precisely those theologians attacked by them have done!) they have managed to find no word, not a single one suitable to win over even a single poor pagan (or a poor member of the Reformed Church), and to bring him to their side, to strengthen, to bind and to direct a Christian engaged in battle in the year 1936. They defend, instead of testifying and advancing in the consciousness of victory, and so their articles and writings have about them an unutterable tedium so that one is glad to finish reading them and waits until they at last understand that the Lutheran confession is badly served as long as the misrepresentation of other ideas and confessions is thought necessary for its defence. Anyone who calumniates individual theologians or whole denominations for views and statements which are not theirs only proves the suspicious nearness of confessionalism to a confessional politics in which the eighth commandment occurs as little as it does in the rest of politics.

We should be thankful that the Lutheran churches – roused from their long paralysis – allowed themselves at Barmen to be brought to an audible, pertinent confession of their faith and that in this they joined with the confessing remnant of the other denominations. In view of such a gift, we should not allow ourselves to be misled by people who again put the law before us as did the Jews in John 5. 10: 'It is not seemly that you should hold a synod with the Reformed church and join in a confession with it!' The Gospel preached by Martin Luther has made us understand this confession better than before. At this we rejoice. The Lord of the church does not subject us to any 'It is not seemly'; he turns away from the Jews and says to the lame man whom he has healed, 'See, you are well! Sin no more, that nothing worse befall you!' (John 5. 14).   G.S. II pp. 245–55

Much of the debate was of little value, but it served to show the arrangement of the battle in Germany over the nature of the true church. Bonhoeffer sums up the debate in a series of questions which, as he says, must be answered clearly by a synod.

QUESTIONS TO BE ANSWERED

Instead of entering straight away into discussion with all the statements and attacks which have been called forth by my article on the question of church union, I would first like to put just a few more quite simple questions. I can only ask those who have hitherto been content with arbitrary abbreviations and misrepresentations of my article to read all of it, and until they have done so I can simply leave aside all those debates from the green letters of Herr Eger to the purely German Christian press. As far as serious theological questions and hesitations have been expressed, for instance by Gollwitzer, Künneth, Sasse, etc., they will provisionally be taken up in the questions that follow. I am, however, of the opinion that these questions may not remain undiscussed between us and that we must also demand a completely clear answer to them if ambiguity is not to do away with all true fellowship. They are so simple that every layman understands them. They are so urgent that they cannot be left unanswered any longer without serious damage to the church. They will first become the subject of theological discussion, and then they must be answered by a synod.

First, *What is the Confessing Church?* Is it the Church of Jesus Christ in which the Word of God is preached purely and the sacraments are duly administered? Is it the place where brotherly love is practised, where prayer is made with promise, sins are forgiven and men suffer for Christ's sake? Is it the city on a hill, which cannot remain hidden, whose good works people see and praise their Father in heaven for them? Is the Confessing Church the church in the New Testament sense of the word, the church to whom the Spirit of God is promised and given? Is it the church which distributes the gift of salvation in the power of the Holy Spirit? Is it the church whose true communion makes us certain that we partake of salvation, the visible church in the world, but not of the world, the visible body whose members we are as long as we remain in it, from which we may not cut ourselves off for our souls' sakes? Is the Confessing Church therefore Christ's body with his own members, with proper church order, proper officers, proper church government? Has the government of this church been commissioned by Jesus Christ? Has it been entrusted with the care of souls? Is this Church government therefore authorised to undertake theological examinations, ordinations, institutions? Is it obliged for Christ's sake to bind pastors and congregations to itself? May and must it expect pastors and congregations to undergo suffering and persecution for this acceptance of the true church government? Is the Confessing Church therefore obliged to exercise doctrinal discipline and church discipline? Everything depends on the answer to these questions. If the answer is 'Yes', then the path of the Confessing Church from Barmen to Oeynhausen is consistent and inwardly necessary, its fight for the government of the church is a fight for the true church itself, i.e. for the salvation of the souls of the faithful; compromise at this point is a denial of the *status confessionis* and therefore the surrender of the church and its congregations to its enemies. The Confessing Church will of course always meet enemies in its free spreading of the glad tidings of the Gospel, who cut themselves off from it, whose communion it will seek, by the preaching of the Gospel, with intercession and hope, until its last offer of communion which can only consist in the fearless revelation of the full truth that they have cut themselves off from the true Church of Jesus Christ and are without promise. If the answer to these questions is 'No', then the struggle for the government of the church is flagrant selfishness; it would be impossible to see why young theologians should risk their existence to be examined, ordained and made pastors of the Confessing Church; the suffering of the imprisoned and expelled brethren for this cause would no longer be suffering for Christ and his cause and our intercession for them would be without promise; even discipline of doctrine and life would be impossible and the question of church communion does not exist as a responsibility and a decision for the Confessing Church at all; the Confessing Church can make no doctrinal decision, it is given over to false doctrine and into the hands of its foes, the Holy Spirit must have departed from it.

Or is the Confessing Church an alliance of Confessing Churches governed by a confession? Is it then not a church, but an organised association, the sort of alliance in which churches possibly mutually exclusive are joined together in doctrine and preaching? Or does such an alliance imply the equal rights of the churches which it comprises? How then are these equal rights justified by the confession? Where is the criterion of which churches have equal rights and which do not? Is it possible for this church to act and speak in common, and if so what guarantee does the confession provide? What is the significance of a common government of such an alliance, which cannot in any case have the character of church government?

Or is the Confessing Church a fighting fellowship, which has joined together for common confession and common action? Are we to understand by it that in view of the common enemy a common front has arisen, a 'confessing front'? Or does this expression merely hint that the existence of the Confessing Church is in many respects still so questionable that no more than this can or may be said about it?

Or is the Confessing Church really a Confessing movement, analogous to the manifold movements of our day? Is the Confessing Church the 'Confessing fellowship' of all those who want to make the confession effective in a 'Confessing movement'? In that case it would be a more or less private affair within or alongside the church, which in any case did not have any church authority and therefore no right to claim exclusiveness. It would exist as a movement, as a trend alongside other trends, and would have to content itself with that status; it would be a church political group. True, it would fight against the German Christians, but it could never deny their membership of the church. It would content itself with the strength of its influence and comfort itself with the fact that the few German Christians would be finished off in a free play of forces, but it would by no means understand that by the one single, perhaps quite honourable, spiritual, pious German Christian to whom this church accords an office the church would forfeit its promise as it would through the one, single non-Aryan Christian or pastor whom it knowingly let fall. A Confessing movement would never understand that the church in truth never rests on the ninety-nine Confessing pastors who will prevail against the one German Christian, but on the promise of God which can be taken even from the ninety-nine Confessing pastors if they knowingly make room for one false teacher in the church. Even a Confessing movement is at root German-Christian.

Secondly: *What is the confession of the Confessing Church?* Is the theological declaration of Barmen a confession binding on all members of the Confessing Church because it is a correct exposition of the Reformation confessions grounded in Holy Scripture, just as the Formula of Concord is a correct exposition of the Augsburg Confession? Is an obligation towards the Declaration of Barmen justified and necessary for members of the Examining Commission, for the teachers of the theological colleges of the Confessing Church or even at ordination – as is the practice in the Rhine province? Can a Lutheran refuse the Declaration of Barmen its character of a confession because it gives itself out to be only a 'Declaration', although even the *Solida Declaratio* of the Formula of Concord, the 'Declaration of some articles of the Augsburg Confession . . .' is numbered among the Lutheran Confessional writings? Are the Synods of the Confessing Church true Synods of the Church of Jesus Christ in so far as they stand by Scripture and confession in a right ordering? On this presupposition is their confession the testimony of the true church? Is it then not also the testimony of God, of the Holy Spirit himself, which requires obedience? Either the Declaration of Barmen is a true confession of the Lord Jesus Christ which has been brought about through the Holy Spirit, in which case it can make or divide a church – or it is an unofficial expression of the opinion of a number of theologians, in which case the Confessing Church has been for a long time on the wrong track. Is not the relative authority of the synods in the face of the Word of Scripture and the possibility of their error given full expression by the statement that their word in any event always remains 'under the Word' if it is to be a right word? Or is it true that 'of course God has not spoken either through Barmen or through the message of Dahlem differently from the way in which he speaks through all events of history' (Sasse)? Is

God's Word in his church and in the world – the all too German Christian world – really to be taken as the same here?

In what sense does the Confessing Church appeal to the Confessional writings and in what sense do the Lutherans of the Confessing Church appeal to the Lutheran Confessional writings? The letter of the Confessional writings rejects not only the Zwinglian, but also the Calvinistic eucharistic doctrine (*Formula of Concord sol. decl.* VII 2) and the Calvinistic doctrine of predestination (*Formula of Concord sol. decl.* XI) as both are still taught today by the Reformed brethren. To the Lutheran Confessional writings the Lutheran and the Reformed church are never churches whose confessions are of equal importance. The question is: Is the Confessing Church ready to revise individual judgements of the Lutheran Confessions by new research and new knowledge of Holy Scripture? Is it ready to inquire at all what Holy Scripture has to say on the matter? Is it further ready to give a decision different from that of the Confessional writings about matters of schismatic significance on the basis of new learning? Is it willing to recognise that a decision on church union has not been made once and for all, but that it must be made afresh at any given time on the basis of Scripture and the testimony of the church? Or is the word of the Confessional writings regarded as the unalterable basis of the church? Is the letter of the Confessional writings the only rule and norm for the exegesis of Scripture, against the view of the Confessing writings themselves? Or does the Confessing Church take the Lutheran Confessions seriously precisely by allowing itself to be referred back by them to Scripture as the only rule and norm? Is the Confessing Church ready to tolerate the charge of heresy from a false Lutheran orthodoxy, the charge which has been heard by everyone who has put Scripture above the confessional writings? In that case is it willing to bring up the Confessional differences in concrete form in a new examination of Scripture, instead of remaining in the realm of principles? Will it confess its doctrine of the eucharist, of predestination, and of the person of Christ?

Is the union of confession with the Reformed churches a way finally forbidden for Lutherans? Does the Word of God forbid once and for all the tolerance of differences between Reformed and Lutherans which cannot be got rid of in the one Confessing Church? Or does precisely this possibility of a right understanding of the Lutheran confessions remain open for the Word of God itself? If it remains finally closed, then the Confessing Church is really not a church, but one of the many factors mentioned which makes room for untruthfulness and falsification of the Gospel.

Thirdly: *What is church union?* Is church union and fellowship in the Word and Sacrament created by the Holy Spirit, or is it the union of all well-disposed, honourable, pious Christians whether their observance be German Christian, that of the church committees or that of the Confessing Church? Is church union founded only on the truth of the Gospel or on a love uncontrolled by the question of truth *Doctrina est coelum, vita est terra* (Luther). Is church union a question of preaching and the administration of the sacraments, or is it a question of personal sanctification? Does the union of prayer, intercession, forgiveness, repentance and discipline still have the promise if the union of the right faith has not been given? Is such union without this last anything but pious human work? Is the description 'false teacher' a moral or a religious value judgement, or is it the judgement of the Word of God on truth and untruth, which we can only pronounce with fear and trembling? Is the false teacher still our Christian brother? Does the distinction in the New Testament between the erring brother and the false teacher mean anything other than that the latter remains stubbornly in error despite brotherly warning and admonition and thus excludes himself from the brotherhood in the body of Christ? Is there true Christian communion and brotherhood in the New Testament sense without discipline of truth and life? Is there fellowship in the Holy Spirit without the Holy Spirit at the same time having the power to separate and to divide? Are we ready to hear what was justified in detail in the previous article, that the dissolution of fellowship is the 'strange' work of the church which it does in order to be able to fulfil its proper function, that the dissolution of fellowship is the last offer of fellowship? And vice versa: what is the significance of a union in Word which will not become a union in sacrament? What can the goal of union in the Word be if not union in the sacraments? What is the significance of a discipline which is exercised outwardly but neglected inwardly? How can the Gospel be strong enough to divide if it is too weak for union, for the *consolatio fratrum*, for forgiveness, repentance and penance?

What difference is there in the light of the confession between the church government of the German Christian National Church which contradicts the confession, and the church committees? If according to the statement of the Synod of Dahlem, obedience to the German Christian church government which contradicts the confession was disobedience to the Lord Jesus, we must ask how far obedience towards a church government of the committees which is also contradictory to the confession, is to be at all a venture of faith, a Christian freedom, a free decision of conscience? If the separation from the German Christian National Church that was demanded was not an impermissible law which was laid on the individual, why should the same demand made about the committees all of a sudden be 'unevangelical legalism'? Granted we find ourselves facing a different situation as far as people, experience and good will is concerned. In essentials, however, the situation is completely unchanged, namely in the way in which the claim of the church government contradicts both Scripture and confession. If anyone who despite the message of Dahlem remained obedient to the German Christian Church incurred the guilt of destroying the true Church of Christ by precisely this obedience to a false church government, it is hard to see how the person who is obedient to the church committees does not also fall under the same judgement. Any distinction made here on understandable personal or church-political considerations without justification from Scripture and confession in the end gives false teaching a place in the Church of Christ.

It is not an easily understood will of God that so rends us inwardly at a time when a common defence against the outside enemy would be so necessary. We cannot go against this will. Only one thing is to be left us, his word, his sacrament, his promise. We ask for nothing else. For from this gift derives the incomparable gift of true fellowship in faith, in prayer, in intercession, in brotherly service, in forgiveness, in penance, in discipline, in the recognition of our sins and the mercy of Jesus Christ. Here lies our proper work, the proper work of the church.

G.S. II pp. 255–63

It is clear that Bonhoeffer is here fighting a battle on two fronts. Since the Synod at Bad Oeynhausen on which he had already commented,[1] he had a battle with the Confessing Church to bring it to a realisation of what it had done at Barmen and at Dahlem. In August 1935, he had shown something of what this meant in his paper on, 'The Confessing Church and the Ecumenical Movement'.[2] A year later, he is in the midst of the same controversy, having committed himself even further with such outlandish statements as, 'Whoever separates himself from the Confessing Church in Germany, separates himself from salvation.' This battle raged. But again referring back to the August 1935 paper, the battle raged equally on the ecumenical front.[3] He had obtained the support of the ecumenical movement at Fanö and he pressed this home. The conference planned for this year in Chamby was important, not only because both the Confessing Church and the National Church Council would be represented, but also because this might well be the last ecumenical conference at which the Confessing Church would be present. It had special importance because of its task, to prepare for Oxford 1937. Bonhoeffer assessed all this with the mastery of a statesman and insisted on the importance of remaining in Switzerland with

[1] The last national Synod of the Confessing Church held at Bad Oeynhausen 17th–22nd February 1936.

[2] *No Rusty Swords,* pp. 326–44.   [3] *No Rusty Swords,* pp. 292–5.

Bethge for at least two weeks after the conference. He intended to help draft a message from the council to be addressed to Hitler. He attended to practical difficulties explaining to Bethge how he might manage about money. 'I've got no money. That's dreadful. Now I must travel on invitation. That holds good for the two of us, but not for more than two! . . . You must get your mother to send 10 RM in your name *poste restante*, Basel, Switzerland. Only parents can do that. I'm also having two lots of 10 RM sent' (*from a letter of 13th August*).

Bonhoeffer and Bethge went to Chamby and stayed on. Their mission accomplished, they spent a short holiday in Italy. The memory of that holiday remained with Bonhoeffer through his difficult and dark days ahead and he refers to it in his letters from prison to Bethge. During his time in Switzerland, he had not managed to contact Karl Barth. This led to a third exchange of correspondence between the two warriors.

Finkenwalde, 19th September, 1936

BONHOEFFER TO BARTH: When I was in Switzerland recently, I very much wanted to visit you, not having seen you for so long. I gather that my friend Sutz had already said that I was coming, unfortunately at a time which I did not suggest to him at all. I have now heard that you waited in vain for Sutz and me one Sunday afternoon. I'm dreadfully sorry. I always find it overwhelming to think that I am taking up a great deal of your time by visiting you when you are already being deprived of it on all sides. And I certainly would not do it if I did not have something of the utmost importance. This time I really would have been glad to do it and then it was too late. It grieved me very much. Now I must at least write to you, as I have really kept silent for long enough. Our last encounter was a telephone conversation in which I was to invite you to Berlin for Jacobi. Since you wrote to me in England that time that I was to return by the next ship[1] or failing that by the ship after next, you have heard nothing from me in person. I must ask you to excuse me

[1] *No Rusty Swords*, pp. 237–40.

for that. But the arrow did strike home! I think it really was the ship after next on which I came home. Now I have been back here eighteen months; in many respects I am glad that I was over there, but I am still more glad that I am back here again. There are all sorts of reasons for my not having written since then. I have always thought that if I write to you I ought to have something reasonable to write, and I never had anything reasonable, at any rate, anything that I thought it worth while bothering you with. Nor have I even now.

Then I really wanted first of all to come to some sort of conclusion about the questions which the Bible raised for me and which kept on bothering me, though of course I also recognised time and again that in some respects I was probably departing from your views. The whole period was basically a constant, silent controversy with you, and so I had to keep silence for a while. The chief questions are those of the exposition of the Sermon on the Mount and the Pauline doctrine of justification and sanctification. I am engaged in a work[1] on the subject and would have asked and learnt a very, very great deal from you. Most of us who feel that they had to keep away from you for a while for theological reasons of some sort seem to find that afterwards, in a personal conversation with you, they learn that once again they have seen the whole question in far too crude terms. Now I am earnestly hoping for another opportunity of seeing you and talking to you at length. Finally I must say for the sake of clarity – I have said it to no one else – that I felt myself somewhat excluded from your circle by not taking part in your Festschrift. I would very much have liked to write a contribution for you; please do not misunderstand that. I simply took it as an objective verdict that I was not counted as one of the theologians associated with you. I was sorry about it, as I know that it is not true. So, those were the reasons why I kept silent for so long.

Work at the seminary gives me great joy. Academic and practical

[1] *The Cost of Discipleship*, SCM Press, 1959.

work are combined splendidly. I find that all along the line the young theologians coming into the seminary raise the very questions that have been troubling me recently, and of course our life together is strongly influenced by this. I am firmly convinced that in view of what the young theologians bring with them from the university and in view of the independent work which will be demanded of them in the parishes – particularly here in the East – they need a completely different kind of training which life together in a seminary like this unquestionably gives. You can hardly imagine how empty, how completely burnt out most of the brothers are when they come to the seminary. Empty not only as regards theological insights and still more as regards knowledge of the Bible, but also as regards their personal life. On an open evening – the only one in which I shared – you once said very seriously to the students that you sometimes felt as though you would rather give up all lectures and instead pay a surprise visit on someone and ask him, like old Tholuck, 'How goes it with your soul?' The need has not been met since then, not even by the Confessing Church. But there are very few who recognise this sort of work with young theologians as a task of the church and do something about it. And it is really what everyone is waiting for. Unfortunately I am not up to it, but I remind the brothers of each other, and that seems to me to be the most important thing. It is, though, certain that both theological work and real pastoral fellowship can only grow in a life which is governed by gathering round the Word morning and evening and by fixed times of prayer. And it is in fact only the consequence of what you have made very clear in 'Anselm'. The charge of legalism does not seem to me to fit at all. What is there legalistic in a Christian setting to work to learn what prayer is and in his spending a good deal of his time in this learning? A leading man in the Confessing Church recently said to me: 'We have no time for meditation now, the ordinands should learn how to preach and to catechise'. That seems to me either a complete misunderstanding of what young theologians are like today or a culpable ignorance of how preaching and catechism come to life. The questions that are seriously put to us today by young theologians are: How do I learn to pray? How do I learn to read the Bible? If we cannot help them there we cannot help them at all. And there is really nothing obvious about it. To say, 'If someone does not know that, then he should not be a minister' would be to exclude most of us from our profession. It is quite clear to me that all these things are only justified when alongside them and with them – at just the same time! – there is really serious and sober theological, exegetical and dogmatic work going on. Otherwise all these questions are given the wrong emphasis. But I do not mean to ignore these questions about everything in the world; they are what I am concerned with! And these are just the things that I would most have liked to discuss with you.

Unfortunately I am at the moment involved in a big battle over my article on church union. They are getting frightfully excited about it. And I thought that I was writing something obvious. I would very much have liked to have heard a word from you on the matter. But I really won't trouble you with it. We must now fight it out ourselves. That is also probably a good thing. But I would like to make one large request of you. I think it would be very important for the present situation if some of the questions of substance which divide Lutherans and Reformed could be brought into the open and discussed. But as far as I know there is no one in Germany who could do it, as Sasse's arguments are always completely formal and so too are all the statements of our opponents. No one knows enough. The overall view is lacking and still more the time in which to acquire it. There is the need of a worthy successor to Schneckenburger's book (*Vergleichende Darstellung des lutherischen und reformierten Lehrbegriffs*, Stuttgart 1855). Oughtn't you to get the conversation going again? In its present form it is simply wasting time. That is a great deal to ask. But I believe that it would also be a great service. I certainly do not mean to underestimate the significance of the periodic appearance of *Theologische Existenz Heute*. But you yourself know the danger that many theologians now get everything from it. It is imperative for them to be confronted once again with some really hard, solid stuff in the form of such a book.

Now I will stop. There is much that one can only discuss in person. I am looking forward to that very much.

Bergli, Oberrieden, 14th October, 1936

BARTH TO BONHOEFFER: After my brief acknowledgement from Hungary you will now have a rather more appropriate answer to your letter of 19th September.

On that Sunday afternoon I did in fact expect you here from one minute to the next until a telephone call with Sutz cleared up the matter. So I was all the more pleased to hear from you by letter in such detail. You could have written to me with a quiet conscience long ago, even if in the meanwhile you were describing some theological curves which did not run quite parallel to my own. What claim do I have on you, that you should owe me a solemn reckoning? Do you know the only thing I knew about you for a long time after that business of the 'ship after next'? The strange news that you intended to go to India to take over from Gandhi or some other friend of God there a spiritual technique, for the application of which in the West you promised great things! But then a year ago your Inspector Rott was here with me and saw to it that the picture became a bit more exact.

You should not draw such tragic conclusions from the fact that you were not invited to contribute to the Festschrift! I am quite sure that Wolf had no intention at all of exercising anything like a censorship on the invitations which he sent out then. For some reason you were not just in his line of vision, or in more concrete terms, he had probably forgotten you; there was certainly no question of an 'objective verdict'. Besides, I did not think that there was much reason for speaking of a 'circle' particularly associated with me. On the one hand I would find it very difficult to say where (within the possibilities that can be considered, i.e. leaving aside German Christians, Papists, etc.) this circle ceased, while on the other hand I would also find it very difficult to say where it began in a rather more definite sense. As far as I am concerned you are certainly nearest to me when you do not make the question whether you are 'inside' or 'outside' a matter of special reflection but cheerfully leave it open from day to day.

So now I also hear from you in person that you are particularly concerned both theoretically and practically with the inexhaustible theme of justification and sanctification. I am all agog for your results, both as regards your intended book and also as regards the new possibilities your seminary will bring to light. You will not expect me to do other than look at the matter openly, but not without concern. Openly, because it is clear enough to me that new questions must continually be raised in life and doctrine, and attempts must be made, because we really cannot imagine that in the church's preaching and the form of its life we have even from a distance found our way to the truth which bears in on us in almost incomprehensible abundance from Scripture and confession. Not without concern, because for the past fifteen years now I have been under an almost ceaseless hail of objections, 'concerns', suggestions for expansion and improvement, precisely in respect of this theme whose basic rightness I could not or would not ever dispute, but in the concrete realisation of which I would immediately have to see a return to the fleshpots of Egypt. I am thinking of the Religious Socialists, the Wuppertal pietists in the decade before the church struggle and most recently of the Oxford people with Emil Brunner. You will understand that I have gradually developed the impression of there being a common denominator here, resignation in the face of the original Christological-eschatological beginning in favour of some kind of realisation (in fact becoming more and more abstract) in a specifically human sphere. You will also understand that I have become more and more critical in this direction – without being able to deny the rightness of the question in principle – and am watching more and more closely to see whether these ever repeated announcements, of better solutions, do not once again amount to giving up the sparrow in the hand in favour of the dove on the roof. And now I can already see that particularly among the present young men of the Confessing Church a further wave of this nature is in the offing in which all the earlier stuff will acquire a new topicality and it may well be that you are the very ones who are called and are capable of being leaders and spokesmen here. If this is no blind uproar, I hope that I am not too old to learn this time what there is to learn and to correct my books where necessary, as I have already done in another respect. But you must understand also if I temporize at first. There are reasons why on occasions I could point not unemphatically to the Tholuck possibility – the thing then meant quite a lot to a certain group of my students at whom I was aiming – but have not now become a second Tholuck. If I see it rightly, you are now in the process of as it were bringing that statement into a theoretical-practical system. I have every sympathy with that. I cannot say straight away that it is impossible. But I must look very carefully to see how the hare runs so that perhaps I shall be able to say to you that I too feel what you are thinking of to be possible. Unless I am mistaken, it was Rott who showed me this summer the advice on scriptural meditation which was adopted in your seminary.[1] I read it carefully, but I can hardly say that I am very happy about it. I cannot go with the distinction in principle between theological work and devotional edification which is evident in this piece of writing and which I can also perceive from your letter. Furthermore, an almost indefinable odour of a monastic eros and pathos in the former writing disturbs me; true, it would represent a new possibility compared with previous experiences in this field, but at the moment I still have neither a positive feeling nor a use for it. Do not regard this as a

[1] Cf. pages 57 ff.

criticism of your efforts, simply because the basis of my knowledge and understanding of them is still far too scanty. But you will at least understand from this the questions that I would put to you despite all my sympathies.

I doubt if I shall get round to the improved edition of the Schneckenburger work in the foreseeable future. Would it be at all possible to avoid the formalism in the treatment of the confessional problem up to now, which you so rightly bewail, if we made this problem as such the theme? I expect more of this if both the Lutheran and the Reformed side begin to work out with a totally new seriousness what is peculiar to each of them on the basis of the 'new', or rather completely old, insights, and the decision in the confessional question is left to God, according to the Barmen formula or to the particular importance of what emerges. In addition to this, simple historical studies of the dilemmas of the sixteenth and seventeenth centuries could do good hermeneutical service. As well as this, after the long spell of *Theologische Existenz Heute*, the second volume of my *Dogmatics*, which is to come out D.V. at the end of the winter, should to some extent provide further 'hard, solid stuff'.

Enough for today. Be assured of my warmest sentiment and my serious concern in your work.   G.S. II pp. 283–91

The year 1936 was the only complete year that Finkenwalde had. At the end of that year, in a fashion peculiar to Germans, Bonhoeffer attempted to assess what the year had meant for the seminary. He put most of his conclusions into the annual report sent to former students and friends.

BONHOEFFER'S REPORT FOR 1936

Mark 7. 37. 'He has done all things well'
Finkenwalde, 21st December, 1936

'He has done all things well.' This is what we should say at the end of this year about every week, every hour that is past. We should go to pray with this word until there is no longer an hour of which we did not want to say 'He has done all things well'. Those very days which were hard to us, which troubled us and worried us, days which have left behind in us a trace of bitterness, should not fade from our minds today until we have been able to confess humbly and thankfully even of them, 'He has done all things well.' We should not forget, but overcome. That happens through giving thanks. We should not solve the insoluble riddle of the past and sink into fretful grumbling but leave even the incomprehensible as it is and surrender it peacefully into God's hands. That is done through humility. 'He has done all things well.'

But the most fearful torment still remains: My guilt, my guilt! My negligence in my office, my unfaithfulness in serving the community, my ungratefulness, my anger, my idleness at prayer, my utterly stubborn, despairing, unhappy heart – what about that? The evil fruits of my sin have influence without end. How am I to put an end to it? And yet you are no Christian, but only harden yourself in your sin if you cannot say even of your guilt, HE has done all things well. That does not mean that we have done all things well. Do you believe it? It is the ultimate, the most astonishing recognition of the Christian that in the end he can say even of his sin, He has done all things well. He has helped me to find him even through my sin. He has finally covered all my sin.

Only now do we rightly know the meaning of 'He has done all things well'. He has healed us. He was there and at work all the time. Only now too can we truly thank him for all the good we have received, thank him for the glory of our office, for our work, for the daily Word, for brotherly fellowship, for all kind of personal help and guidance, for the preservation of body and soul from all manner of great evil and danger. Now all the past is swallowed up in the one joy, He has done all things well.

Over the past year God the Lord has deigned to give our Confessing Church great questions, great tasks and great sufferings. Since the intervention of the state church committees in the life of our church, the Confessing Church has suffered great shocks. There have been hard decisions for you, dear brethren, in the parishes. You have had to lead the struggle and in so doing have gone through much questioning, doubt and temptation. Our service here in the house was able to consist chiefly in continuing our work quietly and straightforwardly. Our way was shown clearly.

We have been assembling together every day in the old way to pray, to read the Bible and to praise our God, and as we have done so we have thought of you. Similarly at the end of the day there have been devotions and intercessions for all the concerns of our church for your work and for your struggle. You know that we have joined with you all in our daily time of meditation and have prayed for one another before God. It was a great delight to us that over and above the confines of our brotherhood some members of congregations far and near have also joined our meditations, and we should also keep them in our thoughts. We should also let ourselves be reminded to keep up faithfully the morning half-hour each day of considering the Scriptures and interceding. Each of us knows the needs, the inner contradiction, the laziness, which keep on wanting to hold us up, and how to search out what we have recognised as our salvation. We have still been given time and admonition. If one person goes astray, that is a visible or an invisible weakening of every one else in the fellowship of prayer. Let us not despise God's gift.

As well as meditation, however, daily, plentiful reading of Scripture must keep its place. No day of our life in office may go past without our having read the Bible on it. The very controversies of the last months have once again clearly shown to our shame how unversed in Holy Scripture we still are. How ready people were to make the decision for or against the church committees dependent on all sorts of contingencies of this or that kind, instead of asking for and seeking out only the evidence of Scripture. Indeed, how little did people so often listen when the Bible was read out, and how readily did they swallow all the novelties. This must be changed. We must make it a rule to look for the scriptural evidence for every decision that confronts us, and not to rest until we have found it. Our confidence in dealing with the Bible must increase year by year. And there is something else. We know that it was quite a long time before some of the brothers who were arrested were given Bibles. Weeks like that can prove whether we have been faithful in our reading of Scripture and whether in our knowledge of Scripture we have acquired a great treasury.

Lectures and exercises stand now, as ever, under the shadow of biblical work. After dealing with the 'Discipleship of Christ' in the first course, the theme 'The Visible Church' followed in the second, 'The New Life in Paul' in the third and 'Concrete Ethics in Paul' in the present semester. It would take too long to tell you about the Old Testament, homilectic and catechetical work. A great deal of theological work has been done, from the first course onwards, but I believe that a certain climax has been reached in it with the present course. While I am writing this report, a two and a half day long disputation is going on, from morning to evening, on 'The preaching of the Law'. For some weeks a chosen group of brothers has been working in all its free time to prepare this disputation. We can be grateful for the clarification and the furthering of our knowledge and our insights in many important spheres. But at the same time, our community is knit more closely together by this common work on a question which is so significant for our church today.

We have made music, as ever, with great joy. In default of any instruments in Zingst, the first course was predominantly active in singing. The second course at Finkenwalde had two grand pianos and tremendous soloists! The third and fourth sing and make music together. On the third Sunday in Advent we had a musical evening for the parish and the friends of the house, which was repeated in the church at Podejuch. We were able to assemble quite a respectable orchestra for it. It was a great delight to all of us, and I for one cannot imagine our common life here without daily music-making together. We have certainly driven out some evil spirits that way.

Although the quietness of domestic life and work must be the real purpose of the short time at the seminary, each course has also had a glimpse of life beyond our walls. In the spring, we accepted an invitation to Sweden. For most people this trip was the first encounter with the Church of Christ beyond the borders of Germany, with the ecumenical world. We were given a most hearty welcome, and ten days were almost overfilled with seeing, hearing and meetings. The friendship and the love we found there enriched us on our return. Thanks for this time will be equally alive in all of us. For another purpose, the summer course went from the house for almost the same time to a popular mission together in the Belgard district. Four brethren each were housed in six villages; they preached on four evenings of the week and on Sunday. In the evenings these four each expounded a text for ten minutes. This combined proclamation, which derives from shared daily work in the parish and shared prayer, commended itself to all the brethren involved and, we hope, to the parish. After long weeks of silence it is a special delight to be able to preach the Gospel again. So this popular mission week has strongly influenced the whole semester. One special benefit from this week has been that since then we have kept close contact with several parishes and a number of people, and that we are continually given indications of Christian love and readiness to help. We have much reason for gratitude.

Several missionary weeks have been requested for this winter semester; the brethren of the community have already held some and will hold more. We hope to have another popular mission to one of the districts here with the whole seminary at the end of January.

It was a special delight to have the older brethren with us again for their annual reunions at the beginning of the last two semesters.

Despite some abnormality and unrest which this produces at the beginning of the semester, it is good for the older and the younger brethren to get to know each other in this way, and it makes settling in much easier for the new course. We had busy and happy days of reunion. Time at the seminary is so short, and the gap between life in the seminary and the solitariness of work in a village is so great and brings with it such important questions, that this yearly meeting is an urgent necessity and a real help. Of course there are individual letters and visits in between. The reports of brethren on their work have already grown into quite a large volume, and are studied thoroughly by brethren who visit us from time to time. We also try to serve the brethren in parishes by the circular letter which goes out from the house each month, by the short report on the house, the goings-on of the older brothers, the notification of texts for meditation and preaching aids. But all this only gains its full value through the annual reunions. Let us keep to them.

During this year almost all the brethren of the first and second courses have been ordained. We have been thinking of you particularly on these days. God grant you a great love for your parish and the strength to preach the uncurtailed Gospel.

We do not want to end this survey without thinking of the three brethren who during the course of this year have cut themselves off from our church and have put themselves at the disposal of the church committees. This has been a great grief to us. Our words here have no longer been enough. And in their life and their office we commend them to the grace of God in prayer.

The group of parishes and friends which gives regular help to our house has grown. We recognise here the gracious guidance of God, who by this leads us even more to recognise our own failings and to give thanks. Many gifts have shamed us. We have been done great services. They summon us to be even more faithful to our work than before.

There is the report. Much has happened, and yet we recognise that we have done nothing worth mentioning before God. We acknowledge that everywhere we have lagged far behind what should have been done. We owe much to our office and to each other. So once again we will let ourselves be surrounded by his forgiving love and thankfully confess: Not we, but HE has done all things well. And as we look to the New Year we hear, 'Commend your ways to the Lord and hope on him, HE will do all things well.'

G.S. II pp. 506–12

3. The Beginning of the Fateful Year 1937

The year 1937 was a year of destiny for the Confessing Church and for that reason also for Bonhoeffer. He saw the difficulties likely to arise and prepared for them at Finkenwalde. The need to remain in touch with the churches abroad came out again in a memorandum he drafted for the exchange of students.

MEMORANDUM ON AN EXCHANGE OF ORDINANDS AND THEOLOGICAL STUDENTS BETWEEN THE CONFESSING CHURCH AND FOREIGN CHURCHES

The encounter of the Confessing Church with the churches of the world is no chance one. The more a church is left to find itself afresh on its own basis, the more openly it seeks community with all churches with which it may know itself to be one in faith, love and hope. The more deeply a church comprehends its own nature, the more genuine will be its urge towards the ecumenical movement. The Confessing Church seeks in the ecumenical movement brothers in faith, with whom to believe, to pray, to fight and to suffer together. Christianity is forced by God as never before into a common responsibility by the present onslaught of world powers and new religions. The same powers and the same questions trouble churches far and wide. In this struggle, with which the churches are faced and in which they are to some extent already taking part, the churches must, for the sake of the Christian faith, listen to one another more and learn from one another more than they have done previously. As a result of this recognition, the desire has grown in the Confessing

Church for a regular exchange of young theologians of other churches with those of the Confessing Church.

The following suggestions might be made:

1. *Exchange of ordinands and young ordained ministers*

For this purpose, first consideration is to be given in the Confessing Church to the five preaching seminaries.[1] The Confessing Church invites young theologians of other churches (from England, as soon as possible after the end of the theological course, from Scandinavia as soon as possible after the practical course; the German ordinands have not only their theological study but also one and a half years' practical work behind them) to take part in a seminary course. This would include full participation in the common life of the brotherhood of the seminary. The way of life is extremely unpretentious. There is a fixed order of services throughout the day. Lectures are given on NT, OT, homiletics, catechism, pastoral work, dogmatics, music. About three hours per day, lectures and classes are taken by the director and inspector of the seminary, and also on occasions by theologians from outside. The greatest benefit from time spent at the seminary lies in the close common life of a brotherhood of theologians who are in the last stages of training for ordination together. It is a quiet time, but at the same time a very lively one. Foreign students would acquire a quite personal knowledge of the life and nature of the Confessing Church here. There are two semesters a year, from 15th April to 1st September, and from 15th October to 3rd March. During time at the seminar there are occasionally missionary preaching trips on which a foreign brother would have the opportunity to gain practical knowledge of church conditions and church work in Germany. For this purpose we recommend the preaching seminary at Finkenwalde, in which ecumenical interests are especially catered for. It is desirable that the foreign guest should have some knowledge

[1] Blöstau, Naumburg, Elberfeld, Bielefeld, Finkenwalde.

of German so as to be able to make better use of the short time available.

On the other side, we would ask for invitations to young German ordinands to go to a theological college or to one of the theological schools attached to the religious communities (like Mirfield or Kelham). But our invitation is not being made dependent on a reciprocal invitation from abroad.

11. *Exchange of students*

For this the two theological colleges of the Confessing Church in Berlin and Elberfeld are to be considered. Here, pastors and lecturers of the Confessing Church teach the following subjects: NT, OT, church history, history of dogma, dogmatics, ethics, and practical theology. It is possible here to be lodged either privately or in a seminary for students of the Confessing Church. Both Berlin and Elberfeld offer foreign students the possibility of acquiring a comprehensive knowledge of church life.

We would ask for invitations to German theological students to one of the institutions already mentioned.

We are very much concerned to bring about such an exchange as soon as possible, and herewith invite foreign students to the preaching seminary at Finkenwalde for the coming semester, 15th April to 1st September, 1937.   G.S. I pp. 268–70

The circular letters for the early months of 1937 contain several telling phrases. On Bonhoeffer's birthday, the students express the two hopes: that 'The Cost of Discipleship may be published before we retire!' and that a journey to England may be a possibility. 'We promise to obviate the language problem – we speak only English in the corridors!' A note not so lighthearted is, 'We have to tell you that Br. Koch is no longer in Berlin, but in Sachsenhausen "conversion camp". It is now more difficult to reach him!' (G.S. II p. 514).

On 19th February Bonhoeffer was in London for the Universal Christian Council for Life and Work. The minutes of this meeting show his increasing difficulties and his separation from those not belonging to the Confessing Church. (In many of the documents of this period, written in English, the word 'Bekennende' is wrongly translated 'Confessional', as in the following it should read 'Confessing'.)

MINUTES OF THE MEETING OF THE YOUTH COMMISSION

World Alliance for International Friendship through the Churches, Universal Christian Council for Life and Work

In London 19th February, 1937

Members present: Archdeacon Hunter (in the chair), Messrs. Bonhoeffer, Craske, Espy, Guillon, Henriod, Toureille, Zernoff.
By invitation: Messrs. Burlingham, Fenn, Oldham, Schönfeld, Miss Sichtig.

Apologies for absence were received from Signorina Rossi, Captain Bach, Pastor Udo Smidt, Rev. Sparring-Petersen and Dr. Strange. . . .

II. . . . With regard to the participation of youth at Oxford, Mr. Espy referred to the principle underlying the selection of the 100 youth visitors, ten of whom are to be co-opted by the Youth Commission, 50% of the remainder to be chosen from the Youth work of the actual churches, and 50% from the three international Christian Youth Movements of the YMCA, the YWCA, and the WSCF. The selection on this basis has required considerable organisational clarification in many countries, but it has met with general approval and the selections under the respective categories are going forward satisfactorily . . . Dr. Bonhoeffer expressed his regret that it has not been possible for him to do as much as he would have liked to, due to the conditions obtaining in Germany. He stated that he did not feel in a position to work on the same platform with other youth groups than those of the Confessional Church. Within his own circle, however, as Director of a Seminary of the Confessional Church he has been able to talk with the students about ecumenical problems, to give them lectures on the subject, and to discuss these questions regularly in private conversations. Talks are possible only in very small groups, but they are composed of people on whom one is able to rely and they feel the need of increased ecumenical understanding.

Dr. Bonhoeffer stated that he had been in touch with Pastor Udo Smidt to see whether he could take over the work of his field. He has not finally decided but has expressed his willingness at any rate to help, through his own organisation, in the preparation for the Oxford Conference.

As to the field of work, Pastor Bonhoeffer expressed the opinion that it seems almost impossible to combine under one secretary the work in Germany with that of other countries. Therefore the question of appointing another secretary for the regions outside Germany (Scandinavia, Austria, Hungary, Holland) should be seriously taken into consideration. Dr. Bonhoeffer expressed his especial thanks to Dr. Winterhager for his active assistance in the work in Germany....

VII. . . . The Commission gave special attention to the situation in Germany, where Dr. Bonhoeffer declared the differences between the churches to be so great that he would be unwilling to secure a German youth delegation in which the Reichskirche would be represented. The Commission maintained that this was contrary to the policy of the churches in Germany for official delegates, the decision having been reached at Chamby between the Reichskirche, the Lutherischer Rat and the Bekennende Kirche that each would contribute seven delegates towards a single German delegation of twenty-one persons. The Commission proposed that for the German Youth delegation of three persons representing the youth work of the actual churches, one be chosen from each of these groups. Upon Dr. Bonhoeffer's unwillingness to make the nomination for Germany on this basis, the Commission asked if he would obtain the nomination of one each from the Lutherischer Rat and the Bekennende Kirche, leaving the Youth Commission, through its Chairman, Secretary and M. Henriod, to negotiate direct for the third member. Dr. Bonhoeffer agreed to take the proposal under consultation with his colleagues in Germany, and to report his decision at an early date. The Commission authorized the Chairman, Secretary and M. Henriod to act as they found best, in the light of developments in Germany, after receiving Dr. Bonhoeffer's reply....

R. H. EDWIN ESPY, *Secretary*
G.S. I pp. 271–1

Bonhoeffer saw Herr Henriod of the Geneva staff on 19th February and later dictated a letter to him, which was sent from London after he had returned to Germany.

London, *24th February, 1937*

BONHOEFFER TO HENRIOD: In the not very enjoyable session on Friday, 19th February, you based the whole of your argument for the representation on the Youth Conference on your interpretation of the agreement made in Chamby. You stated as final that according to this agreement either all three groups of the German delegation had to be present or none at all. I already had to cast doubts on this interpretation of the agreement at the time. You insisted on it. I now consider it of prime importance that you should know that according to my present information through the Bishop of Chichester, who in fact carried on negotiations at the time, your interpretation is not acceptable. The view was rather that one German delegation, consisting of twenty-one delegates, should come; to fit in with the necessary internal German agreements, membership was fixed in the ratio of 7:7:7. It was not said that if one German group fell out another should be excluded from coming. The agreement about the composition of the delegation is regarded by the Bishop of Chichester as a purely internal German concern. I regret that our whole debate therefore began from an incorrect presupposition and must accordingly think out afresh my attitude towards the Youth Conference.

G.S. I p. 273

From Bonhoeffer's point of view, it was inconceivable that the national, the then central, group should be treated as a church! The attitude of Henriod must have seemed reasonable to most people at the time, but he had not understood the basis of Bonhoeffer's view. This is borne out by two further letters from Henriod.

10th March, 1937

HENRIOD TO BONHOEFFER: I was much surprised by your letter of 24th February, the more so as your report of the interpretation of the situation with regard to the German participation at the Oxford Conference by the Bishop of Chichester: 'The view was rather that one German delegation, consisting of 21 delegates, should come; to fit in with the necessary internal German agreements, membership was fixed in the ratio. 7:7:7', is exactly what I have repeatedly stressed at the meeting of the Youth Commission, according to the principle of the threefold representation and the choice on this basis to be made in Germany itself.

The Council was and is anxious that not one party but the three main parties within the German Evangelical Church be represented at Oxford.

The representation of the younger generation at the Oxford Conference cannot be regarded as an independent Youth Conference, but should preserve a similar representation from young people from the churches which have agreed to send official delegates to Oxford. This applies particularly to the 50 persons that the Youth Commission has been asked to nominate; the choice of the other 50 having been entrusted to the International Christian youth organisations, YMCA, YWCA and WSCF.

In view of the new situation created by the election of a synod it becomes necessary to postpone any final decision. This applies also to all the other delegates from Germany and we shall take up the question of the youth representatives direct from Geneva with the Church authorities after the election. This should not prevent you from consulting with Dr. Lilje and sending in any suggestions you may have as agreed upon at the Youth Commission meeting...

17th April, 1937

HENRIOD TO BONHOEFFER: Thank you for your letter of 24th March ... A discussion on the matter by letter is unsatisfactory and cannot prove fruitful. There never was and there is no question of a delegate from Heckel for the youth part of the conference. The youth representation at the conference cannot be regarded as an independent conference. It must be related to the churches which have accepted to take responsibility for it, and to such personalities as can best further work for 1939. We can only look at the whole preparation in terms of a great effort with a definite object and in terms of people who can best serve the task which we feel entrusted to us by God. The church situation is no more what it was when we discussed the matter in London at the Youth Commission. We do not want to put you into difficulties nor to have you do anything against your conscience. Therefore, in agreement with Espy, as administrative secretary of the Youth Commission I am asking you finally to nominate the one most qualified young person who can best serve the conference and later the home constituency. The other two will be taken from among the list of young people whose names we have received and who are engaged already in the preparations for Oxford. Please let Espy have your nomination by the end of April. It is necessary for the preparation of delegates that they know as long in advance as possible that they will be able to participate, and we cannot keep indefinitely places open at Oxford for hospitality, etc.

For any further exchange of correspondence concerning the Youth Section of the conference please deal with Espy.

G.S. I pp. 274–5

In April, a reunion was held at Finkenwalde of those students who had started two years before in the first course Bonhoeffer held after his return from London. It was to be the last reunion of its kind, because the seminary was closed in September 1937 by order of Himmler. The whole year was ominous with restrictions and arrests. It was not without a sense of drama that Bonhoeffer met his pioneers during the week 12th–17th April.

THE JUDAS SERMON

On 14th March in this critical year, Bonhoeffer had preached on the theme of Judas.

Matt. 26. 45b–50

Jesus had kept one thing from his disciples right up to the Last Supper. He had left them in no doubt about the path of suffering he was to tread. Three times he had told them that the Son of Man had to be delivered into the hands of sinners. But he had not yet revealed the deepest mystery to them. Only in their last hours together at the Passover meal could he say to them, The Son of Man is delivered into the hands of sinners – by treachery. 'One of you will betray me.'

By themselves, the enemy can have no power over him. It takes a friend for that: a close friend to give him up, a disciple to betray him. The most fearful thing of all happens not from outside, but from within. Jesus' path to Golgotha begins with the disciples' betrayal. Some sleep, that incomprehensible sleep in Gethsemane, one betrays him, and in the end 'all the disciples forsook him and fled'.

137

The night of Gethsemane comes to an end. *'Behold, the hour is at hand'* – the hour which Jesus had prophesied earlier, the hour of which the disciples had long known and at whose advent they trembled, the hour for which Jesus was so ready and for which the disciples were so utterly unprepared, the hour which nothing in the world could postpone any longer. 'Behold, the hour is at hand, *and the Son of man is delivered into the hands of sinners.'*

'Delivered,' says Jesus. That means that it is not the world that gets him in its grasp. Jesus himself is now handed over, surrendered, given up by his own. He is refused protection. No one will bother with him any more – Leave him to the others. That is, Jesus is thrown aside, the protecting hands of his friends are lowered. Let the hands of the sinners do what they will with him now. Let them assault him, those whose impious hands should never have touched him. Let them make sport of him, mock him, smite him. We cannot change that now. This is what delivering up Jesus means, no longer to take his part, to surrender him to mockery and the power of the public, to let the world take its feelings out on him, not to stand by him any more. Jesus is handed over to the world by his own. That is his death.

Jesus knows what is before him. Firmly and decisively he summons his disciples, *'Rise, let us be going.'* Often his threatening foes had to fall back before him, he went out freely through their midst, their hands fell. Then his hour had not yet come. Now it is here. Now he goes out to meet them of his own free will. And so that there shall be no doubt, so that it is absolutely clear that the hour has come in which he is to be delivered up, he says, *'See, my betrayer is at hand.'* Not a glance at the great crowd approaching, at the swords and clubs of the enemy. By themselves they would have had no power! Jesus fixes his gaze solely on the one who has brought to pass this hour of darkness. His disciples too are to know where the enemy stands. For a moment everything, the history of salvation, the history of the world, lies in the hands of one man – the traitor. 'See, my

138

betrayer is at hand' – and in the darkness the disciples recognise him with horror – Judas, the disciple, the brother, the friend. With horror, for when Jesus that selfsame evening had said to them 'One of you will betray me', none had dared to accuse another. None had been able to imagine another capable of such an action. And so each had to ask the other 'Lord, is it I? Lord, is it I?' Each in his own heart was more capable than his brother of such an action.

'While he was still speaking, Judas came, one of the twelve, and with him a great crowd with swords and clubs.' Now we see only the two persons concerned. The disciples and the mob fall back – both do their work badly. Only two do their work as it had to be done.

Jesus and Judas. Who is Judas? That is the question. It is one of the oldest and most troublesome questions in Christianity. First of all let us keep to what the Evangelist himself tells us about it: *Judas, one of the twelve.* Can we feel something of the horror with which the evangelist wrote this tiny clause? Judas, one of the twelve – what more was there to say here? And does not this really say everything? The whole of the dark mystery of Judas and at the same time the deepest shock at his deed? Judas, one of the twelve. That means, it was impossible for this to happen; it was absolutely impossible – and yet it happened. No, there is nothing more to explain or to understand here. It is completely and utterly inexplicable, incomprehensible, it is an unfathomable riddle – and yet it was done. Judas, one of the twelve. That does not just mean that he was one who was with Jesus day and night, who had followed Jesus, who had sacrificed something, who had given up all to be with Jesus, a brother, a friend, a confidant of Peter, of John, of the Lord himself. It means something far more incomprehensible: Jesus himself called and chose Judas! That is the real mystery. For Jesus knew who would betray him from the beginning. In St. John's Gospel Jesus says, 'Did I not choose you, the twelve, and one of you is a devil?' Judas, one of the twelve, and now the reader must look not only at Judas, but rather in great bewilderment at the Lord who chose him. And those whom he chose, he loved. He shared his whole life with them, he shared with them the mystery of his person, and in the same way he sent them out to preach the gospel. He gave them authority to drive out demons and to heal – and Judas was in their midst. Nowhere is there a hint that Jesus had secretly hated Judas. On the contrary, by his office of keeping charge of the disciples' purse, Judas seemed to have been marked out above the others.

True, John once says that Judas was a thief. But is that not meant to be just a dark hint that Judas was a thief in the case of Jesus, that he stole and surrendered to the world Jesus, who did not belong to him? And are not the thirty pieces of silver too simply a sign of how common and small the gift of the world is for him who knows the gift of Jesus? And yet Jesus knew from the beginning who would betray him! John has one more completely mysterious sign of Jesus' closeness with Judas to tell. On the night of the Last Supper, Jesus offers Judas a sop dipped in the dish, and with this sign of the closest community Satan enters into Judas. Thereupon Jesus says to Judas half as a request, half as a command, 'What you are going to do, do quickly.' No one else understood what was happening. Everything remained between Jesus and Judas.

Judas, one of the twelve, chosen by Jesus, taken by Jesus into his company, beloved – does this mean that Jesus wills to show and to demonstrate all his love even to his betrayer? Does it mean that he too is to know that there is really nothing at all to betray in Jesus? Does it mean even this, that Jesus loves with a deep love the will of God which is being accomplished in his path of suffering; that he also loves him by whose betrayal the path is made clear, indeed, who now for a moment has Jesus' fate in his hand? Does it mean that he loves him as the fulfiller of the divine will and yet knows 'Woe to that man by whom it comes to pass?' It is a great, unfathomable mystery – Judas, one of the twelve.

But it is also a mystery on the part of Judas. What does Judas want with Jesus? It must be that the evil one cannot get away from the innocent, from the pure. He hates him, and because nevertheless he cannot get away from him, he also loves him with the dark, passionate love with which even the evil one, the devil, still knows of his origin in God, in the pure one. The evil one would be the disciple of the good. The evil one is the most passionate disciple of the good – until he betrays him. The evil one knows that he must serve God, and loves God because of his power which he himself does not have, while at the same time having only the one urge, to get God in his grasp. So he is a disciple and yet must betray his Lord. Jesus chooses Judas, Judas cannot leave Jesus. Jesus and Judas belong together from the beginning. Neither lets the other go.

And now we see this in the actual account: Jesus and Judas joined by a kiss. Listen to the monstrous words: *'Now the betrayer had given them a sign, saying, "The one I shall kiss is the man: seize him." And he came up to Jesus at once and said, "Hail, Master!" And he kissed him, Jesus said to him, "Friend, why are you here?" Then they came up and laid hands on Jesus and seized him.'* And *'Judas, would you betray the Son of Man with a kiss?'* Once again we are assailed by the question: Who is Judas, who betrays the Son of man with a kiss? It is certainly superficial to say that the kiss was just the usual form of greeting. This kiss was more than that! This kiss was the end of the road for Judas, the deepest expression of the community and the abysmal separation between Jesus and Judas.

'Friend, why are you here?' Do you hear how Jesus still loves Judas, how he still calls him his friend at this hour? Even now Jesus will not let Judas go. He lets himself be kissed by him. He does not push him away. No, Judas must kiss him. His communion with Jesus must reach its consummation. Why are you here? Jesus knows well why Judas is here, and yet, 'Why are you here?' And 'Judas, would you betray the Son of Man with a kiss?' A last expression of a disciple's faithfulness, coupled with betrayal. A last sign of passionate love, joined with far more passionate hate. A last enjoyment of a

subservient gesture, in consciousness of the superiority of the victory over Jesus which it brings. An action divided to its uttermost depths, this kiss of Judas. Not to be able to be abandoned by Christ, and yet to give him up. Judas, would you betray the Son of Man with a kiss? Who is Judas? Should we not also think here of the name that he bore? 'Judas', does he not stand here for the people, divided to its uttermost depths, from which Jesus came, for the chosen people, that had received the promise of the Messiah and yet had rejected him? For the people of Judah, that loved the Messiah and yet could not love him in this way? 'Judas' – his name in German means 'thanks'. Was this kiss not the thanks offered by the divided people and yet at the same time the eternal renunciation? Who is Judas? Who is the traitor? Faced with this question, are we to be able to do anything but say with the disciples 'Lord, is it I? Is it I?'

'Then they came up and laid hands on Jesus and seized him.'

> *'Tis I, whose sin now binds thee,*
> *With anguish deep surrounds thee,*
> *And nails thee to the tree;*
> *The torture thou art feeling,*
> *Thy patient love revealing,*
> *'Tis I should bear it, I alone.'*

Let us now see the final end. At the same hour as Jesus accomplishes his redemptive suffering on the cross on Golgotha, Judas went and hanged himself, damned himself in fruitless repentance. What terrible community!

Christendom has always seen in Judas the dark mystery of divine rejection and eternal damnation. It has recognised and borne witness with fear to the earnestness and the judgement of God on the traitor For precisely this reason, however, it has never looked on him with pride and arrogance, but has in trembling and in recognition of its own tremendous sin sung 'O poor Judas, what is it that thou hast done?' So we too would say no more than this today, 'O poor Judas, what is it that thou hast done?' and would take refuge with him who hung on the cross for all our sins and brought about our redemption, praying,

> *In thy most bitter passion,*
> *My heart to share doth cry,*
> *With thee for my salvation*
> *Upon the cross to die.*
> *Ah, keep my heart thus moved*
> *To stand thy cross beneath,*
> *To mourn thee well-beloved*
> *Yet thank thee for thy death.*

G.S. IV pp. 406–13

PART TWO

The Years of Decision

1937   *1st July* – the arrest of Martin Niemöller.

       End of September – Finkenwalde closed by order of Himmler.

       November – 27 of the men from Finkenwalde arrested.

       (*12th–26th July* – Ecumenical conference on 'Church, Community and State' meets at Oxford without a German delegation.)

1938   *February* – Bonhoeffer's first contact with the leaders of the political resistance – Sack, Oster, Canaris and Beck.

       12th March – Hitler annexes Austria.

       20th June – Finkenwalde reunion at Zingst – Bible study on *Temptation*, published posthumously.

       17th August – retirement of General Beck.

       September – *Life Together* written at Göttingen.

       29th–30th September – 'Munich'.

       1st October – Hitler annexes Sudetenland as agreed.

       9th November – 'The Crystal Night.'

1939   *March–April* – Bonhoeffer in London with Bell, Niebuhr, Leibholz and Visser 't Hooft.

       15th March – Hitler annexes the rest of Czechoslovakia.

       23rd March – Hitler annexes Memel.

       4th June – Bonhoeffer's departure for London and then the U.S.A.

       15th June – arrival in the U.S.A.

       1st July – Britain declares that she cannot tolerate further territorial demands by Hitler.

       27th July – Bonhoeffer's arrival back in Berlin.

       23rd–24th August – German/Soviet Pact.

       1st September – Hitler invades Poland.

       3rd September – Britain and France declare war on Germany.

1. The Attempt to Destroy the Confessing Church

Until 1937, the church struggle had been theological and the only politics with which it was concerned were church politics. The struggle had been with the German Christians. Finkenwalde was a theological seminary and its community was conscious of serving the church. Most of the disputes that bordered upon politics had really been about the nature of the church and consequently its relation with the state. Bonhoeffer found himself reluctantly pushed into a political struggle. He was as unwilling to take this step as he had been to enter the church struggle at all.[1]

In April of 1937, Bonhoeffer prepared some notes on 'War and Peace' for the ecumenical conference to be held in Oxford in the July. The theme of the conference was 'Church, Community and State' and this would inevitably raise political issues. Bonhoeffer in his notes went farther than the pacifist position, which was popular at the time. He saw that something must be said about the role of the ecumenical movement if war came.

WAR AND PEACE

(The last section of a report from the preparatory committee for Oxford, 1937 – almost certainly written by Bonhoeffer.)

1. The Gospel is the message of peace. 'Christ is our peace.' This peace may be a hidden peace, peace with God, but it must emerge and make an open appearance in the ordering of human society, because Christ's claim to dominion extends over the world.

2. The Church of Christ must affirm this message before the whole world, not only before the Lord's community, but also before the world of nations. The church may never surrender this

[1] *No Rusty Swords*, pp. 212–17.

world-wide commission, as it is contained in the Gospel, to anyone. 'You are the salt of the earth.'

3. Because of this commission, the church bears witness to Christendom that in all tensions and all divisions it must allow itself to be guided and supported by faith in the one Lord of the church and by the commandment, 'If possible, so far as it depends upon you, live peaceably with all.'

4. The church must recall the nations from worshipping false gods to obedience towards the only God, the Father of Jesus Christ. The church must show them that the cross is the sole deliverance from all helplessness, anxiety and sin, and that it is the place from which come new ways of peace.

5. As the church fulfils this commission today, it must above all remember that even among the 'Christian' nations the national consciousness is being widely developed into a new national religion and a state cult. On the other hand, not only economic questions, but political, racial and class ideologies of all kinds threaten to tear the world of nations further apart.

6. The church has shown itself to be fully conscious of its obligations and duties towards the people and the state on the basis of its assessment of them. But it is in love and mercy bound to point out that a new world war would not only bring unprecedented suffering and misery on sorely tried peoples, but also destroy the ethical foundations of international life by its slaughter and by doing away with obedience to all God's commandments.

7. The church welcomes the serious attempts of statesmen to seek peaceful solutions to conflicting national interests and also to find ways of providing international aid in basic necessities, all of which serve to keep the peace.

8. The church, then, appeals to Christendom and to the nations for peace. But for the sake of true peace and to make clear the issues involved, the church must also point out that an external peace alone cannot represent the fulfilment of God's will. Even in struggling for

148

peace, we can be threatened by the temptation of arbitrary and god-less thought and action, and by the demonic character of our time. The church knows that the fulfilment of the message 'peace on earth' will always be the subject of Christian hope until the appearing of Jesus Christ.

9. A war is always a severe trial for the church. At the same time it is a call for the church to prove its faith and obedience towards its Lord. For this very reason, even if war comes, the ecumenical alliance of the Church of Christ must not collapse. It must bear its witness in the fellowship of faith, love and intercession. The bonds of the Holy Spirit are stronger than the bonds of the created world.

G.S. I pp. 276–8

In the following month in a retreat arranged at Finkenwalde for ministers of the Confessing Church, Bonhoeffer turned his attention towards church discipline and the authority of the church. It was as though he knew the main attack was about to begin and wished to see the congregations of the Confessing Church ready for it, disciplined and knowing their power. He turned to the New Testament and drafted a paper which listed a number of theses on 'The Power of the Keys and Church Discipline'.

STATEMENTS ABOUT THE POWER OF THE KEYS AND CHURCH DISCIPLINE IN THE NEW TESTAMENT

1. Christ has given his church power to forgive and to retain sins on earth with divine authority (Matt. 16. 19; 18. 18; John 20. 23). Eternal salvation and eternal damnation are decided by its word. Anyone who turns from his sinful way at the word of proclamation and repents, receives forgiveness. Anyone who perseveres in his sin receives judgement. The church cannot loose the penitent from sin without arresting and binding the impenitent in sin. The key to loose does not itself have eternal significance, unless the key to bind also has eternal significance. If the church wants to forgive sins at the command and in the authority of Jesus Christ, it must call sin

149

sin, not only when it forgives, but also where it cannot forgive. If the church wants to use only the key to loose, then it can find no faith with its forgiveness of sins; for in that case the declaration of the forgiveness of sins has become a general principle; it is no longer the living, saving intervention of God himself. If the church wants to use only the key to loose, then it is depriving those who believe of the certainty of forgiveness; for what sort of forgiveness is it that is not also a deliverance from damnation? If the church wants to use only the key to loose, it is contradicting the command of its Lord and thus loses its whole commission and its promise.

2. The church's office of the keys includes two aspects: public preaching and private confession with absolution or retention. Public preaching uses both keys in promising forgiveness to those who repent and believe, and judgement and damnation to those who do not repent. Forgiveness can therefore never be preached authoritatively without definite preaching about repentance and judgement. Here the key to bind shows itself to be subordinate to the key to loose. For the fact that the word arrests and condemns the hearers in their sins is at the same time the call to repentance, i.e. to forgiveness and fellowship. Here the judgement of the key to bind is a divine judgement and holds for eternity unless the sinner repents. Only those who hear the word are bound, until they repent through the word and may be saved. Private confession (James 5. 16; Matt. 18. 18) is added to public preaching to make absolution certain. Because the promise of forgiveness is linked in preaching to penitence and faith, the individual runs the risk of despairing of his penitence and his faith, and thus of himself, or, alternatively, of forgiving himself. In private confession he is bidden to confess his sins personally before God and to mention them by name, to allow them to be corrected by God's word and to receive personal absolution through the brethren. The individual needs private confession to be certain of forgiveness. The church needs private confession to be able to pronounce absolution over the individual with authority, and to be sure

that his penitence is sincere. 'Therefore pastors are to be solemnly forbidden to absolve the people together, in groups; if anyone pronounces the absolution over his people, in groups, without being certain, and does not desist after due warning, the superintendent is to depose him from his preaching office as being an unfaithful hireling' (Pomeranian Church Order). The word of forgiveness may not be wasted.

3. 'Do not give dogs what is holy; and do not throw your pearls before swine, lest they trample them underfoot and turn to attack you' (Matt. 7. 6). The promise of grace is not to be squandered; it needs to be protected from the godless. There are those who are not worthy of the sanctuary. The proclamation of grace has its limits. Grace may not be proclaimed to anyone who does not recognise or distinguish or desire it. Not only does that pollute the sanctuary itself, not only must those who sin still be guilty against the Most Holy, but in addition, the misuse of the Holy must turn against the community itself. The world upon whom grace is thrust as a bargain will grow tired of it, and it will not only trample upon the Holy, but also will tear apart those who force it on them. For its own sake, for the sake of the sinner, and for the sake of the community, the Holy is to be protected from cheap surrender. The Gospel is protected by the preaching of repentance which calls sin sin and declares the sinner guilty. The key to loose is protected by the key to bind. The preaching of grace can only be protected by the preaching of repentance.

4. There is a distinction between mission preaching and preaching in the community. It is already quite clear in the New Testament. The office of the keys is exercised in both, but in different ways. Mission preaching is a call to join the community. Anyone who repents and believes has the door to the community opened to him through baptism. The door is shut for anyone who is bound. The word has no power over that man except to forbid his being accepted for baptism. Baptism involves confession of sins, absolution and the

acknowledgement of Jesus Christ. The proclamation of the word in the community of those who are baptised uses the keys in proclaiming grace to those who are penitent and the discipline of the community to those who are not. To proclaim grace means to have a full part in the fellowship of the body of Christ. Community discipline is the way which leads to partial or total exclusion from the community. Community discipline then, is the exercise of the church's power to bind on the members of the body of Christ. Just as the preaching of repentance safeguards the proclamation of the Gospel, so the proclamation of the word safeguards baptism and community discipline safeguards the eucharist.

5. Community exists only where both word and sacrament are to be found (CA VII). The community is the body of Christ only through baptism and eucharist. The word has missionary character; the community of the word is not limited as long as both keys are preached. The community of the sacrament is the community of believers who have been won by the word. The unbeliever, too, has access to the word, but not to the sacrament.

6. Baptism is incorporation into the body of Christ (Gal. 3. 27 f.) It is once for all, and cannot be repeated. The community is the body of Christ (I Cor. 12. 12 ff.; Rom. 12. 1 ff.). Entry into the community of salvation can be made only once; it cannot be repeated. So complete exclusion from the community would mean eternal damnation. For that very reason, community discipline cannot be exclusion from the community of the baptised; it must always be only from the fellowship of the community of the baptised. Baptism presupposes the hearing of the word, repentance and faith; in accordance with the practice of the church, it assumes that there is instruction, confession of sins, absolution, acknowledgement of Jesus Christ (Acts 8. 5, 35; 2. 38; Rom. 6. 2, etc.). So infant baptism, whether it is present in the New Testament or not, is never baptism of unbelievers, which is impossible, but baptism of those who are to come to faith in the community. Infant baptism therefore exists only as

a special gift of God's grace in the confessing community. The community is responsible to the sacrament, the child and itself, for the child to be brought to instruction by the community (godparents).

7. The eucharist is the repeated feeding of the confessing community of the baptised with the true body and blood of Christ. The faithful are assured of their physical communion with the Lord and with each other, and receive forgiveness of sins through Christ's body. The eucharist is not missionary, but a community meal in the strict sense. In this, it presupposes no narrower circle than the community of the baptised. But there is one condition for receiving the eucharist. Anyone who comes to the eucharist must be able to distinguish (*diakrinein*: I Cor. 11. 29) between the body of Christ and any other meal, i.e. he must come in order to receive truly the body and blood of Christ. Anyone who does not 'discern' here, receives the meal unworthily and eats judgement to himself. It is not his false attitude, but the body and blood of Christ which work judgement in him through his eating and drinking. Because body and blood remain what they are in eating and drinking in the holy eucharist, whether they are eaten worthily or unworthily, the community must take care that they are not received unworthily. Now worthy reception presupposes 'discernment' of the gift, i.e. as far as community practice is concerned, *instruction* about the holy eucharist (not natural food, not symbolic, not a memorial meal, but the true body and blood of Christ for the forgiveness of sins and the fellowship of his body. I Cor. 11. 24; 10. 16).

From this follows the *trial of faith*; examination (*dokimazeto heauton*), whether one is ready to receive the sacrament for what it is, i.e. desiring the forgiveness of sins, whether one renounces one's sins. The truth of the self-examination of which Scripture speaks can be removed beyond all doubt by *confession before the brethren*. Where the community has any doubts about the self-examination, it can insist on examination by the community (notice, etc.). The community must exclude from the eucharist any who do not discern the body, for the sake of the sanctity of Christ's body, for men's sake and for its own sake. There is a difference between one who sins against the Word and one who sins against the body of Christ. The unbaptised person who does not hear the word remains outside Christ's body and can still be called by the community; the person who receives the sacrament in unbelief is guilty against the body of Christ itself; there is no more help for him because he has misused the help. True, the community can never protect itself from hypocrites, but in order to protect a man from his own hypocrisy it safeguards the holy through the discipline of the Word and of the community.

8. Church discipline is the necessary, visible consequence of the right exercising of the office of the keys within the community. The New Testament community has a wide range of disciplinary measures. The origin of all disciplinary measures is the preaching of the Word in accordance with both keys. The minister 'who walks in the house of God' (I Tim. 3. 15) is never released from his charge. 'Preach the Word, be urgent in season and out of season, convince, rebuke and exhort, be unfailing in patience and in teaching' (II Tim. 4. 2). The minister who exercises the power of the keys is to exercise discipline as a guardian of souls in daily contact with his community. That is part of his office. It is *the beginning of church discipline*. It is clear that, unlike the power of the keys, community discipline can only punish sins which have become manifest. 'The sins of some men are conspicuous, pointing to judgement, but the sins of others appear later' (I Tim. 5. 24). So community discipline also spares a man from punishment at the last judgement. Now if a gap can already be discovered at this first stage, the whole question of community discipline can be put in question; for how can the *second stage* (mutual brotherly admonition of members of the community) be a living force if the minister neglects his office? Scripture demands, 'Teach and admonish one another' (Col. 3. 16; I Thess. 5. 11 and 14). Only in this way can sins and apostasy in the community be prevented. Admonition also involves comforting the timid, supporting the weak, being

patient to everyone (I Thess. 5. 14). Unless the office of the keys continues a living force in the community, the *third stage* will hardly be reached. If a brother falls into open sin in word or deed, the community must have the power to institute proper disciplinary measures against him. These have three parts: The community must have power to cut itself off from the sinner. 'Have nothing more to do with him' (Titus 3. 10). 'Avoid them' (Rom. 16. 17). 'Do not even eat with such an one' (eucharist? I Cor. 5. 11). 'Avoid such people' (II Tim. 3. 5; I Tim. 6. 11). 'Now we command you, brethren, in the name of the Lord Jesus Christ, that you keep away from any brother who is living in idleness and not in accord with the tradition that you received from us' (II Thess. 3. 6). This conduct of the community is intended to make the sinner be 'ashamed' (II Thess. 3. 14) and thus to win him back. Such avoidance of the sinner certainly also includes his temporary exclusion from the affairs of the community. But at the same time, this avoidance of the manifest sinner should not already be the abolition of all fellowship. The community which separates itself from the sinner should also meet him with a word of warning. 'Do not look on him as an enemy, but warn him as a brother' (II Thess. 3. 15).

The sinner still remains a brother and for that reason undergoes the punishment and the warning of the community. It is brotherly mercy which makes the community exercise its discipline. The rebellious ones must be punished, the evil ones tolerated, with all gentleness. 'God may perhaps grant that they will repent and come to know the truth, and they may escape from the snare of the devil, after being captured by him to do his will' (II Tim. 2. 25 f.). The way in which this warning is given will differ, depending upon the sin and the sinner, but it will always have the same aim, to bring him to repentance and reconciliation. If the sin can remain hidden between you and the sinner, you should not reveal it, but punish it alone and call the sinner to repentance. In this way, 'you have gained your brother'. But if he does not listen, and perseveres in his sin, once again you should not immediately reveal the sin, but should look for one or two witnesses (Matt. 18. 15 f.). Witness is needed both because of the circumstances of the sin – i.e. if it cannot be proved and is denied by the member of the community one commends the matter to God; the brethren are witnesses, not inquisitors – because of the stubbornness of the sinner towards repentance. The secrecy of the discipline should make repentance easier for the sinner. If even now he still does not listen, or the sin is in any case manifest before the whole community, it is the concern of the whole community to warn the sinner and to call him to repentance (Matt. 18. 17; cf. II Thess. 3. 14). If the sinner holds an office in the community he should only be accused on the indictment of two or three witnesses. 'As for those who persist in sin, rebuke them in the presence of all, so that the rest may stand in fear' (I Tim. 5. 20). Now the community is called upon to exercise the office of the keys along with its minister. Public statements need public representation of the community and the ministry. 'In the presence of God and of Christ Jesus and of the elect angels I charge you to keep these rules without favour, doing nothing from partiality' (I Tim. 5. 21), for now God's own judgement is to be passed on the sinner. If he sincerely repents and openly acknowledges his sin, he receives forgiveness for all his sins in God's name (cf. II Cor. 2. 6 ff.), but if he perseveres in his sin the community must retain his sin in God's name. But that means his exclusion from all the fellowship of the community. 'Let him be to you as a Gentile and a tax collector. Truly, I say to you, whatever you bind on earth shall be bound in heaven, and whatever you loose on earth shall be loosed in heaven . . . For where two or three are gathered in my name, there am I in the midst of them' (Matt. 18. 17 ff.). This exclusion from the community only confirms what is already a fact, namely that the impenitent sinner is 'self-condemned' (Titus 3. 11). The community has not condemned him, he himself has spoken the verdict. Paul describes this complete exclusion as 'handing over to Satan' (I Cor. 5. 5; I Tim. 1. 20). The

156

guilty one is returned to the world in which Satan rules and death does its work. (A comparison of I Tim. 1. 20 and II Tim. 2. 17; 4. 15 shows that an act of punishment with death, as in Acts 5, is not envisaged here.) The guilty one is expelled from the fellowship of the body of Christ because he has cut himself off; he has no longer any claim on the community. Nevertheless, even this last act is still meant for the salvation of the person concerned, 'that his spirit may be saved in the day of the Lord Jesus' (I Cor. 5. 5), 'that they may learn not to blaspheme' (I Tim. 1. 20). The aim of church discipline remains either the man's return to the community or his salvation. It remains pedagogical action. The saying in which the sinner is deprived of his salvation is simply the last possible offer of the fellowship of the community and of salvation, as surely as the community's decision will last for ever unless the other repents.

If we look back again at the basis for the exercise of community discipline, we shall see that the charge to use both keys occupies first place. The key to bind must be used because of the holiness of the Gospel; from the human point of view that means that the sinner must be punished to be saved, and from the community's point of view it means that the unclean vessels must be removed for the community to be pure (II Tim. 2. 21). The community which gives fellowship to the sinner without exercising discipline shares in the responsibility for his sin (II John 10). It must therefore be particularly careful before it gives a member of the community a responsibility in the community for which he is not adequate (I Tim. 5. 22).

Beyond all exercising of community discipline, which always stands at the service of mercy, even beyond the deliverance of the stubborn sinner to Satan, the New Testament has the most fearful punishment of all: the solemn curse, the anathema. It is no longer meant to lead to salvation. It appears as an anticipation of the divine judgement. It corresponds to the Old Testament *herem*, which is carried out against the godless. It represents definitive separation from the community. The person under the ban is killed. This indicates two things: the community can under no circumstances tolerate and absolve the person under the ban any longer. So he is surrendered to God alone. Now in this way the person under the ban is at the same time cursed, and still holy; holy, because he has been handed over to God. But because, in being cursed, he belongs to God alone, the community can no longer make any attempts to save him. Rom. 9. 3 proves that anathema means being deprived of salvation. I Cor. 16. 22 suggests that the anathema has an eschatological reference. Gal. 1. 8 f. says that the person who deliberately destroys the very Gospel by his preaching is anathema. It is certainly no coincidence that the only place which pronounces the anathema over specific people refers to false teaching. *Doctrina est coelum, vita erra* (Luther).

9. Teaching discipline differs from the community discipline in that the latter follows from correct doctrine, i.e. from the right use of the keys, whereas the former is directed against the misuse of doctrine. The source of community life and community discipline is destroyed by false teaching. Therefore to sin against doctrine is more reprehensible than to sin in one's conduct. Teaching discipline primarily extends to those who exercise a teaching ministry in the church. It is assumed in the first place that when an office is conferred there is some guarantee that the minister is *didaktikos*, capable of teaching (I Tim. 3. 2; II Tim. 2. 24; Titus 1. 9), 'able to teach others also' (II Tim. 2. 2), that hands will not be laid on anyone suddenly, because otherwise that man's guilt falls on the person who appointed him (I Tim. 5. 22). So teaching discipline already begins before a person is called to a teaching office. The life and death of whole communities depend on the utmost certainty here. But teaching discipline does not end with the call to the teaching ministry; that is only its beginning. Once the minister has been proved – Timothy – he must still be admonished incessantly to abide by true, saving doctrine. He is asked specially to read the Scriptures. The

danger of deviation is too great (II Tim. 3. 10 and 14; 4. 2; 2. 15; I Tim. 4. 13, 16; Titus 1. 9; 3. 8). In addition he must also be warned to live an exemplary life: 'Take heed to yourself and to your teaching' (I Tim. 4. 13 f.; Acts 20. 28). It is no dishonour for Timothy to be admonished to be chaste, humble, impartial, assiduous. So before the church exercises discipline all its officers are themselves subject to discipline. It is the task of the person in office to propagate correct doctrine in his community and to combat all perversions of it. If doctrinal differences appear in the community, the community should be told that certain differences in the mode of proclamation are unavoidable. But whether it is Apollos, Paul, or Peter, the one undivided Christ should be served in all things (I Cor. 1. 11 f.). Any deliberate formation of schools is, of course, to be avoided, because here each one simply seeks his own and becomes puffed up. In this way the formation of a school becomes a brute state of disobedience towards Christ (I Tim. 6. 5, 20; II Tim. 2. 26; 3. 7 f.; Titus 1. 10). In addition, there is the difficulty of differentiating between permissible differences between schools and inadmissible false doctrines (cf. e.g. Rev. 2. 6 and 15). Where manifest false doctrine appears, the minister is to command the teachers 'not to teach any different doctrine' (I Tim. 1. 3); for he holds the teaching office and can so order. He is also to warn and to remind the community to avoid disputing about words (II Tim. 2. 14). If a person is manifestly a false teacher he is to be 'warned once and for all'. If he does not listen, the community must have nothing more to do with the heretical man (Titus 3. 10; I Tim. 6. 4 f.); for he is leading the community astray (II Tim. 3. 6 f.). 'Anyone who does not remain in Christ's teaching has no God.' Such a false teacher is not to be received into the house or to be given greeting (II John 10). Antichrist comes in the person of the false teacher. Only the false teacher, and not the sinner with his way of life, is called Anti-Christ. The anathema of Gal. 1. 9 applies only to him.

The relationship between teaching discipline and community

discipline is as follows: there is no community discipline without teaching discipline. But at the same time, there is no teaching discipline which does not inevitably lead to community discipline. Paul accuses the Corinthians of wanting, in their arrogance, to cause schisms without exercising community discipline (I Cor. 5. 2). This separation of the doctrinal question from the question of the community way of life is impossible.

10. Community discipline presupposes not only an intact teaching ministry but also a right ordering of the offices in the community. The ordering of the community must help towards the proper use of the keys and all the actions of the community which stem from that. The community is the body of Christ in which every single member is guided by his Spirit. The New Testament affirms that the offices of the church were appointed by God himself (I Cor. 12. 28), by Christ (Eph. 4. 11), by the Holy Spirit (Acts 20. 28), by the community with the help of the Holy Spirit (Acts 6. 5; 13. 2), by the apostles and ministers after careful examination (Titus 1. 5; I Tim. 5. 22). Is is inconceivable for the New Testament that people should be appointed to offices in the church from outside the community. For the community is the body of Christ. True, there are no firm rules for the structure of the ministry in the community. The Jerusalem community was not ordered in the same way as those of Asia minor. There is freedom here, so that 'all things may be done for edification' (I Cor. 14. 26), i.e. so that the body of Christ is built up rightly through the power of the keys.   G.S. III pp. 369–81

The attack came in June. On 9th June, a law forbade collections for the Confessing Church and it also forbade teachers at the church college in Berlin to teach; on the 14th, the Gestapo raided the offices of the church of the Old Prussian Union and Niesel was arrested; on the 23rd, eight members of the Council of Brethren were arrested in Berlin.

On 24th June, Bonhoeffer began his circular letter with a full awareness of the seriousness of the situation:

BONHOEFFER TO THE BRETHREN: In these days when the homes of our Confessing Church are being searched, we think often and with stronger prayer of you all, especially those of you who are alone and perhaps deeply troubled by all the things that are happening. Especially now, we must rejoice in our fellowship and be true in our intercessions for each other. Make sure that you have the names of all the brethren who were with you here, and bring them out in your meditations, lest any of the brethren should be cut off from this common prayer together. At the same time, let us give special thought to those who have already separated themselves from us. Let us learn in this difficult time to say again the first petitions of the Lord's Prayer: Hallowed be thy name; thy kingdom come; thy will be done . . . Last Tuesday, Brothers Kühn, Lent and Martiwe were ordained in Berlin. That is a cause of rejoicing for all of us. It shows that our church is still sending labourers into the harvest even in this time of our greatest trial . . .

G.S. II pp. 516–7

A week later, on 1st July, Martin Niemöller was arrested. The state was clearly trying to destroy the Confessing Church, and as Bonhoeffer could only think of it as the true Church of Jesus Christ in Germany, this meant more than the suppression of a movement; it was an attempt to destroy the Church of Christ. Bonhoeffer was compelled into resistance. The storm clouds gathered that summer.

On 29th July, the following news letter went out to the brethren:

BONHOEFFER TO THE BRETHREN: Brother Niemöller was again interrogated for several hours by the police while his house was searched. Apparently, he gave 'offence by holding Bible study in private houses'. . . . Brother Kanitz is in danger again . . . These and all the other men from Dahme are guilty of the collection of 18th July. Brother Seydel is now in Neuruppin, looking after Brother Klapproth's congregation. He was able to give us news of Brother

Klapproth's arrest while he was in the interrogation prison at Neuruppin. Meanwhile he has been released again. Brother Hofmann was arrested at a youth conference and taken to the prison at Kolberg. The reason given for his arrest was: *Words used in a previous sermon!* Brother Hofmann is now released . . . Brother Carras of Berlin has been arrested again. Brother Koch is in concentration camp . . .

G.S. II pp. 519–20

On 18th August, a service of intercession arranged in Christ Church, Dahlem, to pray for Martin Niemöller, was banned by the police. This led to demonstrations in the adjoining streets and 250 people were arrested. The battle was in earnest. Meanwhile the men of Finkenwalde were kept informed about their brethren. On 26th August, Horst Lekszas sent round the following letter:

LEKSZAS TO THE BRETHREN: The first word must be for the brethren in prison. After Brother Danicke and Brother Schrader, now also Brother Mickley and for the second time, Brother Giese have been arrested. Brother Mickley is in Potsdam prison, Lindenstr. 54, Brother Schrader and Brother Danicke are in the same prison – visiting hours, Monday and Wednesday, from 1 to 3 in the afternoon. You are allowed 10 minutes and several of the brethren have already visited. It's not known where Brother Giese is. Brother Grosch was also arrested – on the famous Dahlem Sunday.[1] Here are a few words from the letters of these brethren: 'It's not always easy to bear!', but also, 'Be still and humble yourself a while, because our King will stir himself and turn away our anguish'. To that must be added another quote from one of the other letters. 'You should know that we have learnt to feel secure here. One does not always know from whence this patience comes. Just remain true in your intercessions and we shall have no fear in the struggle! Exod. 17. 11. . . .

G.S. II p. 520

[1] 8th August, 1937.

The summer semester at Finkenwalde ended on 11th September with strange forebodings. Bonhoeffer went on holiday to Bavaria and on his return it was only a matter of weeks before, at the end of September, the seminary was closed by order of Heinrich Himmler, leader of the Nazi SS (Hitler's Black Guards). This followed naturally and fairly quickly upon Himmler's announcement of the banning of all substitute colleges and institutions of the Confessing Church.[1] Some twenty-seven of the Finkenwalde men were arrested, and a little later Iwand and his seminary at Blöstau suffered the same fate. Bonhoeffer was not arrested.

The Cost of Discipleship[2] was published that autumn and Bonhoeffer wrote in the dedication:

> To Pastor Niemöller,
>   Advent 1937, with thanks,
> A book which he could have written much better
>
> G.S. II p. 307

That Christmas, Bonhoeffer sent to Mrs. Niemöller the first of a series of presents which he never failed to send each Christmas until he was himself imprisoned. The influence of Martin Niemöller was considerable. Bonhoeffer recognised this in a letter he wrote to Mrs. Niemöller during Holy Week:

BONHOEFFER TO MRS. NIEMÖLLER:'This Holy Week, the thoughts of many men and especially of many young theologians who look to your husband for inspiration and pray daily for him, go out to you and your children. God has so directed it that a special blessing goes out from your house to the parish and to the whole church. It is surely to the glory of God that those of us who are still free can look to you and see how you stand firm in trouble and remain patient in affliction. That is the grace of God for which we are grateful. It is a great joy to see how men keep asking after your

[1] 30th September, 1937.
[2] E.T. SCM Press, 1959.

163

husband wherever one goes and how quite simple churchgoers are able to be true and bear witness to the same faith for which he suffers when they are summoned before the authorities. All this will greatly strengthen the church. May God grant you and your children a truly joyful Easter.

With deep respect and thankfulness, in the unity of our common intercessions, I greet you . . .
G.S. II p. 307

It is surprising how many did look to Martin Niemöller as a symbol of the resistance. Paul Schneider, the first martyr of the Confessing Church, who was arrested in 1937, kept a picture of Martin Niemöller in his cell in Buchenwald until his death in July 1939.[1] 1937 had been a fateful year and as it drew to a close, Bonhoeffer tried to assess it in a number of papers and letters. In January 1938, he wrote to the younger theologians of Pomerania.

THE CONFESSING CHURCH IN POMERANIA AT THE
BEGINNING OF 1938

During the past few weeks, letters and personal comments have reached me which make it clear that our church, and in Pomerania particularly our group of young theologians, has come to a time of sore trial. It is no longer a question of the troubles of one individual, for a great many people are being threatened by one and the same temptation, so I hope that you won't mind if I try to give a common answer to you all. Of course, the letter is still meant for each of you personally. I shall try to take up all the points that you have severally made, in the course of it.

We have to cover a great deal of ground. We shall all agree that when we embraced the cause of the Confessing Church we took the step with a supreme faith which was, for that very reason, a boldness beyond human understanding. We were glad, certain of victory, ready for sacrifice. Our whole life, both our personal life and our ministry, had taken a new turn. Of course I don't pretend that there weren't all sorts of purely human overtones to our feelings – who

[1] *The Pastor of Buchenwald*, SCM Press, 1956.

knows even his own heart? – but there was one thing that made us so joyful and ready to fight and even ready to suffer. Once again we knew that a life with Jesus Christ and his church is worth staking everything on. We believed that in the Confessing Church we had not only found, but through God's great goodness had also actually experienced, the Church of Jesus Christ. For individuals, for pastors and for communities, a new life began in the joy of God's Word. As long as God's Word was with us, we no longer wanted to worry and fret about the future. With this Word we were ready to fight, to suffer, to undergo poverty, sin and death, so as finally to reach God's kingdom. Young people and the fathers of large families stood here side by side. What was it that united us then and gave us such great joy? It was the one, age-old recognition which God himself had granted us again, that Jesus Christ wants to build his church among us, a church which lives only by the preaching of the pure, untainted Gospel and the grace of his sacraments, a church which obeys him alone in everything that it does. Christ himself will stand by a church like this; he will protect and guide it. Only a church like this can be free from all fear. This, and nothing else, was acknowledged by the synods of the Confessing Church at Barmen and at Dahlem. Was it an illusion? Did the synods speak under the pressure of external circumstances, which seemed favourable to a 'realisation' of this faith? No, it was supreme faith, it was the biblical truth itself that was clearly acknowledged then before the whole world. The witness of Christ conquered our hearts, made us glad, and summoned us to act obediently. Dear brothers, surely we are at least agreed on this much, that this was the case? Or do we now want to abuse the grace of God which he has so richly given to us?

That, then, was the beginning of the fight for the true Church of Christ. Or do you perhaps think that the devil took all that trouble to annihilate a band of rabid idealists? No, Christ was in the ship, and so the storm was stilled. The battle demanded sacrifice from the beginning. Perhaps everyone did not always realise how much both individuals and communities would have to give up so that the members of the Councils of Brethren would be able to fulfil their duty to the church. But the sacrifices were joyfully made for the cause of Jesus Christ. Who could hold back as long as Jesus still called, 'Be the church. Be the church that serves none but me'? Who could take his leave as long as no one released him from his responsibility to preach the pure Gospel and to build up the communities in accordance with Scripture and the confessions of our church?

If we are still in agreement here, too, then let us ask in all openness what has happened between those beginnings and our present situation. Perhaps we might put it another way. What is the difference between the church in those provinces where men still live and work and fight as they did at the beginning, and the church in our province? Why has there been incessant lamentation in Pomerania for several months that our church is paralysed, that it is under a curse, that an inner narrowness and stubbornness is preventing us from doing fruitful work? How has it happened that brethren who were convinced members of the Confessing Church are now saying that all their joy has gone? That they see no good reason why they could not do their work as well under the Consistory of the National Church as under the Council of Brethren? And can we deny that the witness of our church in Pomerania has recently been growing weaker and weaker? Can we deny that the word of the Confessing Church has largely lost its power to awaken belief and thus call for a decision? Who can deny that the real theological decisions of the church are continually being obscured by considerations of expediency? And has not all this had its effect on our own preaching, too? We ask why all this happens. I don't think that the answer is as hard as people make out. The so-called paralysis in the Confessing Church, the lack of joy, the weak witness, comes from our own disobedience. We should not be thinking about other people now, but about ourselves and our work. What has become of the first clear decisions of the Confessing Church in our communities? Have our communities taken a really lively part in the church? Have we a parish council or a local Council of Brethren unshakeably devoted to the cause of the Confessing Church and to us as its pastors? One which supports us and helps us to try new methods in the community? If we haven't, why not? Are the congregations solely responsible for that? There are those among them who are of a contrary opinion. Are the congregations still too 'immature'? As though a congregation could be too immature to hear God's Word and act in obedience to it and yet could be 'mature' enough to act outside the church! Who taught us to think so contemptuously of our congregations? Who made the cause of the Confessing Church a concern of 'the mature'? As if the maturity of a community did not develop precisely from its days of distress before God! Where are the district Councils of Brethren formed from the parish Councils of Brethren, to help the district pastors with their great responsibility? Where is the Confessing Synod of Pomerania, which could only have been formed properly as we went along, and which should have shown the Pomeranian Church the way? In other words, why have we in Pomerania not taken the decisions of the Synod of Dahlem seriously? And if we did not do that, have we ever taken Barmen seriously at all? Other provinces, with much less of a church, fought the battle of the church of the Gospel, with all its promise, on the basis of clear, theological decisions made by the church. And in all their sufferings they were glad of it. Why do we so often miss the mark? Why is theological conversation so meaningless among us? At this moment it is really not a question of one accusing another, but of each acknowledging for himself that through our disobedience we have often all too readily despised the grace of God which we received when the Confessing Church came into being. Our words and our actions have often been very different. And now, when we reap our due reward, we begin to accuse one another, indeed we mutter against the way which has been spoilt through our own disobedience and which consequently no longer gives us any joy.

Let me try to put it in a different way: the church struggle can be law or gospel. At the moment it has largely become law as far as we are concerned. We rebel against it. It has become a threatening, angry law which strikes us down. No man can support and direct the church struggle as law without succumbing to it and failing completely. As law, the church struggle is without joy, without certainty, without authority, and without promise. How is that? It is just the same here as in our personal lives. If through our disobedience we evade the gracious Word of God, it becomes a harsh law for us. What is a gentle and easy yoke when done in obedience becomes an insupportable burden when done in disobedience. The more we have hardened ourselves in disobedience against the gracious Word, the harder it is to change, the more obstinately we rebel against God's claim. But just as in our personal life there is only one way, the way of repentance, of patience under God's Word, in which God restores to us our lost communion, so too it is in the church struggle. Without penitence, i.e. unless the church struggle itself becomes our penitence, we shall never receive back the gift we have lost, the church struggle as Gospel. Even if the obedience of penitence is harder now than it was then, because we are hardened in our guilt – it is the only way by which God will help us back to the right road.

My dear brethren, if I may so address those of you who still have no permanent appointment in the church, I know that you are perhaps least of all to blame. Indeed things have happened to you, which the pastor could avoid. But must you not accept them with particular joy, and gratitude that the church expects you to go the way that is quite clear? That today *you* have perhaps a greater responsibility than has ever been laid on a generation of young theologians in our church? First, the Confessing Church in Pomerania must come into being. It will, humanly speaking, also depend on you whether it can come into being or not. In the past week we have shared a meditation text from Haggai 1; it runs: 'This people say, "The time has not yet come to rebuild the house of the Lord". Then the Word of the Lord came by Haggai the prophet, "Is it a time for you yourselves to dwell in your panelled houses, while this house lies in ruins?"' (Haggai 1. 2–4). It is none of my business, as they say, to 'straighten you out', to talk you over. But everything does of course depend on our re-awakening in you, with God's Word, the courage, the joy, the faith in Jesus Christ who is and will remain with the Confessing Church, whether you go along with it or not. You ought to know that the faith which threatens to become extinguished among you still lives as it did in the beginning in many communities and many pastorates, that solitary brethren, in Pomerania and outside, in lonely out-posts, bear witness to this faith with the greatest joy. The Church of Jesus Christ, which lives only from his Word and which means to be obedient to him alone in all things, still lives and will live, and calls you back from temptation and trial. It calls you to penitence and warns you of the unfaithfulness which must ultimately end in despair. It prays for you, that your faith may not fail.

But now once more to your own questions. You say that the situation today is not what it was in the beginning, so we should have acted differently. I can think of only one change in the situation which might also alter our actions, and that is if the Consistories of the church relieved us of the responsibility of governing the church in accordance with its Confessions. Only someone who is throwing dust in his own eyes could doubt that there is no question of this in the present composition of the church administration. But the fact that outwardly the situation seems more threatening than before, that the encroachment upon the church by outside forces increases, could only make us gather more closely together in those places where the invasion could not yet take place, i.e., in the Confessing Church.

You say that the Confessing Church is losing the chance of getting into the parishes, i.e. of preaching the Gospel. Do you remember how the German Christians argued in just the same way, and the disastrous results that that had? Don't you see that by putting yourselves under the Consistory of the National Church you make yourselves instruments of the secular powers, who really want to give not the Gospel, but a quite different teaching, to the parishes?

You say that under the Consistory you would stick to the creed and the confessions. Do you remember who said that before you did? And even supposing that it were possible – which it is not – are you not forgetting that the church is greater than your congregation? Are you not forgetting your brethren and their congregations? Don't you know that by going over to the Consistory you would provide the most effective support for the fight against the Confessing Church? Don't you realise that a Council of Brethren which exercised merely spiritual direction, as you recommend, would lead a phantom existence and be swept away in a moment? If the Confessing Church is destroyed in that way, the responsibility will be yours. For you to go to the Consistory is the strongest conceivable confirmation of the verdict of the anti-Christians on the Confessing Church.

You complain about the Council of Brethren. Do that, if you must, at the Council itself. But please also ask yourselves whether you came into the Confessing Church because there was a good Council of Brethren. Ask too whether you would have been prepared to embrace the cause of the Confessing Church even if there had not been a Council of Brethren at all. Indeed, ask whether you are ready to bear witness for the Confessing Church and to suffer for it all by yourself, before God and man, cut off from all church government and brotherly fellowship. No, your choice is not a simple one, between two church régimes. You cannot take a positive attitude to what you once rejected on grounds of faith for some completely different reason without also destroying yourselves and your belief. God's Word calls you to more faithful work in the Confessing Church, under the direction of the Council of Brethren, however weak both of them may be.

You no longer hope for the success of the Confessing Church. You cannot see any way out. Indeed, who among us *can* see a way out? Only God can do that, and he will show it to those who humbly wait for it. Perhaps we once hoped that the Confessing Church would gain public recognition in Germany. But was this hope ever promised? Certainly not. Now we have learnt to believe in a church which follows its Lord beneath the cross. That is more like the promise. Finally, you say that you would be ready for all kinds of sacrifice both personally and in your ministry, if only you knew why they were necessary. Why, dear brethren? For no reason that men can see, not for the sake of a flourishing church or of a convincing church government, but simply because the way of the Confessing Church must also be followed through desolate stretches of desert and wilderness and because you do not want to stay in the wilderness. So for the sake of the poor church, which will of course go on under the guidance of its Lord even without you, for the sake of your faith, for your certainty, you should remain with the Confessing Church.

What is to happen now? There are so many reasons, and theologians can prove anything. Everything will depend on whether God gives us his testimony afresh in our hearts. Jesus Christ alone can lead the way. But we should have some tasks clearly in mind. There will never be a renewal of our Confessing Church unless we plead for it before God with vigorous prayer. An hour of prayer for our church and for those who lead it should unite us, and at the same time clean and clarify our thoughts. God will then again lead us by the right way. Then we should go on to what we have neglected. We must struggle for complete theological clarity about the decisions of the Confessing Church. We must not stop until we have firm ground under our feet. We can all too easily neglect questions of truth for questions of daily routine. But how can we have clear guidance for a community or a church without a clear theology? False fronts of the church struggle always develop when the question of truth has been passed over. Let us once again take up our conversation with those who confront us with questions. But let it be a conversation in the ultimate truth! The discipline with which the pastors of other districts do theology, preach and teach, does great credit to these churches and their pastors. Shouldn't discipline also be possible, not least among the younger brethren of our church, for mutual help and strengthening? All this is simply so that we serve our communities. The real need here is for us to prepare to form a Pomeranian Confessing Synod. For this we need local Councils of Brethren and District Councils of Brethren. And once we get that far, the never-ending work will begin: ordering the church's life for baptisms, arranging godparents, instruction, confirmation, confession and the eucharist, visiting, and so on. There are already groups in the Confessing Church which are beginning to attack these questions seriously. But there is no authority which could do this work under the sole guidance of the Word of God but the organs of the Confessing Church. There is work enough. We must now at last get down to it. 　　　　　　　　　　　　　　　　G.S. II pp. 297–306

It is clear from this that the Confessing Church, at least in Pomerania, was in low waters, and one can see why Bonhoeffer repeatedly insisted that the decisions of Barmen and even more of Dahlem be adhered to. His battle against the Consistory and the Church Committees is incessant. He will not have the Confessing Church reduced to a spiritual movement. This was the most crucial period for the life of the Confessing Church. Leaving aside the political events of 1938 which will be followed later[1] it will be instructive to jump ahead a bit and follow the way in which Bonhoeffer helped the younger theologians of Pomerania to respond to this call to be true. In October 1938 he addressed a conference of these 'illegal' younger theologians

[1] See pp. 194 ff.

who met with the Council of Brethren, including Reinhold von Thadden-Trieglaff. The lecture, which was given on the 26th October, was later circulated.

OUR WAY ACCORDING TO THE TESTIMONY OF SCRIPTURE

These remarks are meant to provoke you to serious reflection and renewed joy over the way of the Church of Jesus Christ. Only Holy Scripture can guide our reflections aright and give us utter joy and confidence. So we would ask you to examine with us what our church has done in the light of the testimony of Scripture and so to allow yourselves to be set upon the firm ground of the divine Word. The question we must consider again today is this: was the teaching of the Synods of Barmen and Dahlem in accordance with Scripture? The fact that this question has to be discussed afresh after four years must certainly make us think. It could indeed be that we really have been working and acting for four years without deciding this question before God, that you have allowed yourselves to be trained, tested and ordained by the Council of Brethren without being compelled to by the Word of God. In that case, our situation now would in fact be the same as that of 1934. Were that so, at least the position would be clear, and the question whether Barmen and Dahlem were commensurate with Scripture would be a belated, but nevertheless a real, question. It could also be that at one time we allowed ourselves to be led by Scripture along the way of Barmen and Dahlem and that today we are once again compelled by Scripture alone to raise objections to our former decisions. In other words, that we have a better knowledge of Scripture to set alongside Barmen and Dahlem. In that case, we would have to recall you from a course contrary to Scripture to a course in accordance with it. You would then have moved towards the Council of Brethren not thoughtlessly, but wrongly. But this situation too would be clear, and our present question about Scripture would be a real one. But it could also be that while we were once convinced of the scriptural character

173

of the Confessing Synods, today, in view of a number of circumstances, for example, the failure of the church government, the departure of brethren we admired, hindrance and oppression from all sides, we have been overcome by wholesale doubt and now, to avoid all further theological, ecclesiastical, and personal difficulties, we resign ourselves to take the only positive step we can, the only one that seems to offer some support, some work, some security, namely the step to a pastorate under the Consistory of the National Church. But in any case, we have to be quite clear today what we are really doubtful about. Have we become doubtful whether we weak men could carry out what has been laid upon us? Or have we become doubtful whether the Confessing Synods are in accordance with Scripture? Or have we gone so far as to doubt whether Holy Scripture can still show us God's will if we look for it?

You will understand that there will inevitably be different answers, depending on the way our questions are put to the Scriptures. If we doubt whether we shall be able to carry out the course that has been laid upon us, we shall have to look for the promise which Scripture gives to those who are uncertain and despondent, the strength and comfort it offers to hearts and hands that have grown weary, and we shall hear that with God all things are possible. If we doubt whether God is still giving us clear knowledge of his will today through Scripture, and as a result say that these days we must allow ourselves to be guided only by our own personal assessment of any particular circumstances, we would then have to ask Scripture whether God has ever left his people in this way, whether he has not always dealt out severe punishment to those who make this complaint, and has pointed to his eternal covenant. In that case, the whole question of our personal attitude to the Bible and to salvation would be at stake. But if at the present moment our doubt is not in fact directed towards men and God's word in general, but is simply a doubt whether Barmen and Dahlem were in accordance with Scripture, we shall have to prove once again from Scripture something that has been untiringly affirmed for four years in the Confessing Church, and yet still needs to be asserted again and again.

All the questions I have mentioned could be genuine ones, but they cease to be authentic the moment they are confused. Anyone who doubts whether the Confessing Synods are in accordance with Scripture because he is concerned about the Council of Brethren or because he understandably longs for a peaceful ministry, will not be able to get any answer from the Scripture because he is not really looking for one. Anyone whose whole faith in God's revelation in the testimony of Scripture is in peril and who throws the decisions of the Confessing Church into the melting pot for good measure really needs all the comfort and all the patience of Scripture, but a scriptural proof for Barmen and Dahlem cannot really help him. Perhaps everyone in the Confessing Church ought to talk about these things. We shall now turn to the question whether the Confessing Synods of Barmen and Dahlem are really in accordance with Scripture.

What is a Scriptural Proof?

1. Only the truth of a doctrine can be proved by Scripture.

2. A scriptural proof is successful where a doctrine is based both on individual texts and on Scripture as a whole, in other words, where it corresponds to the so-called formal and material principles of our Church.

The first thing that Christians had to prove from Scripture was the statement, 'Jesus is the Christ'. Only the Old Testament was Scripture at that time. Then there followed scriptural proofs of the dogmas of the early church. Our present scriptural proof can only extend to the truth of the doctrines of the Synods of Barmen and (more particularly) Dahlem. Only the truth of a doctrine can be proved by Scripture, never the rightness of a particular course. This rules out two dangerous misunderstandings.

1. Scripture can never prove that a particular course of action was justified. Only God, who sees our faith, knows whether our ways are right. But whatever does not proceed from faith is sin (Rom. 14. 23), even if it is following Dahlem to the letter. Our ways will never be justified except through faith. So Scripture vindicates the truth which was expressed and affirmed at Dahlem, not what we did there. What we do is not particularly interesting except in so far as it is done in the truth, i.e. for the sake of the truth that is affirmed in it. The Bible does not know the pathos and the problems of the question, 'Which way?' Our way follows quite clearly, simply, necessarily, from the truth that we affirm. It is not important, problematic, tragic, in itself. Our way is simply 'doing the truth' (John 3. 21) and the accent lies completely on 'the truth'. Because we know that any course we take needs forgiveness, we should not be concerned so much with the question 'Which way?' as with the question of truth. If we remain in the truth and only in the truth, our way will be right.

The question 'Which way?' should therefore suggest only the question of whether the Confessing Synods of Barmen and Dahlem were true according to the witness of Scripture. Only in this truth is our way justified. Christ is the way. He is also our way. Strictly speaking, there is no other way. The Bible is not interested in the abundance of human ways and ends.

It is our way to let Jesus Christ find us in this way. Christ is the truth. The sole truth of our way is that we should be found in this truth. Anyone who looks to the Bible to justify his own way looks for justification by his own works.

2. The other misunderstanding about scriptural proof comes from the same source: we seek to justify our way, not for the past, but for the future. We expect Scripture to give us such clear instructions that it absolves us from acting in faith. We want to see the way before we go along it. We need to be certain that the way also pleases God before we go along it. People say, Were we quite certain from

Scripture that the way of the Council of Brethren pleases God, we would go along it. Show us that from Scripture and we will follow. I want a proof from Scripture in my pocket as a guarantee of the course I am following. But the Bible will never fulfil even this request, because it is not meant to be an insurance policy for our ways, which might possibly be dangerous. It does only one thing: it calls us to faith and obedience to the truth once recognised in Jesus Christ. The Scriptures do not prove courses of action, but the truth of God. Scriptural proof does not free us from believing; it first takes us to God's Word in the venture of faith and obedience, and it strengthens us in it. It is not by Scripture that one first knows the right way, surveys it, and then decides to go along it; only when the journey has begun does one know whether one is on the right way. Knowledge comes only in action, in decision. Only a man who is in the truth knows the truth. Jesus says, 'If any man's will is to do God's will, he shall know whether my teaching is from God' (John 7. 17). So ultimately a proof from Scripture can be given only to those who are on the way, i.e. to believers.

Anyone who expects to justify a past or a future way from Scripture looks for justification by his works before God. He is not ready to live by faith. Scriptural proof is addressed to the believer. There is therefore an attitude which rules out proof from Scripture from the start. It is the sort of attitude which is characterised by sentences like, 'You can prove anything from the Bible', or, 'The Bible gives us no advice about our present situation', or, 'Yes, that's quite right in theory, but in practice . . . , the community, financial matters, the state, and so on . . .' Anyone who talks like this is steeped in unbelief about God's revelation in Scripture, perhaps without knowing it. He undermines the only ground on which he can stand. He robs Scripture of its force. How is a proof from Scripture going to help him? But anyone who approaches Scripture for advice in faith will never find that it remains dumb.

Let us now pay special attention to the decisions of the Synod of

Dahlem. It has become the custom to criticise Dahlem while at the same time asserting one's assent to Barmen. This is a contradiction which rests largely on a simple ignorance of the decisions of Barmen and Dahlem, and no attempt has yet been made anywhere to point out the theological difference or contradictions between Barmen and Dahlem. Dahlem is simply the implementation of the third and fourth clauses of Barmen. Without question, an attack on Dahlem is an attack on Barmen. Dahlem rightly appeals to Barmen, and Barmen itself clearly gave the scriptural basis for the decisive clause of Dahlem: Eph. 4. 15, 'Rather, speaking the truth in love, we are to grow up in every way into him who is the head, into Christ, from whom the whole body is composed.'

By this, Barmen has affirmed that in its order the church is bound solely to Jesus Christ, and as a result it has rejected the heresy that the order of the church can be left 'to its discretion or to suit convictions dictated by politics or the climate of opinion'. Barmen rightly held to the central New Testament concept of the church as the body of Christ. The church is not a community of souls, as people want to make it today, nor is it simply the proclamation of the Gospel. In other words, the church is not just the pulpit, but the real body of Christ on earth. It is an ordered and well-defined life together which is founded and established by God on this earth. Just as Jesus Christ was not a truth or an idea, but flesh, i.e. a man with a body, so too the church is the earthly body of the heavenly head. The whole body, with all its members, obeys the one head. It grows in all its parts to the one who is the head. So there is no area of the church which is not wholly and exclusively subject to Christ. It is a dreadful reduction of the New Testament concept if today the church is often seen to have its existence only in preaching and the administration of the sacrament. The church is essentially a gathering round the Word and sacrament, but in addition it is also the whole fullness of gifts, offices and powers which are at work in the community. Finally, it represents the life of the community in accordance with

178

God's commandments. The church is thus the sphere of proclamation, the sphere of order, the sphere of the Christian life. It is all this as the body of Christ. If the preaching is falsified, the church must be responsible for the right sort of preaching; if the order is destroyed by force, the church has to be concerned for a right order; if the church is prevented from practising the Christian life or Christian love, it must nevertheless follow God's commandments and nothing else.

The Synod of Dahlem was faced with the destruction of the church's preaching and order by German Christian despotism. So it took from God's Word the commission to appeal for right preaching and for the right church order. That could not be done in theory alone, it also had to be practised. Dahlem did precisely this. Appealing to Barmen, the synod restored a right church order by appointing the Council of Brethren to guide the church so that it could grow in all parts to him who is the head, Christ. That is the simple fact. All the anxious questions which I am sure you have been wanting to put for a long time: What about the reactions of the state, the Consistory, the pastors and the communities? What will be the consequences for the placing of the younger generation, finance, discussion with the neutrals, and so on? All these questions were not asked by the Synod of Dahlem on purpose, simply because it wanted to say 'Yes' in obedience to the call of its Lord, which had become clear and extremely simple. If this was really God's call, then all further worries could confidently be left to him.

If one wants to give further theological clarification to the simple, basic decision of Dahlem, one might do it in the following clauses:

By its declaration, Dahlem had expressed the following convictions:

1. We are one church.
2. The church needs a church government.
3. The church government can only be appointed by the church

179

itself; and its sole purpose is to proclaim the Gospel and further proper community life.

4. Proclamation in the church is bound up with the church's task.

5. To obey the heretical church government is to disobey Christ.

6. The church leaves concern for the future to its Lord, who is its only leader.

1. *We are one church*

Dahlem acted representatively for the whole church. It spoke 'in the church's cause' and thus indicated that the whole church is not made up by adding the individual communities together, but is the church in itself. Each individual community is merely a part or member of the whole church, just as the Confessing Church is a part of the one Christian church. So Dahlem, being responsible to Scripture, did not think congregationally, i.e. in terms of the individual communities, but in terms of the whole church. The church is originally and essentially one. The members do not come before the body; they are members only as members of the one body. Paul writes to 'the church of God which is in Corinth' (I Cor. 1. 1). He sums up the community to which he writes with his own, 'saints together with all those who in every place call on the name of our Lord Jesus Christ' (I Cor 1. 2). For the sake of the church's unity, Dahlem did not leave the struggle against destruction to the individual communities, but acted in responsibility for the whole church. The whole church was threatened, so action had to be taken on its behalf. Let us notice one thing: we met for the sake of the unity of the church, to prevent separation and schism. But who are the ones who are causing the schism, those who break up and destroy the teaching and order of the church or those who maintain it and restore it? Let us put an end to the perverse self-accusations that the Confessing Church has caused divisions. We are ready to be penitent where we have sinned. But that is a false call to penitence, it comes from the mouths of the German Christians. We are concerned with 'one body and one spirit', but how can that be possible unless there is 'one Lord, one faith' (Eph. 4. 5)? The Church of Jesus Christ can only be truly one where the one faith corresponds to the one Lord, and at present there is only one place where this is, and has been, the case. All self-made unity, whether it is based on organisation, or temperament, or expediency, was revealed as heresy. Dahlem called for the true unity of the church on the basis of the saying, 'Every one who acknowledges me before men, I also will acknowledge before my Father who is in heaven' (Matt. 10. 32).

From this standpoint, Dahlem had to advance the claims of the newly appointed church government upon the whole church and in so doing to set itself against all congregationalist, free-church tendencies from the start. Since the Confessing Church meant to be the one, true church of the Gospel, it could not (and cannot ever) become a sect, surrendering its claim to be the whole church and only looking for and caring for its own life. As long as the church holds to the decisions of Dahlem, it may be a persecuted, suffering church, but it can never go the way of self-sufficiency, by separating itself from the whole church. It will not be lured or forced into that. But as soon as the church abandons the decisions of Dahlem, it must become a sect; for in so doing it separates itself from the one true Catholic Church. Indeed, it will be lucky if it gets away with its life. By appealing to the confessions of the church recognised in the church constitution, the church government must make its claim upon the whole church, just as the Apostolic Church once decided for the whole church.

Because the matter at stake was the true unity of the church in the sense of John 17, because a word for the whole church had been spoken here, it had to be matched by fellowship in action and in suffering. God has made the church one body, 'that there may be no discord in the body, but that the members may have the same care for one another' (I Cor. 12. 25). Suffering together and rejoicing together corresponds with this reciprocal action. 'If one member suffers, all suffer together . . .' It is in the nature of a body that no question, no problem, no reflection can be raised as to whether one member should care for another or suffer with another; such a question is itself the end of membership of the body. Among members of a body, one cares entirely of its own accord for the others, and suffers and rejoices with the others. Being for one another and with each other is simply taken for granted. Anyone who wants to get out of that gets out of the body. It has been asked whether action within the church must always be in common. The New Testament is not conscious of this question. It knows that in any case, members can act for one another only as long as they are members. Isolated action, action which is not for one another, cuts men off from the church as the body of Christ. For the New Testament, to be for one another means that the members are also one in *nous* and *gnome* (I Cor. 1. 10). They should say the same thing, think the same thing (II Cor. 13. 11; Rom. 15. 5; Rom. 12. 16.) The common decision at the Apostolic Council arose from the concern of Jewish and Gentile Christians for one another. It is clear that this mutual responsibility can and will have different forms. The weak act differently from the strong. But the limits of the difference are clear. All act in obedience to the one Lord. Disobedient action cuts men off from the fellowship of the body. I shall discuss what constitutes disobedience later.

We should also add a word here about the often misunderstood saying about 'brotherly solidarity'. The word is not important here. We speak of active and brotherly love. It is so remarkable that we theologians keep forgetting that our obedience to Jesus Christ also demands simple, brotherly love to our brethren in office, to those who suffer and to those who are in the front line. It is almost too obvious to be worth mentioning that we do not leave a brother in distress, that we stand by a brother who is attacked for the sake of the Gospel, even if by chance we ourselves are not attacked, that we side with one another in danger, battle and suffering. Every question, even if it is put unconditionally, already makes this situation problematical and can only lead to evasion. We are again asking about good works instead of doing this work ourselves in such a way that the left hand does not know what the right hand is doing. Let us remember that splendid witness of the Old Testament about the East Jordanian tribes, though as an example, not as a scriptural proof. The Promised Land is being conquered. Reuben and Gad want to remain and settle East of the Jordan. They come to Moses and ask for permission. But Moses lays conditions upon them. They must first help their brothers to settle in *their* land, and so must go before them into battle. Then they may occupy their own lands. We should read Numbers 32. 5–6, 16–23 and Joshua 22. 3–4 thoroughly once more.

We ought also to remember the cry of the prisoner Paul to Timothy, to come to Rome to him, to suffering, not to be ashamed of his fetters but to suffer with him. 'Suffer with' – that is in the end what II Timothy is all about, and it is the last appeal we have from the Apostle Paul. So much for the question of 'solidarity'. We spoke of true unity and the true fellowship of the church; now we come to the second clause.

II. *The church needs a church government*

For the sake of the unity of the church, Dahlem put a true church government in place of one that had become heretical. It did this because of its responsibility for the whole church. Why, and in what sense, does the church needs a church government? Just as each individual community needs direction, so does the whole church. The New Testament community already knows the beginnings of such a common church government. Everything that was part of the Jerusalem church, and this included a number of communities (Acts 21. 20, 'thousands of believers', Samaria, Galilee,

Damascus belonged to it) was under the leadership of James. Similarly, the direction of the community at Ephesus will have involved the care of wide areas. It is quite clear how Paul directs his communities (I Cor. 11; I Cor. 14. 34 and 6. 1; I Tim. 3. 2 ff.; II Cor. 10. 6 and 13. 10, etc.). The clearest example of a comprehensive church government is the Apostolic Council, at which the Jewish ceremonial law was officially declared not to be binding on all the Christian communities. The church needs a church government so that it can be directed as a unity in accordance with the Word of God, and so that schism may be prevented. The situation was particularly clear and simple for the Synod of Dahlem in so far as the individual communities had already relinquished particular rights (training, testing, ordination of preachers) to the whole church. So only the most local rights of the communities themselves had to be considered.

Should the church have tolerated the heretical church government of the German Christians as being the 'overbearing masters' (I Peter 2. 18)? A man would have to be singularly deficient in judgement to confuse the 'overbearing masters' and the destroyers of the church, i.e. if he could no longer distinguish between the obedience due even to an 'overbearing' worldly authority and the church's task of guardianship. According to the teaching of Scripture, false teachers must be heavily punished and expelled from the community. That is necessary for the sake of the community. Read again those sentences which were on everyone's lips at the beginning of the church struggle, and which today we are all too ready to neglect (Ezek. 33. 2 ff.).

In what sense does the church need a church government? Can it not exist without a government? The church does not live by the church government but by the Gospel, but the church government is concerned for the right preaching of the Gospel. Without church government today, the communities run the gravest risk of having no real preachers of the Christian truth. Without true church government, the holy office of preaching will be made the servant of alien powers. Without true church government, the salvation of the communities, which till the end of time depends upon the full and unfalsified preaching of the Gospel, may easily be endangered. So there must be true church government for the sake of the preaching office and for the sake of the communities.

III. *The church government can only be appointed by the church itself; and its sole purpose is to proclaim the Gospel and further proper community life*

According to the testimony of Scripture, the offices of the community are ordained and appointed by the triune God (I Cor. 12. 28, God has appointed . . . , Eph. 4. 11, Christ has appointed . . . , Acts 20. 28, the Holy Spirit has appointed . . .) The apostles or communities fulfil this will of God (Acts 1. 23; 6. 5; 13. 3). True, the form of the offices can be different (Jerusalem, Ephesus), but common to them all is their institution through the community and their exclusive association with the preaching of the Gospel.

It is therefore of the essence of true church government that it binds the community and its offices solely to Jesus Christ. It is of the essence of a heretical church government that it binds community and offices to itself. Dahlem condemned the German Christian church government for binding the offices of the church to the church government instead of to Christ (Dahlem 1. 5). The church government of the Confessing Church is not an end in itself, but exclusively a means to an end. It serves towards redemptive preaching. An attack on the means to the end is an attack on the end itself. The attack on the right church government is an attack on the church's proclamation. The church government is the bulwark of true proclamation in the community. If it is breached, the proclamation and the community itself are endangered. Where concern for the true proclamation is hindered, the proclamation itself is obstructed. For the sake of this proclamation, the offices of the Confessing Church must continue their service to the body of Christ.

IV. *Proclamation in the church is bound up with the church's task*

The proclamation of the Gospel is not a matter of a man's own choice and inner compulsion; he is commissioned to do it. Everything depends on the name, or the authorisation, in which I preach. The most burning love for nation, for community, for the office of preaching can never replace this commission. Preaching is not meant to be *my* word about God, however serious, however honourable, however faithful, but God's own Word. So there can be preaching only where there is a divine commission, i.e. where there is an office in the proper sense. The *vocatio interna* can never replace the *vocatio externa*, otherwise we are led into enthusiasm and sectarianism. This is the very danger which lies in wait for all those who enter office without the right *vocatio externa*, who seek the legal pastorate, but not the legitimate spiritual office of preaching. At this point we must look at the great significance of the concept of 'sending' in the Old and New Testaments. Anyone who preaches without being sent misleads the community. It is said of false prophets that 'I did not send the prophets, yet they ran; I did not speak to them, yet they prophesied' (Jer. 23. 21) and, 'I am against those who prophesy lying dreams, says the Lord, and who tell them and lead my people astray by their lies and their recklessness, when I did not send them or charge them, so they do not profit this people at all' (v. 32) and, 'How can men preach unless they are sent?' (Rom. 10. 15). When Jesus sees the people and has compassion on them, because they are harassed and helpless, like sheep without a shepherd, he does not make his disciples offer to preach and he does not appeal to their love of people and community, but he says, 'Pray the Lord of the harvest to send out labourers into his harvest' (Matt. 9. 38). In a situation which looks very like our own, Jesus does not call his disciples to act in their own power but to pray that God will send preachers. This is because we do not know what is good for the community; God alone in his providence should act with the community. The fire that is to burn in the community is not the fire that burns in us. Only God knows what will really serve the community. God himself will kindle the fire on the altar. The fire which the sons of Aaron wanted to kindle by themselves upon God's altar must consume them, for it is 'unholy fire, such as the Lord had not commanded them' (Lev. 10. 1 ff.). Miriam's rebellion against Moses, whom God has sent, 'Has the Lord indeed spoken only through Moses? Has he not spoken through us also?' (Num. 12. 1) is punished with leprosy. The desire of the Levites, Korah, Dathan and Abiram, for the priesthood, because 'all the congregation are holy' is called a rebellion against the Lord and leads to their downfall (Num. 16. 11). God appoints prophets and priests. 'Then some of the itinerant Jewish exorcists undertook to pronounce the name of the Lord Jesus over those who had evil spirits' (Acts 19. 13), and they are exposed and punished.

The Word may not be spoken without a commission, for the Word is God's own. When Paul goes through Phrygia and Galatia, he is forbidden by the Holy Spirit to preach the Word (Acts 16. 6). Jesus forbids his disciples to go into the cities of the Samaritans, who, in the disciples' view, would certainly also have needed the Gospel (Matt. 10. 6). But Jesus knows why it must be so, and only much later do the disciples see the reason. God will fulfil Matthew 28. 19 himself, in his own way, even if times should come in which Amos 8. 11 becomes true: a hunger and thirst for God's Word come upon the land which will not be quieted, and men seek, but find nothing. God builds his kingdom, we do not. Nowhere in the whole of Scripture does anyone take up an office to which he was not called, because here we are concerned, not with pious actions, but with God's own work. Why did Jeremiah delay, why did Jonah refuse to accept God's commission? Why must James advise, 'Let not many of you become teachers, my brethren, for you know that we who teach shall be judged with greater strictness' (James 3. 1)? Do we want to become preachers of the Gospel in our own power? Do we know what that means? Do we want to dare to snatch at this office? Do we want to do what no man in the Bible did, to take on our own shoulders the responsibility for doing what is really God's work? And do we also want to take the blame for what we have done if it should not please God? Do we want to send ourselves because we are unwilling to pray and wait for God to send us? In the ministry, everything depends upon our being sent, on our commission, and so we should take it upon ourselves only when we receive it quite certainly from God's hand, namely, when we receive it in the name of his true church, where we have been properly instructed in the true Gospel, where we have been rightly tested and proved in our preaching (cf. I Tim. 3. 10; 3. 2; II Tim. 2. 2); these things not only help the church to decide, as it must 'not be hasty in the laying on of hands' (I Tim. 5. 22), but also make us sure. We should not want to become preachers at all unless we have a proper knowledge of the truth and our service has been tested. To receive the office of preaching the Gospel from the hand of a heretical church government is a dangerous thing, it is high-handed, it is a slight on God's commission. But what if we cannot come into office any other way? Must we not make the sacrifice of submitting ourselves again to the Consistory for the sake of the community? Scripture says, 'Obedience is better than sacrifice' (I Sam. 15. 22), for in obedience you leave the power to God alone. It says, 'I will give you shepherds after my own heart' (Jer. 3. 15). God knows his own will. So what are we to do? 'Pray the Lord of the harvest . . .' That is the first thing. It is more certain, for the sake of the Gospel and the community, to receive a minor office from the hand of, and in the name of, the church of God, than an assured office from the hands of the enemies of the church; for in all the responsibility and difficulty of our office there is one thing of which we want to be quite certain – that Christ has sent us.

188

v. *To obey the heretical church government is to disobey Christ*

In recognition of this, Dahlem appealed for a general withdrawal from the German Christian church government and from cooperation with those who still wanted to obey that régime. A church government is inevitably heretical if it recognises other demands on its ministry than those of the Gospel. It then becomes necessary to suppress those who are bound only by the Gospel, and as a result the church becomes a furtherer of false teaching and lies. The fact that individual members of the church government may make a desperate, hopeless stand against these restrictions laid upon them, against their commission, does not affect the office of the church government as such.

We are not so much interested in the personal question as in the false commission, the misuse of office. In bearing an office not of the church, they must be enemies of the church, whether they wish it and realise it or not; indeed through their inability to distinguish between truth and lies, they themselves must be false teachers. Jeroboam's hidden sin leads inevitably to the open sin of Ahab. You should read I Kings 12. 25–33 again very carefully, and then go on. Saul, who no longer asks God for wisdom in all things, but acts from the thoughts of his heart, must in the end go to the witch and have his downfall prophesied. But the Church of Christ should remain undisturbed by false teaching and by those who introduce and excuse it, for the sake of the will of God, the salvation of the communities and the redemption of their souls. 'Avoid a heretical man' (Titus 3. 10), for he leads the community astray (II Tim. 3. 6 f.) 'Anyone who does not abide in the doctrine of Christ does not have God' (II John 9). A church which no longer takes the rejection of false teaching seriously no longer takes truth, i.e. its salvation, seriously, and ultimately no longer takes the community seriously, no matter how pious or well organised it may be. Anyone who follows false teaching, indeed who simply supports it and furthers it, no longer obeys Christ. We read, 'You cannot serve two masters, you cannot serve God and mammon' (Matt. 6. 24), and mammon has always been in the hands of this world. 'Do not be mismated with unbelievers. For what partnership have righteousness and iniquity? What accord has Christ with Belial?' (II Cor. 6. 14 ff.). To obey a heretical church government is to disobey Christ. For Christ's sake we must disobey the heretical church government, even if it has been appointed by the state. But disobedience to the false church régime must be matched by true obedience to the right church government. The latter must be supported for the sake of the Gospel. True, the church government is not the Gospel; in any given form it is an *adiaphoron*. But where it is to be subjected by outside force to a law which is alien to the church it may not yield, but must bear witness in word and deed to its freedom from the alien law and its sole obedience to Jesus Christ. *In statu confessionis nihil est adiaphoron* (cf. Paul and Titus, Gal. 1. 3 ff.). And let anyone who thinks that with a free conscience, and in obedience to Christ, he can obey a heretical church government know the straits into which he is leading his brothers. Let him take to heart the words of Jesus, which give such a fearful warning against causing one of the little ones to be offended.

Now where this presupposition is clear once and for all, that the way to the heretical church government is forbidden us by the Word of God, we can fruitfully consider the new ways that are open to us. If we continually toy with the idea that we might still get back in the end, then the future can only depress us, for we have taken it into our own régime.

VI. *The church leaves concern for the future to its Lord, who is its only leader*

It may be that only now have we reached the point which most concerns us today. 'What is to be done?' we ask. Worry goes the rounds, and has become a terrible power. Dahlem could abandon care for the future to God, because it wanted to obey him alone. We shall only be free from care if we remain firm in the truth that we know and allow ourselves to be guided only by that. But we stare at the waves, instead of looking to the Lord, and so we are lost. It is a great temptation – we must confess it – for us and for many when brethren keep on demanding earnestly, 'Look at the waves! Look at the storm! All cannot be well'. That is a temptation to unbelief. We will not and cannot deny that there are waves, but we do not want to look at them, but at Christ, who is stronger than they. I wish people would only understand that. It is different in the world, but that is the only way it can be in the church.

From the other side, since the beginning of the church struggle people have been recalling Jesus' saying about counting the cost before one begins a thing (Luke 14. 28 ff.). But they tend to forget what it means. Jesus is not talking about deciding on a particular course here, but about the whole of discipleship. Jesus compels no one to follow him, he asks everyone to think what he is doing if he wants to be a disciple. If a person reflects, and then decides against it, it is then impossible for him to take another easier, say a consistorial, way. Everything is at stake. There is a straightforward answer. 'You cannot be my disciple' (v. 33). Jesus does not ask them to weigh up a number of possibilities. He demands a decision. Wholly with him or wholly without him. This is the question that we face today.

People ask, 'Have you really nothing more to say in addition to Barmen and Dahlem? We must go further!' 'We need something new!' Only a person who stands completely by the decision of the Confessing Synods can talk like that, and one thing is certain: we, at any rate, are not in that position. What, then, is the real position? Not that we have taken Barmen and Dahlem too seriously, but that since 1935 we have not taken them seriously enough! We see and acknowledge a great fault of the Confessing Church: we have largely rejected God's grace and God's call. We thought that we would be able to get on without them. What do Barmen and Dahlem mean? Concern for true proclamation and for the proper development of the congregations. Where is that now? We have taken too little notice of God's gracious offer and it is unspeakably difficult to begin again. Only God himself in his forgiving grace can once again lead us to the right way. Our guilt has become particularly manifest in two things: we have taken the way of Dahlem seriously only as far as the young theologians were concerned. We have not dared to stand completely by Dahlem. So we have laid too heavy a burden on you young brethren. But it was still the right way, and for that we would wholeheartedly thank God the Lord with you today. And secondly: since 1935, we have often asked how we can win back those who are faltering, restrain those who are leaving us, make a broader front, instead of how we can continue faithfully and in practice on the way of Barmen and Dahlem. As a result, concern for the preaching of the Confessing Church and the development of the congregations, despite the urgency, has often remained too much in the background. Instead, the question of church government has time and again become the centre of our thoughts and conversations. That was not only an unhealthy development, it was a fault. It gradually became an almost intolerable burden for all those who wanted to continue along the way of Barmen and Dahlem in faith that the question, 'Council of Brethren or Consistory?', continually dominated discussions and sessions. We allowed ourselves to remain on a course which we had to continue. The trouble with it all was not that we carried out the decisions of Dahlem but that we did not carry them out. We have been shown this by a number of provinces, districts and congregations. Some of them have spent a lot of time on practical questions of preaching and developing the congregational life and are doing fruitful work in it. Would it not be more welcome to you (and we could start today) to talk at last about what really oppresses us, instead of the continual discussion of the old question? We could think about what the Confessing Church has to say about Gospel and Law, proclamation and youth, church and synagogue, baptism and godparents, penitence and the eucharist, popular mission and discipline in the community. Why can't we do this? Because we continually let ourselves be held back by doubt about the truth we once recognised, because for a long time we have not 'done' the 'truth' of Barmen and Dahlem. If we don't begin to do the truth, we shall have plenty of time for all the practical questions over there in the ranks of the Consistory. There we have lost all inward authority, because we have not remained in the truth. We must go the whole way, even today, as we did at Barmen and at Dahlem.

But anyone who does go will be free from all care for the future. He will learn that the way of the church is a joyful way. He will learn that the yoke of Jesus is easy and light to those who do not press against it.

'Listen, ye servants of the Lord. You can be suspended, removed, refused acceptance, be deprived of office, forfeit home and hearth, but you will again be preachers. That is the word of promise. And if a man is deposed at twelve places and gets one more new place, he will be a preacher in thirteen parishes. For in all the previous ones our innocence, our cross, our faith, will preach more strongly than if we were there ourselves.' (*Zinzendorff, On Jeremiah 15*)

Dear brethren, be sure of God's promise!

God does not leave us without instruction (Deut. 30. 11 f.)

God will give the churches shepherds after his own heart (Jer. 3. 15)

God has ways and means of sustaining his own (Matthew 6. 32)

God makes us joyful and certain (Joshua 1. 8)

God gives us constancy and patience (James 1. 12)

God grants us the victory (Luke 12. 32)

G.S. II pp. 320–45

With that word to the younger ministers of Pomerania, we need now to return to the progress of events during 1938. In February, Bonhoeffer made his first contact with the leaders of the political resistance. There are naturally enough no documents to support this, but there is clear evidence that he met with Sack, Oster, Canaris and Beck during that month. There was some talk of Niemöller being released early in March, but this came to nothing, or rather he was taken to concentration camp instead. Then on 12th March came the annexation of Austria. Hitler's extension of the greater Reich had started. It was a gloomy Easter for many in Germany as well as Austria, now part of Germany. On the church scene, efforts were being made to reconcile the Confessing Church with, or rather within, the German Evangelical Church. The oath of loyalty, required of all government officials, was demanded of church officials also. Bonhoeffer was in the thick of this fight. Then, in June, came the reunion of former Finkenwalde students at the original site in Zingst.[1] Bonhoeffer circulated a personal letter after this reunion.

PERSONAL LETTER FROM BONHOEFFER TO THE BRETHREN:[2] We still have vivid memories of those days of holiday together. Seldom have I experienced so rich a time. After sharing these days together, we certainly understand better than ever those remarks in the two Johannine letters on which we were meditating recently. John not only wants to communicate with his brethren 'with pen and ink', but desires to speak with them 'face to face', 'so that our joy may be complete' (II John 12). The spoken word strikes us more, involves us more, strengthens us more than anything else. The Lord Jesus Christ was among us in those conversations which never stopped from morning until late evening, and he has bound us firmly together once again. We could listen to one another, discuss and contribute to the decisions of the brethren, and we could again tell one another

[1] *No Rusty Swords*, p. 297
[2] In the place of circular letters which were banned.

of Jesus' call to faith and obedience which is our sole help. So once again we also know something of how our joy is made complete by such meetings. Only during these days did it probably dawn on many of us how poor we had become, how often our prayer for one another had grown empty and thoughtless over the time in which we did not see each other. One of the many gifts of these days has been the completely different reality which our intercession for one another has taken on, and I also hope that after these conversations 'face to face' the correspondence with 'pen and ink' will now gain new life.

Once again, I thank those who were there with all my heart for coming. Some sacrificed a great deal of time and money for the sake of the brethren. To come from the Rhine and the most eastern parts of East Prussia was no small thing. But I am sure that each of you went home as enriched as the rest of us. May I tell those of you who were not there how much we missed you. Many faithfully sent a brotherly greeting. We thank them especially. In this way they were in our company with 'pen and ink'. We know that they too had to make a sacrifice in not coming. Questions were asked about some people about whom we unfortunately did not know a great deal. But the many greetings cards which were sent to the absent brethren in themselves gave a sure sign of the comradeship which still exists.

Forty-five brethren came. The photographs, which we are still waiting for, will serve to remind us of the time. It is certain that we shall do everything possible to be together again next year. We are grateful that despite everything it was possible this year.

I greet you all in the fellowship of intercession for your health in body, soul and spirit (III John 2), for your homes, your ministry and your communities. Do not be led astray by the numerous negotiations and plans in which we are once more involved. 'Look to yourselves, that you may not lose what you have worked for, but may win a full reward' (II John 8).

Bonhoeffer attached the following report by one of the participants to his circular letter.

HOLIDAY IN ZINGST

The older brethren can at least imagine the outward scene: bathing, games on the shore, conversations behind the dunes, and everything that has made this place so familiar at other times . . . The day began, of course, with prayers in the usual form, and meditation after breakfast, which was immediately followed by the singing. We also sang for half an hour before supper. Brother Bonhoeffer took the Bible study in the morning on the concept of temptation, an exegesis of the sixth petition of the Lord's Prayer. It is to be hoped that this work will later be made available to all the brethren . . .[1] After coffee, we had discussions together, introduced by brief reports from individual brethren about preaching, pastoral care and the instruction of confirmands. In the discussions about preaching we were principally concerned with the question of being single-minded and yet going right to the heart of the text, with the need for a concrete approach, and with the right way of preaching the paraenetic texts of the Gospels. Pastoralia discussions dealt with the difficulty which almost all of us find in helping members of our congregations who want to be Christians but will not accept the way of the Confessing Church either because of fear or mistrust. We decided that the liberating power of the glad tidings must be proclaimed in all its strength to enslaved consciences as well as the commandment of the 'first step'. We must remember that red cards and participation in the service of intercession is already hard food, which all cannot take while on the other hand the personal responsibility of the individual for home and congregation is 'the milk' which must first be given to such men . . . In the evening, we had reports by the brethren from their churches and then discussed the situation of our Confessing Church in general and that of the younger brethren in particular.

[1] *Temptation*, SCM Press, 1955. It was not published in Germany until 1953.

The report of a brother from Saxony about work in his province was a joy to us. Recently, a number of brethren have stayed with their congregations under express prohibition, until they have been ejected by physical force. Brethren who are available have made the first beginnings of a regular popular mission, an itinerant preaching of the Word. We were clear that even if the way to the pastorate is largely barred, the rumour of our being out of work must never be allowed to arise, and that even if a Council of Brethren neglects its tasks of spiritual direction, we must all attempt to stay in the churches to which we have been appointed, and so through our obedience to the Council of Brethren lead them to give us proper instructions. The fact that in some leading church circles stagnation seems to have set in, that here and there simple obedience and joy threaten to disappear, that instead of this a concern for numbers, for winning over the outsiders, the bishops, the neutrals, etc., is sapping so much useful strength, has caused us to write a letter to the leading men of our church. It is to be taken in person by some of the brethren. We know that some of the leading brethren are grateful for such voices from the group of brethren. We were conscious of another urgent task and obligation, the pastoral care which we owe to those brethren who have left us for the Consistory. Two brethren will visit each of them in the near future. While we have been here, we have also become clear about the absolute necessity of taking seriously the job of visiting each other and all the brethren in our group of churches. The decisions which we face now and in the near future are difficult to bear alone. We have decided together on one more thing: to help us towards popular missions in the near future, brethren who live closest to each other are to work together in groups of four. The list of addresses will tell us who lives nearest to us and whom we can ask to help in a popular mission in the way that we have worked out.

We very much want to let you know that we have thought of you all each day in our prayers, and particularly of the two brethren,

Lohmann and Wichmann, who are sick. Also about Brother Koch and all those who are in prison. We thank you for all your letters and greetings. All the brothers greet you.   G.S. II pp. 533–7

Bonhoeffer wrote to his parents with enthusiasm of this reunion: 'The days in Zingst, where I met with all the former students, were wonderful. Now we are taking a few days' rest before throwing ourselves again into the work. I hear that we are not to expect any further hindrances for some time. Perhaps that depends upon Uncle Rudi . . .'[1]

G.S. II p. 533

Bonhoeffer's personal letters continued to circulate and it is evident from them that he was concerned about the troubles in Czechoslovakia. The resistance to Hitler received a heavy set-back on 17th August when General Beck, the senior military member of the group Bonhoeffer had contacted, was retired. The situation was dark, but the letters show that he did not falter. His meditation text for the letter of 23rd August is, 'Let no man disqualify you!' (Col. 2. 18). In September he wrote up what had been the basis of the community life at Finkenwalde in a little book called, 'Life Together'.[2] His mind was very much on Czechoslovakia. This was hardly surprising with Chamberlain at Berchtesgarten on the 15th to discuss the Sudeten crisis, Karl Barth's letter to Hromadka on the 19th, the Lutheran liturgy of prayers for Czechoslovakia appearing on the 27th, and the infamous Munich conference on the 29th and 30th. This was Czechoslovakia's month! It needed only the condemnation of the 'Lutheran liturgy' by bishops Marahrens, Meiser and Wurm to complete the picture. This declaration by the three bishops was made to Kerrl on 29th October. By then, Hitler had annexed the Sudetenland and had his eyes on the rest of Czechoslovakia. The horror of the régime was clear to everybody by now, and the 'Crystal Night'[3] when Jews were cruelly attacked confirmed the

---

[1] 'Uncle Rudi' was the code name for war or war preparations.

[2] SCM Press, 1954.

[3] 9th November, 1938, when Jewish homes, shops and synagogues were ruthlessly smashed by the Nazis. The name in German has the same macabre poetical tone as in English.

nature of the Nazis. Bonhoeffer was confirmed in his resistance and his political contacts increased. He continued to send his 'personal letters' and on 20th November we read:

ADVENT LETTER, 1938

At the end of the old church year and the beginning of the new, my first greeting to you is the saying from last week's meditation text: 'May the God of steadfastness and encouragement grant you to live in such harmony with one another, in accord with Christ Jesus' (Rom. 15. 5). We have been doing a great deal of work here recently, thinking together about the New Testament concept of patience, during which it has become quite clear to me that all along the line we have got to the point where there is only one fundamental question. Do we want to learn the meaning of patience from the Gospel? In my opinion, we do not need to take the numerous questions about which we get impatient so seriously. The only serious thing is that our impatience always wants to play nasty tricks on us, by giving itself out as a special sort of obedience, and leading us into unfaithfulness. Somehow, I'm not quite sure how, we have largely got into a way of thinking which is positively dangerous. We think that we are acting particularly responsibly if every other week we take another look at the question whether the way on which we have set out is the right one. It is particularly noticeable that such a 'responsible reappraisal' always begins the moment serious difficulties appear. We then speak as though we no longer had 'a proper joy and certainty' about this way, or, still worse, as though God and his Word were no longer as clearly present with us as they used to be. In all this, we are ultimately trying to get round what the New Testament calls 'patience' and 'testing'. Paul, at any rate, did not begin to reflect whether his way was the right one when opposition and suffering threatened, nor did Luther. They were both quite certain and glad that they should remain disciples and followers of their Lord. Dear brethren, our real trouble is not doubt about the way upon which we have set out, but our failure to be patient, to keep quiet. We still cannot imagine that today God really doesn't want anything new from us, but simply to prove us in the old way. That is too petty, too monotonous, too undemanding for us. And we simply cannot be constant with the fact that God's cause is not always the successful one, that we really could be 'unsuccessful' and yet be on the right road. But this is where we find out whether we have begun in faith or in a burst of enthusiasm.

The significance of patience in the New Testament is quite striking. Only the patient man receives the promise (Matt. 24. 13), only the patient man brings forth good fruit (Luke 8. 15). A faith which does not become patience is inauthentic, unusable. Faith must be proved. It can only be proved in suffering. Only suffering and endurance, will produce the 'perfect work' (James 1. 3 ff.). If we remember that the word faith *(pistis)* already contains the element of faithfulness, we shall not be surprised at the close connection between faith and patience. There is patience only 'in Jesus' (Rev. 1. 9) for Jesus was patient as he bore the cross. Hebrews 12. 2 describes Jesus' way of the cross as a way of endurance, of patience. For us, endurance means to stand in the fellowship of Christ's suffering (I Cor. 1. 6 ff.), and thereby to gain assurance. If we share in the patience of Jesus, we shall ourselves become patient and we will finally have a share in his kingdom (II Tim. 2. 12). The way to patience leads through discipline (II Peter 1. 6). The freer we are from ease and indolence and personal claims, the more ready we shall be for patience.

Our text tells us that we can remain united only if we remain patient. Impatience makes for division. And unfortunately it cannot be denied that all those who have already gone their own way through impatience, have made the struggle and test of patience still more difficult for the other brethren. Impatience disrupts fellowship. In the view of the Gospel, it is not just a minor, venial, bad habit; it is a failure in the testing of faith. 'Now the God of patience' – the God who himself endured in Jesus Christ and helps us to endure –

give you 'one mind' – to stand by one another in these hours of testing, to come closer to one another, to strengthen and help one another. It is grim if anyone departs at such a time. But our patience depends, not upon men, but upon Jesus Christ and his patience on the cross. He bore the impatience of all men and so can forgive them. 'One mind', i.e. not this way today and another tomorrow: remain firm by what you already know, remain constant, show yourselves faithful. How little importance we attach to constancy, firmness and faithfulness! In the Scriptures they are right at the top of the list.

God grant them to us by making us patient and promising us his comfort in our endurance. One in patience, one in comfort. We belong together in endurance, we also belong together in comfort and in the final victory. No one fights the battle of proving his faith alone. In the hour in which our patience is tried we are one with those who are of one mind with us. And above all, we know that we are one in the patience and comfort of Jesus. He is our patience and our comfort. And this will also be so in the new church year.

If I may give you some advice, take care and work hard with us at the concepts with which we are so concerned at the moment, temptation, patience, proving, humility, thanksgiving, joy, peace, discipline. We have to learn to hear the Gospel all over again in these passages. We are being led through the Scriptures along almost untrodden paths, but the views are indescribably wide and beautiful. The meditation texts in the next few weeks should also help us here.

During the past few days I have been thinking a great deal about Psalm 74, Zech. 2. 12, Rom. 9. 4 f., and 11. 11–15. That takes us right into prayer.

I have been very glad to hear from many of you and also to have been able to read your sermons. May I ask the brethren to whom I return sermons to let me know, at least by a postcard, whether they arrive safely, and whether you agree with my comments or not? Please do not think that I cannot be reached by letter, but keep writing and telling me what happens. I think that I have become better at answering in the last few months, at any rate. I have taken care in this direction, for one should really not let such comradeship dissolve through idleness. Above all, keep up the links between yourselves, write and visit. That is the most important thing.

I wish you a good Advent with all my heart. God bless your preaching and all your work. May he protect you and your homes. We think of you daily.   G.S. II pp. 541–4

Bonhoeffer is writing with caution and not all the matters deeply concerning him in these terrifying days were recorded in letters. But a few days after this Advent letter, he wrote with enthusiasm to Brother Koch who had been released from his 'conversion camp'.

2. The Second American Visit

As the year 1939 opened, Bonhoeffer was troubled by two things. The Confessing Church was rapidly being cut off from contact with churches abroad. This had the effect of turning its interest inward as well as misrepresenting its struggle abroad. The other matter was personal and he was at pains to separate it from the first. The personal issue concerned his attitude to military service which became a real issue as his age group was due to be called up. He knew that he could not serve in Hitler's armed forces and would be unable to take the oath. He was never lacking in courage, but he was afraid for the Confessing Church. If he was condemned as a pacifist, that might put a pacifist label on the Confessing Church and again confuse the real issue at stake in the struggle.

Both matters which concerned him in 1939 could be helped by his departure from Germany at this critical moment. He was too conscientious to mix the two and faced grave moral questions as he sought to solve both his personal and his more official problems separately. He resolved to explain the situation clearly to the Bishop of Chichester; but could hardly do this in a letter from Germany. He waited until he made a visit to England in March, when he stayed with his sister and her husband who had been refugees there since the previous year. His letter to Dr. Bell was dated 13th March from London.

23 Manor Mount, London, S.E.23 13th March, 1939

BONHOEFFER TO CHICHESTER: May I just let you know that I have arrived in London last night. I am so happy to be here once again for a short time and I am looking forward very much to seeing you soon. A friend of mine, Pastor Bethge, has come with me and wishes to bring you a special message from the Provisional Adminis-tration. There are so many things which I should like to discuss with you, that I should be very grateful, if you could let me know when and where I could see you. I have found the Leibholzes well and full of gratitude for all your goodness and help. It makes me so happy to know that. I am afraid the political situation is just now becoming more tense and precarious. In deep gratitude for all you are doing for us.   G.S. I p. 279

This letter said very little, but a few days later Bonhoeffer heard that Visser 't Hooft was coming to England and he saw an opportunity for wider discussion with this leader of the ecumenical movement. He wrote again on 25th March, this time going into details about his problems.

BONHOEFFER TO CHICHESTER: Dr. Rieger just tells me that Visser 't Hooft will come to London next week and stay with you at Chichester. I also understand that the next week-end does not suit you well for our visit to Chichester. May I now ask a great favour from you? Would you kindly tell Visser 't Hooft that I am very anxious to see him during his stay in London? Any time except Wednesday when I have to be at Oxford would suit me well. Would you also be so kind as to let me know any time when I could see you once more before I go back to Germany?

In order not to take too much of your time when we meet, I should like to put before you the two questions which I am very anxious to discuss with you before my return to Germany. The first question concerns the Confessing Church, the second one is very personal. Please excuse my troubling you again and again and my placing one burden after another on your shoulders.

With regard to the position of the Confessing Church we feel strongly in Germany that – mainly owing to travelling difficulties – the relationship of our church to the churches abroad is not as it ought to be. The responsibility which is placed upon us makes it more and more necessary to have a permanent exchange of opinion and the advice of other churches. We are fully aware of and gratefully appreciate what is continuously being done for us from individuals to individuals. But I think, we must try to go a step farther and to come to some sort of regular cooperation with and to a better representation of the Confessing Church in the ecumenical movements. If we are not going to take a decisive step forward in this direction I am afraid we shall very soon be cut off entirely from our brethren abroad, and that would at any rate mean a tremendous loss to us. What I therefore think we should try to get, is a man who could devote all his time to establishing the necessary contacts, to cooperating in the ecumenical meetings and conferences, learning and contributing. I think we failed in earlier years to give our full assistance in advice and fellowship to the Russian Christians; now a similar situation is clearly developing in Germany. Do you not think, my Lord Bishop, it is urgently necessary to avoid a similar failure? Frankly and with all due respect, the German representatives in Geneva simply cannot represent the cause of the Confessing Church. So there is a real vacancy which must be filled up sooner or later. This is the first question which I should like to raise and to discuss with you before I go home again to see the men of the Brethren Council. I have also an idea in my mind for the eventual financial difficulties.

The second point is of entirely personal character and I am not certain if I may bother you with it. Please, do take it quite apart from the first point. I am thinking of leaving Germany sometime. The main reason is the compulsory military service to which the men of my age (1906) will be called up this year. It seems to me conscientiously impossible to join in a war under the present circumstances. On the other hand, the Confessing Church as such has not taken any definite attitude in this respect and probably cannot take it as things are. So I should cause a tremendous damage to my brethren if I would make a stand on this point which would be regarded by the régime as typical of the hostility of our church towards the state. Perhaps the worst thing of all is the military oath which I should have to swear. So I am rather puzzled in this situation, and perhaps even more because I feel, it is really only on Christian grounds that I find it difficult to do military service under the present conditions, and yet there are only very few friends who would approve of my attitude. In spite of much reading and thinking concerning this matter I have not yet made up my mind what I would do under different circumstances. But actually as things are I should have to do violence to my Christian conviction, if I would take up arms 'here and now'. I have been thinking of going to the Mission Field, not as an escape out of the situation, but because I wish to serve somewhere where service is really wanted. But here also the German foreign exchange situation makes it impossible to send workers abroad. With respect to British Missionary Societies I have no idea of the possibilities there. On the other hand, I still have the great desire to serve the Confessing Church as long as I possibly could. My Lord Bishop, I am very sorry to add trouble to your trouble. But I thought, I might speak freely to you and might ask your advice. You know the Confessing Church and you know me a bit. So I thought you could help me best. It was with regard to this matter that I wanted to see Visser 't Hooft too.

Please excuse this long letter. I hope to see you soon. Leibholz asks me to thank you for your letter to Dr. Lindsay. G.S. I pp. 279–82

Meanwhile he had received an invitation to go to Oxford to talk with Leonard Hodgson, another prominent leader of the ecumenical movement. The following correspondence shows the extent of their discussion.

Westbrook, Westwood Park, London, S.E.23
BONHOEFFER TO HODGSON: I thank you very much indeed for your kind letter and your invitation. On Wednesday the 29th of March I shall come to Oxford and it would be indeed a great privilege to me

if I could see you there. I have been looking forward to an occasion of seeing you ever since we had a short correspondence in Denmark two years ago[1], and I am very happy that I shall have the opportunity of a discussion with you in a few days. The question which I should most of all like to discuss with you is concerning the regular and close contact between the Confessing Church and the 'Faith and Order' movement. The more we are becoming cut off from our foreign friends the more we feel it to be necessary to find a way of a permanent representation in the ecumenical movement and particularly in the department concerning 'Faith and Order'. We need the theological help of other churches in order to be able to bear the burden of responsibilities which God has laid upon us, and we wish to give you a witness of the Christian insights, which God has given us anew during the last years. I feel strongly that something has to be done quickly, practically and effectively in order to establish new relations between you and us. Would it, for instance, not be possible to have a permanent German secretary of the Confessing Church in Geneva or in London, and if not permanent then perhaps for one year or two? Those are the questions which I should like to discuss with you from the theological and practical point of view. The main difficulty might be the financial side of the matter. But I feel, there must be something wrong, if a thing which is spiritually necessary should become impossible for financial reasons. Please excuse this long letter. I thought it to be better to let you know our questions and hopes before we meet.

30th March, 1939

HODGSON TO BONHOEFFER: I was very glad indeed to have the pleasure of seeing you, and I now feel that I appreciate your situation in a manner which would have been impossible without our conversation. I had better try to put down in writing what I said yesterday.

You had written to say that you wanted to discuss the possibility of

[1] Probably a slip of the pen; it should read 'four years ago'.

maintaining contact between the Confessing Church in Germany and the Faith and Order Movement.

i. I began by pointing out the impossibility of our establishing officials relations with the German Evangelical Church at the present moment, the reasons being as follows:

1. By our constitution the churches appoint the World Conference, and the conference then appoints its Continuation Committee, which maintains its existence by co-option until the next conference, when it ceases to exist. There is therefore no direct representation of churches on the Continuation Committee; the committee derives its authority mediately from the churches through the conference.

2. The German Evangelical Church found itself unable to be represented at the Edinburgh Conference, and therefore, when the conference appointed its Continuation Committee, it could not appoint from among its members any representatives of that church. So what it did was to instruct the committee to co-opt eight representatives of that Church when such action should become possible.

3. It is the custom of the Continuation Committee to co-opt to membership those persons whom churches themselves wish to have as their representatives. For this purpose it is necessary to be able to have communication in each case with a central body having full confidence of the whole church, and able to nominate representatives in its name. We are advised that at the present time (in Germany) there is no such church (body), and that we must not attempt to treat the different groups within that church independently as if they were separate churches. Hence for the time being the filling of these places has to be left in abeyance.

ii. I then told you that last summer I was approached by Dr. Wahl asking whether Dr. Krummacher and Dr. Gerstenmaier might attend the 1938 meeting of the Continuation Committee. I replied in a letter explaining the position exactly as I have just set it forth in the preceding paragraph of this letter. I then added that, if they wished to come as visitors, we should be very glad to welcome them, and that they would be given a full part in all proceedings, except that they would not be able to vote on questions which the Continuation Committee alone was competent to decide, and might possibly be unable to be present at any particular session, should the committee wish to confine it strictly to its own members. I wrote individually to Dr. Krummacher and Dr. Gerstenmaier explaining the situation. They both came, were welcomed by the committee, and took a full part in its proceedings, except that they had no responsibility for any of its decisions.

III. It is quite clear that the committee would give an equal welcome on the same conditions to any representatives of the Confessing Church who should be commended to us in a similar way. I understand that for this purpose Dr. Boehm would correspond to Dr. Wahl. If therefore the names of two representatives could be communicated to me by Dr. Boehm, and those two representatives come to St. George's School, Clarens, on Monday 21st August this year, they will be welcomed as visitors and given a full share in our proceedings.

IV. I also asked whether it might not be possible for one or two younger men to come as members of our Youth Group, and I suggested your consulting with the Rev. Oliver Tomkins on this subject. We welcome as visitors to our meetings any persons who are nominated to us by Oliver Tomkins, and therefore we should welcome any of your representatives whom he included in his list.

V. We then discussed the question of finance, and you put before me the difficulty your countrymen have in obtaining foreign currency. I said that if one or two visitors representing the Confessing Church, and one or two members of the Youth Group, could get as far as Montreux station, we would be responsible for their hospitality during the period of the meeting.

VI. I then pointed out that in the next few years I expect the main work of the movement to be done by the Commissions, and expressed the hope that we should be able to have the collaboration of members of the Confessing Church in that work.

I think this covers the ground of our discussion yesterday, and I hope that it gives a satisfactory answer to the questions you raised.

G.S. I pp. 282–5

Copies of this letter were sent to William Temple, then Archbishop of York, and to Tissington Tatlow. Later, copies were sent to Dr. Boehm (13.5.39), the Bishop of Chichester (23.5.39) and to Schönfeld (25.6.39).

Leonard Hodgson had been aware of Bonhoeffer's attitude to the German Christians and he knew his argument concerning representation at ecumenical conferences from correspondence of four years earlier.[1] In the interim Bonhoeffer had not changed, but the situation had and we note a marked softening and understanding on the part of Canon Hodgson! Before he left England, Bonhoeffer wrote his thanks to the Bishop of Chichester.

13th April, 1939

BONHOEFFER TO CHICHESTER: Before returning to Germany I just wish to thank you once again for the great help you gave me in our talk at Chichester. I do not know what will be the outcome of it all, but it means much to me to realise that you see the great conscientious difficulties with which we are faced. I will let you know as soon as I see the situation clearly. Thank you for all your sympathy for our cause.

G.S. I p. 286

Then events moved fast. Bonhoeffer was beginning to realise that the only way his problems could be solved was by an invitation to America. He approached his friend Reinhold Niebuhr of Union Theological Seminary while he was in England. Niebuhr was then giving the Gifford Lectures in Edinburgh. Reinhold Niebuhr acted at once but his letter was either lost or delayed. Bonhoeffer urged him to write again by telling of the urgency. He wrote on 1st May to Henry Leiper in New York.

[1] *No Rusty Swords*, pp. 12, 13.

Edinburgh, 1st May, 1939

NIEBUHR TO LEIPER: Some time ago I wrote Roland Elliot and asked him to transmit the letter to you. It concerned Dr. Dietrich Bonhoeffer whom you know. My letter to Elliot wandered about and finally reached him over here in England. The proposition I wrote him about was this: Bonhoeffer is due for military service in July and will refuse to serve. The Bruderrat of the Confessing Church would like to have him evade the issue and at the same time tell American Christians about their situation. To get him out they need rather formal and formidable invitations from America. I suggested in this letter that the Student Movement might ask him to their June conferences and that afterwards you might get him some engagements at church conferences and church camps during the summer. In the fall, I would secure university engagements for him.

He speaks English so well and embodies the spirit of the struggle over there so well in his person that I believe his coming would be valuable for our sake as well as for his. I have also written to Dr. Coffin asking him to send a formidable invitation for a lecture at Union Seminary.

Much time has been lost because of the loss of my letter. Perhaps by this time the student people have got in touch with you. Today I received word from Bonhoeffer saying that time was short. If he is to make necessary arrangements he ought to have a cable as well as a confirming letter. If you think well of the idea of inviting him would you send him a cable if this has not been done. I shall provide a room for him at the seminary and I think nominal fees will take care of the rest. G.S. I pp. 287–8

Within a few days, Henry Leiper sent the invitation.

11th May, 1939

LEIPER TO BONHOEFFER: It is my pleasure to transmit to you herewith a formal invitation for you to come at once to America to undertake an important piece of service for the churches in the New York area under the general auspices of the Central Bureau of Interchurch Aid and Union Theological Seminary. The nature of your duties would be a combination of pastoral service, preaching and lecturing in the theological summer school at Columbia and Union Seminary, to begin with, and later in the Seminary in the usual term. The term of service is not now fixed although we hope that it can be a permanent thing, and expect that it will occupy you for at least the next two or three years.

The Committee has thought it best not to enter into matters such as salary and other details, but can assure you that we are prepared to meet your reasonable request with respect to salary basis and other terms of service.

We should like to have you come, if possible, to begin service by the middle of June, which will mean your reaching this country at the earliest possible date for consultation and general preparation.

Dr. Samuel McCrea Cavert and Dean Henry P. Van Dusen are associated with me in this request and share with me the very great personal hope that you will find it possible to accept and to come in the very near future, as indicated above.

Copies to Dr. Van Dusen and Dr. Cavert.   G.S. I p. 288

Other correspondence followed and there was soon great enthusiasm for Bonhoeffer to come to America. He was urged to be there by the middle of June and arrived on the 12th.

Before he left Germany a successor had to be found to carry on his work with the young theologians who had continued in community life despite the closing of Finkenwalde. He left a note for his successor, although at the time he wrote the note he was not sure who it would be.

TO MY SUCCESSOR

He will find:

1. One of the finest pieces of work in the Confessing Church.
2. Two colleagues, who have been more than four years in the

work and for the past year and a half have taken full responsibility for the houses, as well as the leadership of the community life during those periods when I could not be there myself.

3. Work already started: N.T.: the concept of *'hamartia'*, which should follow the work done on soteriological concepts; Dogmatics: it will be necessary to continue along the lines already started, which is the Formula of Concord as far as *'de libero arbitrio'*. In the N.T. you will have much more freedom. Some sermon classes in Koeslin, a few lectures on homiletics in both places.'

Matters requested:

1. Apart from N.T. and Dogmatics there should be seminars on pastoral work, in Sigurdshof on catechism and in Koeslin further sermon classes.

2. Above all, one should go for walks with the brethren as much as possible or be with them in other ways.

With brotherly greetings, thanks for continuing the work and my assurance of constant thought and prayer . . .

G.S. II pp. 551–2

That letter gives us some idea of the way in which Bonhoeffer continued to work with his men after the closing of the seminary at Finkenwalde. No successor was appointed, but Helmut Traub continued the work.

Bonhoeffer left Germany on the 4th June and spent a short time in London. From the plane flying over and in London itself, he wrote to Eberhard Bethge.

4th June, 1939

BONHOEFFER TO BETHGE: We are now flying over the channel in a wonderful sunset. It is ten o'clock and still very bright. All is well with me. You will now be going wearily to bed. Thank you for everything. It was splendid that you were there. My regards to Fritz – thank him too. My thoughts alternate between you and the future. Take care of yourself. Greetings to all the brethren; you will now be having evening prayers. God be with you all. I wonder if you will have this card in the morning?

London, 6th June, 1939

BONHOEFFER TO BETHGE: Many thanks for your first brief greeting. Splendid that you went on to celebrate my departure with a film. In town I have often been thinking of the days we spent together here, the National Gallery, the Portrait Gallery, and so on. The readings for these days are a great delight and I am glad to have them from you. A pity that I cannot pay you for them. I have made the necessary arrangements for the invitation in August. But you must let me know whether you want to visit Sabine and me for a short time or Sabine for a long time. Regards to everyone.

G.S. I p. 291

His diary beginning with a letter to Eberhard Bethge shows how his mind was in turmoil during the journey to America. He was far from sure about his decision to leave.

THE JOURNEY TO AMERICA

7th June, 1939

BONHOEFFER TO BETHGE: Many thanks for your last letter which pleased me very much just as it was. I will write a letter to you either during the course of the day or tomorrow. This card is to send you all my last best wishes before we get on the Atlantic and there is no more post. We have just left Southampton and will be docking at Cherbourg in a couple of hours. My cabin is very roomy, and everywhere else there is a remarkable amount of space on the ship. The weather is glorious and the sea quite calm, so we were able to lunch without danger. Now there are five quiet days in front of us in which I shall be thinking of you and all the brethren. I still keep wondering how it has all happened. I'm already very much looking forward to your visit to me. I have seen Uncle George and Julius and have made all the arrangements for the autumn. I hope it comes off. Sabine sends her best wishes and thinks back with great pleasure to our visit together. Every joy and blessing in your work. God keep you and all of you and give you joy.

8th June, 1939

Zech. 7. 9: Render true judgements, show kindness and mercy each to his brother.

Matt. 5. 7: Blessed are the merciful, for they shall obtain mercy. Yesterday evening, shortly after I had written, I met a young American theologian, an old Union man. It was like the answer to a prayer. We spoke of Christ in Germany and America and Sweden, from where he had just come. The task in America!

'Render true judgements and . . .' That is what I would ask of you first, my brethren at home. I do not want to be given special consideration in your thoughts. But before the merciful God, before the cross of Jesus Christ, what is to render true judgement if not to be merciful? No blind mercy, for that would not be merciful, but a seeing, forgiving, brotherly mercy as the true judgement on us.

'Render true judgments and . . .' That is a necessary warning and an indication of the task in America. It forbids any pride and makes the task a great one. We must see in the others brethren who are equally under the mercy of Jesus Christ and no longer live and speak from our own particular knowledge or experience; then we will not be prelatical, but merciful. May God remain merciful to *us*!

9th June, 1939

Isa. 41. 9: You are my servant, I have chosen you and not cast you off.

John 12. 26: If any one serves me, he must follow me; and where I am, there shall my servant be also.

God chooses the sinner to be his servant so that his grace shall be quite plain. The sinner is to do his work and to extend his grace. God gives work to the one whom he has forgiven. But this work can only consist in discipleship. Great programmes always lead us only to the place at which we ourselves are; but we should only be where he is. Indeed, we cannot be anywhere but where he is. You may be working over there and I may be working in America, but we are both only where he is. He brings us together. Or have I missed the place where he is? where he is for me? No, God says, 'You are my servant'.

10th June, 1939

Ps. 28. 7: The Lord is my strength and my shield; in him my heart trusts; so I am helped, and my heart exults, and with my song I give thanks to him.

Eph. 4. 30: And do not grieve the Holy Spirit of God, in whom you were sealed for the day of redemption.

In what can 'the heart exult' but in the daily certainty that God is our loving Father and Jesus Christ is our Saviour? What can be more grief to the Holy Spirit than that we indulge in gloomy thoughts and do not entrust ourselves quite confidently to his guidance, his language and his comfort? until the day of redemption is there, is finally there!

11th June, 1939

Psa. 44. 21: He knows the secrets of the heart.

I Cor. 13. 12: Now I know in part; then I shall understand fully, even as I have been fully understood.

Today is Sunday. No service. The hours have already shifted so much that I cannot share in your service at the same time. But I am altogether with you, today more than ever. If only the doubts about my own course had been overcome. One's own searching into the depths of one's heart which is nevertheless unfathomable – 'He knows the secrets of the heart'. When the confusion of accusations and excuses, of desires and fears, makes everything within us so obscure, he sees quite clearly into all our secrets. And at the heart of them all he finds a name which he himself has inscribed: Jesus Christ. So too one day we shall see quite clearly into the depths of the divine heart and there we shall then be able to read, no, to see, a name: Jesus Christ. So we would celebrate Sunday. One day we shall know and see what today we believe; one day we shall hold a service together in eternity.

> *The beginning and the end, O Lord, are thine;*
> *The span between, life, was mine.*
> *I wandered in the darkness and did not discover myself;*
> *With thee, O Lord, is clarity, and light is thy house.*
> *A short time only, and all is done;*
> *Then the whole struggle dies away to nothing.*
> *Then I will refresh myself by the waters of life,*
> *And will talk with Jesus for ever and ever.*

This afternoon I had a conversation with a former member of the Harnack Seminar, Fräulein Dr. Ferber. She is in charge of an information bureau in the *Bremen*. We had a good talk.

12th June, 1939

Deut. 6. 6: And these words which I command you this day shall be upon your heart . . .

Acts 15. 40: Paul departed, being commended by the brethren to the grace of the Lord.

'Paul departed, being commended by the brethren to the grace of the Lord.' Arrival in New York. To know that brethren have commended us to the grace of the Lord was, in these first few hours, decisive. Rev. Macy from the Federal Council of the Churches met me at the pier. First night in Parkside Hotel. Dr. Sch. called for me in the evening. I began to see all the problems of German emigration . . .

G.S. I pp. 292–6

217

CORRESPONDENCE CONCERNING BONHOEFFER'S APPOINTMENT

Meanwhile arrangements had been made in New York, stimulated by Reinhold Niebuhr from Edinburgh.

Edinburgh, 11th May, 1939

NIEBUHR TO LEHMANN: I have finished eight of my ten lectures here and have done as well as could be expected I suppose. Had a good audience all through but don't know much about how my stuff has been received.

I will not bother you with personal news, however. My concern is in regard to Bonhoeffer. He came to see me shortly upon our arrival and is anxious to come to America to evade for the time being a call to the colors. I secured an invitation for him for the Union Seminary summer school and also asked the Federal Council to arrange for meetings in church camps, etc. He would like to stay through the fall and lecture in colleges and seminaries. As I will not be back until November, I am wondering whether you would be willing to constitute a committee with me, call me the chairman and yourself the secretary and send out a mimeographed letter offering B's services to colleges and universities. Ask them for a nominal fee of $25 to $50 for his services. You could have him give you topics and a description of his activities in behalf of the confessing synod.

I don't like to throw this work on you but I think you could do it best. Be sure and hire stenographers for the job and let me have the bill. Bonhoeffer's present address is Marienburger Allee 43, Berlin Charlottenburg 9. Don't write him too much if you are willing to do this just tell him that you will get in touch with him as soon as he arrives at Union to work out plans which I have suggested. There will be some difficulty in getting him out and if he fails he will land in prison. He has done a great work for the church.

Edinburgh has been very kind to us and we have little time to ourselves. I am staying till May 23 and then will go to Oxford. After June 13 you can reach me at The Moat House, Wivelsfield, Sussex.   G.S. II pp. 349–50

As we have seen, Leiper acted at once and gave the following details to Niebuhr:

22nd May, 1939

LEIPER TO NIEBUHR: I acted at once upon receipt of your letter about Dietrich Bonhoeffer, and was able to cable him a genuine offer of a job with the American Committee for Christian German Refugees in the City of New York, where we hope very much to be able to finance a pastoral service for Germans living here which Bonhoeffer could render superbly. I know him well and am keen about him. I shall certainly be glad to do anything I can to help him.

I hope you are having a good time and that I shall see you soon. Copies to Van Dusen and Cavert.   G.S. II p. 350

Paul Lehmann wrote on 27th May to Berlin, but his letter appears to have missed Bonhoeffer.

27th May, 1939

LEHMANN TO BONHOEFFER: The word that you have been invited to lecture in the summer session of Union Theological Seminary, New York, encourages me to make this urgent request of you. Will you not be good enough to consent and make all possible arrangements accordingly to lecture in the department of Religion here at the college during the forthcoming academic year, 1939–1940? It has long been a concern of mine that your approach to the problems of philosophy and theology should be heard by my students here and by others. Accordingly, I am venturing to plan on your coming and to make arrangements for similar lectures on other campuses of my acquaintance. I am sure you will be eagerly received.

More precise details can be agreed upon while you are in residence at Union Seminary. Meanwhile, I shall look forward to your arrival there. G.S. I p. 289

Henry Leiper wrote to Dr. Cavert on 31st May.

31st May, 1939

LEIPER TO CAVERT: I want to give you the following report concerning the arrangements which have been made under considerable pressure in connection with the Rev. Dietrich Bonhoeffer of Berlin who will arrive here on June 12. Just after the meeting of the American Christian Committee where the presentation was made of the need for a pastor to work with refugees and help to find appropriate church homes for them, I had word from Reinhold Niebuhr in Edinburgh that Dietrich Bonhoeffer was slated to go to a concentration camp unless we could get him out of Germany. Niebuhr stated that he had agreed to let him have residence at his apartment temporarily and would undertake to arrange some lectures for him at Union Seminary and elsewhere.

Knowing Bonhoeffer very well, I was struck with the peculiar fitness of the man for just the thing we had been discussing and immediately called up Dr. Paul Tillich who had been appointed with me as a committee to find a man. Tillich was even more enthusiastic about Bonhoeffer than I and stated his conviction that he was exactly the right person for this delicate and difficult task.

Bonhoeffer was an exchange at Union Theological Seminary, then pastor of an Evangelical German Church in London, and latterly the director of one of the 'peripatetic' theological schools of the confessing wing of the Evangelical Church in Germany. His knowledge of English is excellent and he understands the situation in American churches from first-hand contact. His skill and aptitude in pastoral work are exceptional.

May I ask you to consult with the various church bodies in New

York City, which as I recall had indicated an interest in seeing that some such service was provided for the German refugees. It is my hope that we can supplement the amount made available by the Refugee Committee – £1000 – so as to underwrite a budget of about £3000 for this undertaking. Please let me know if I can supply further data.

G.S. I pp. 289–90

DISAGREEMENTS

The misunderstanding about why Bonhoeffer had come and how long he intended to stay came out at once on his arrival in New York. Henry Leiper had him to breakfast on his first morning and a few days later wrote to Dr. Cavert:

15th June, 1939

LEIPER TO CAVERT: I am attaching hereto a copy of my letter to Bonhoeffer under date of May 11th, which was the basis of his coming here.

I have not yet had any opportunity for a real conference with him, and when I tried to introduce him to you, I found you were out of town.

He is visiting Henry Coffin at the moment, but will be back next week when we must sit down with this matter and work it out. Pit Van Dusen who has had one talk with him seems to discover that he does not feel he can work with the refugees and safely go back to Germany, as he now expects to do. Of course, I thought he was coming to stay. He, apparently, is coming only on a visitor's visa and will be so hampered in his movements on that account that I seriously question whether he can do the thing we had hoped to have him do.

We must talk it over at the earliest possible date which I suppose would be Tuesday, when I get back, if you are here then.

G.S. II p. 351

Bonhoeffer expressed his concern to Paul Lehmann in a letter from New York, half in German, half in English:

BONHOEFFER TO LEHMANN: Now I'm here again! Niebuhr will have written to you about me. There has been some misunderstanding about my trip. I am not a refugee, but I must go back to Germany to take up my work over there. They are in need of teachers. I will remain until late autumn or at the most until the New Year. During the first week in August, I have a series of lectures to give at the summer school in Union. Will I see you at all? I hope so. Do you think there is any chance of lecturing at other universities? – with salary, because I have no money! . . .   G.S. II p. 351

Paul Lehmann was still hopeful that Bonhoeffer would remain, as his letters at the end of June show, but by 27th June there was no further hope of this, and he sent the following letter to forty colleges and seminaries.

Elmhurst College
Elmhurst, Illinois
Department of Religion
27th June 1939

FROM LEHMANN: A committee of which Dr. Reinhold Niebuhr, Professor of Applied Christianity at the Union Theological Seminary, New York, is the chairman, is venturing to bring to your attention, the Reverend Dietrich Bonhoeffer, Licentiate in Theology.

Reverend Mr. Bonhoeffer is one of the ablest of the younger theologians and one of the most courageous of the younger pastors who have undertaken the task of the faithful exposition and perpetuation of the Christian faith in the present critical time in Germany. He comes from a distinguished line of forebears both in the pulpit and in the university. He himself holds a graduate theological degree from the University at Berlin and from the Union Theological Seminary at New York. Among the more notable of Mr.

Bonhoeffer's contributions to theological learning are three brilliant and profound volumes on *The Communion of Saints, Act and Being*, and one published only recently under the title, *Community Life*.[1]

During the academic year, 1930–1931, Mr. Bonhoeffer was a fellow in theology at Union Seminary and after his return to Germany he began a promising theological career as Privatdozent in the theological faculty at Berlin. Political circumstances have interrupted these hopes. After a pastorate in the German Church in London, Mr. Bonhoeffer returned to his country and assumed the difficult responsibility of teaching the future ministers of the Confessing Church. Some time ago his little seminary was closed by the government and he has been continuing his work since then in a private capacity in the parsonages of Pomerania.

Since Mr. Bonhoeffer will be lecturing in theology at the summer session of the Union Theological Seminary, New York, we are anxious to provide him a wider hearing in American academic and theological circles. Accordingly, we are arranging a schedule of lectures at colleges and seminaries during the academic year, 1939–1940. If your institution has a lecture foundation or lecture series on a variety of problems, will you give favourable consideration to an invitation to Mr. Bonhoeffer to appear? He is in full command of the English language and prepared to discuss in a reliable and challenging manner problems of theology, philosophy, and the contemporary situation of Christianity in Germany. The committee is venturing to suggest an honorarium of not less than twenty-five dollars and, wherever possible, of fifty dollars.

I hope very urgently that we may have some word from you at the earliest possible moment. Correspondence either for Mr. Bonhoeffer or for the committee may be addressed to me at the address below. Your active cooperation in this venture will be a real expression of the spirit of ecumenical Christianity and deeply appreciated.

[1] The title of the American edition of *Life Together*.

Elmhurst College
Elmhurst, Illinois
28th June, 1939

LEHMANN TO NIEBUHR: Immediately upon receipt of your letter of May 11, I got started. I wrote at once to Dr. Press and contacted Pauck and Paul Scherer. The enclosed letter which I am sending out today to some thirty or forty places will speak for itself. I hope replies will not come in too slowly.

Meanwhile a letter has come from Bonhoeffer who is already at Union. I don't quite know what to make of it for he speaks already of going back. He says that he is not a refugee and must go back to Germany to take up his work over there, for Germany needs teachers. 'I want to stay,' he writes, 'until late autumn or at the latest, the new year.'

What occurred to me at once was the Eden Theological lectures at Convocation. I ventured to ask Dr. Press to invite Bonhoeffer . . . We are inviting Bonhoeffer for the four Lenten sermons which come just about Eden convocation time. The two would fit beautifully together. As soon as I get replies to the general letter, I shall make up a schedule.

Richter will be teaching with us next Fall. The Board seems to have been surprisingly cooperative, the faculty mildly impressed. But it will be like a cultural tornado which is exactly what this place needs . . . if there is any way at any time that I can do something like this, please never hesitate to write. I'm never too busy or tired for your requests.

Elmhurst College, 28th June, 1939

LEHMANN TO BONHOEFFER: You cannot know with what joy and relief your letter was received. It came to me just when I had to be away for some days and to take part in a conference here for some days, so that I have had to wait until now to reply. Evidently my letter of May 27th, sent to Berlin will not have reached you. Since that time, Marion and I have been eagerly awaiting word of your arrival in Union. Now that you are there, we can scarcely wait until you are here with us.

Whether or not Dr. Niebuhr has been too optimistic, I do not know. But I do know that it is unthinkable that you should return before America shall have the fullest opportunity to be enriched by your contribution to its theological hour of destiny. At least, I like to think of it in this way. The tragic political occasion for these disturbed times may have one great and positive overtone in the widening of the American theological understanding by the present cross-fertilization with the continental tradition. So that you must see this also as a responsibility as well as the German need for teachers.

And besides, Marion and I need very badly to see you again. Surely you would not deprive us of the hope that we have carried with us since the day when we left the café on Unter den Linden. With your anticipated permission, I have already taken steps to bring this about. The enclosed letter will speak for itself. But meanwhile, there is more definite word for you. I am authorised to invite you to deliver the annual series of Lenten sermons which is a part of our campus religious life program. These occur on four succeeding Wednesdays during Lent and seek to interpret the cross to the contemporary student mind. There will be one hundred dollars at your disposal for these sermons and you will live with us. At about the same time, Eden Seminary has a theological lectureship at its annual convocation. This is usually about mid-February. I have written asking that you be invited for these. I hope it will work out.

But whatever happens, Marion and I want you to know that our home is yours in every respect for as long a time as you are able and willing to have it so. There is no limit. And you cannot afford us any greater happiness than by acting with complete freedom on this premise.

Whether or not I shall get to New York this summer, I do not

P

yet know. I am trying very hard to arrange some kind of a brief excursion there, specially to see you. We are leaving here on Saturday for Columbus, Ohio, where we are likely to be until the first of September. The address there is 931 Oakwood Avenue. It should be just about that time that you will be ready to come west and we shall await you here. You will let me hear from you in Columbus, won't you?

Sometime between July 9 and 12, a very good friend of mine and former student, George Kalbfleisch by name, will try to visit you in Union. He is en route to Amsterdam and expects to visit Germany. It was through him that I hoped to send you some word of reply to your earlier letter at Christmas time. Since he expects to visit Germany, there may be some word that you might like to send. I simply mention this in order that you may know that you can have complete confidence in him. I have told him so much of you and am anxious that you meet.

As soon as replies to the letter which I am mailing today to some thirty or forty places come to me, you will hear more. Meanwhile do keep in touch with me and remember how anxious we are to have you with us again. Marion joins me in kindest greetings and highest regard.

New York, 28th June, 1939
BONHOEFFER TO LEHMANN: I wonder if you have received my letter last week. Things have changed for me entirely. I am going back to Germany on August 2nd or even July 25th. The political situation is so terrible. But, of course, I should like to have a word from you before I leave. I am enjoying a few weeks in freedom, but on the other hand, I feel, I must go back to the 'trenches' (I mean of the church struggle). G.S. II pp. 352–6

There is much in the correspondence which shows why Bonhoeffer made this fateful decision, but his diary during that period is the best material.

226

THE AMERICAN DIARY

13th June, 1939

Breakfast with Leiper, who greeted me most kindly and fetched me. First discussion of the future. I am taking as the firm starting point for everything that I want to go back in a year at the latest. Astonishment. But I am quite clear that I must go back. Went to the offices. A whole block is devoted to church offices of all kinds.

After some preliminary conversations and arrangements by telephone, to Union Theological Seminary and the Prophet's Chamber, with a fine view overlooking the quadrangle. I had forgotten a great deal; but it is all coming back again quickly, including the smell of the house. Lunch with Van Dusen. I had a quarrel with him before . . . Here I am beginning to realise for the first time the great change in American theology over the last eight years. The causes we championed, apparently quite hopelessly, in 1930, have established themselves in the course of time. I am still not clear how that has come about. Perhaps just a culture crisis? There is much talk of being lost, of man's 'sin'; optimistic evolutionism is over. But has not perhaps a pessimistic picture of man simply been put in place of an optimistic one? What is there to say about the Gospel, about Jesus Christ himself? That is the question. Met President Coffin at Grand Central about four. I am going to stay with him for a couple of days at his country home. On the train two and a half hours' conversation about the American situation. Strange how critical Coffin is of his own colleagues. I don't think that we can be like that at home any more. Too much binds us together, despite all the difference of opinion. Continuation of the conversation with Van Dusen. Coffin is a straight-forward, practical man. He sees the necessity of preaching the Gospel. He says, 'N . . . preaches for half an hour on the "failure of man" and the last two minutes on the "grace of God"'. If that is generally true, they are now where we were fifteen years ago. The reports about the reunion of Episcopalians and Presbyterians

227

were interesting: mutual recognition, as Churches of Christ, of ordination. (Apostolic succession recognised by the Episcopalians as being guaranteed among the Presbyterians through the presbyteries. Somewhat questionable. It remains an institutional understanding of succession.)

The country house in Lakeville, Connecticut is in the hills; fresh and luxuriant vegetation. In the evening thousands of fire-flies in the garden, flying glow-worms. I had never seen them before. Quite a fantastic sight. Very friendly and 'informal' reception. All I need is Germany, the brethren. The first lonely hours are hard. I do not understand why I am here, whether it was a sensible thing to do, whether the results will be worthwhile. In the evening, last of all, the readings and thoughts about work at home. I have now been almost two weeks without knowing what is going on there. It is hard to bear. 'It is good that one should wait quietly for the salvation of the Lord' (Lam. 3. 26).

14th June, 1939

Breakfast on the veranda at eight. It poured in the night. Everything is fresh and clean. Then prayers. I was almost overcome by the short prayer – the whole family knelt down – in which we thought of the German brethren. Then reading, writing, going out to issue invitations for the evening. In the evening about twenty-five people, pastors, teachers, with wives and friends. Very friendly conversations without getting anywhere.

15th June, 1939

Since yesterday evening I haven't been able to stop thinking of Germany. I would not have thought it possible that at my age, after so many years abroad, one could get so dreadfully homesick. What was in itself a wonderful motor expedition this morning to a female acquaintance in the country, i.e., in the hills, became almost unbearable. We sat for an hour and chattered, not in a silly way, true, but

about things which left me completely cold – whether it is possible
to get a good musical education in New York, about the education
of children, etc., etc., and I thought how usefully I could be spending
these hours in Germany. I would gladly have taken the next ship
home. This inactivity, or rather activity in unimportant things, is
quite intolerable when one thinks of the brethren and of how
precious time is. The whole burden of self-reproach because of a
wrong decision comes back again and almost overwhelms one. I
was in utter despair. In the afternoon I tried to do some work. Then
I was invited for a second trip into the hills of Massachusetts. It was
at quite the wrong time. I still hadn't found peace for Bible reading
and prayer. The trip was splendid. We went through a whole stretch
of laurel wood. The view from above was rather like the Harz
country. But the burden did not leave me all day. Cinema in the
evening: Zuarez with P. Muni. A good film. It occupied my
thoughts for a while. Another letter to Leiper: I must go back
within a year at the latest. How glad I was to begin the readings
again in the evening and find 'My heart shall rejoice in thy salvation'
(Ps. 13. 5).

16th June, 1939

A fortnight ago today I left Berlin and already I long so much for
work. Return to New York. Evening at last. I needed it badly. One
is less lonely when one is alone. The whole afternoon at the World
Exhibition . . . The Russians are too ostentatious and quite bourgeois.
The majority of the others are too commercial. In general no special
impressions. Christians and Jews preach alternately in the 'temple of
religion'. The whole building is dreadful – cinema-like. Other
thoughts: How much cleaner New York is than London! No
smoking in the subway or on the street. Technically more advanced,
too, or more up to date (ventilation in every subway). And how much
more international New York is than London. Of the people to
whom I talked today at least half spoke a dreadfully broken English.

This continual murder of their language must be horrible for the good American. I am waiting for the post! It is almost unbearable. Probably I shall not have to wait long. Today God's Word says, 'I am coming soon' (Rev. 3. 11). There is no time to lose, and here I am wasting days, perhaps weeks. In any case, it seems like that at the moment. Then I say to myself again, 'It is cowardice and weakness to run away here now.' Will I ever be able to do any really significant work here? – Disquieting political news from Japan. If it becomes unsettled now I am definitely going back to Germany. I cannot stay outside by myself. That is quite clear. My whole life is still over there.

Spent the whole day in the library, looking through *The Christian Century*. Instructive articles on 'How my mind has changed in the last decade'. Professors of theology on the change in American theology since 1929. The decisive shift to the Word still does not seem to have been made; instead, the movement seems to be from a belief in progress to nihilism, from ethicism to a philosophy to the 'present', the 'concrete situation'. Account of the last lynching of a negro. Two white people go into the house and pray with the negroes that 'the day may come when such things will not happen in America'. That is a good solution for such happenings. Also a report on the lack of religion among college students – 'disinterested'. That must happen if one doesn't eventually realise that 'religion' is really superfluous.

Sunday, 18th June, 1939

Service in Riverside Church. Quite unbearable. Text: a saying from James (!) about 'accepting a horizon', how one gets a horizon, namely God as man's necessary horizon.

The whole thing was a respectable, self-indulgent, self-satisfied religious celebration. This sort of idolatrous religion stirs up the flesh which is accustomed to being kept in check by the Word of God. Such sermons make for libertinism, egotism, indifference. Do people

not know that one can get on as well, even better, without 'religion'
– if only there were not God himself and his Word? Perhaps the
Anglo-Saxons are really more religious than we are, but they are
certainly not more Christian, at least, if they still have sermons like
that. I have no doubt at all that one day the storm will blow with
full force on this religious hand-out, if God himself is still anywhere
on the scene. Humanly speaking the thing is by no means un-
attractive, but I prefer the rustic preaching of Br. Schutz. The tasks
for a real theologian over here are immeasurable. But only an American himself can shift all this rubbish, and up till now there do not
seem to be any about.

How good the readings are today! Ps. 119, 105; Matt. 13. 8. Work
in the afternoon. Spoke to no one all day. Now I must begin to
learn again how fortunate I have been hitherto always to have been
in the company of the brethren. And Niemöller has been alone for
two years. To imagine it! What a faith, what a discipline, and what a
clear act of God! – Now the day has had a good ending. I went to
church again. As long as there are lonely Christians there will always
be services. It is a great help after a couple of quite lonely days to go
into church and there pray together, sing together, listen together.
The sermon was astonishing (Broadway Presbyterian Church, Dr.
McComb) on 'our likeness with Christ'. A completely biblical
sermon – the sections on 'we are *blameless* like Christ', 'we are
tempted like Christ' were particularly good. This will one day be a
centre of resistance when Riverside Church has long since become
a temple of Baal. I was very glad about this sermon. Why does a
man who preaches like that not notice what dreadful music he has
played? I will ask him. This sermon opened up to me an America
of which I was quite ignorant before. Otherwise I would have
become quite ungrateful in these days for all the protection which
God has given me. With my intention and inner need to think
incessantly of the brethren over there and their work I would almost
have avoided the task here. It began to seem treacherous not to have

all my thoughts over there. I still have to find the right balance. Paul writes that he thinks of his congregation 'without ceasing' in his prayers and yet at the same time he devoted himself completely to the task in hand. I must learn to do that. It will probably only come with prayer. God, grant me in the next few weeks clarity about my future and keep me in the communion of prayer with the brethren.

Without news from Germany the whole day, from post to post, waiting in vain. It does not help to get angry and write that sort of letter. The expected news is there long before the letter arrives. I want to know how work is going over there, whether all is well or whether they need me. I want to have some sign from over there before the decisive meeting tomorrow. Perhaps it is a good thing that it has not come. The news about China is disquieting. Will one be able to get home in time if it gets serious? – Spent the whole day in the library. Wrote English lectures.[1] I have great difficulty with the language. They say that I speak English well, and yet I find it so utterly inadequate. How many years, how many decades has it taken to learn German, and even now one does not know it! I will

---

[1] The following notes are on the leaf of a diary:
Church as a religious province (philosophical-cultural)
as a means to an end (education of the people, moral life, for satisfying religious needs, for harmony of existence, like science, art)
Church submerged, into the world
Religion, Church, Private affair, Private satisfaction
Church as an invention for forgiveness of sins, waste of the word and the sacraments
Outstanding problems of present continental theology:
Doctrine and heresy
  1. Confession and damnation
  2. The Church
  3. The powers ordained by God
  4. Christian life, the meaning of suffering
  5. Church and Synod
  6. Christ and Antichrist
  7. Christlike life

never learn English. That is already one reason for going back home soon. Without language one is lost, hopelessly lonely. In the evening to Times Square, an escape. News-reel there for an hour. Early to bed. What a day! But: 'The name of the Lord Jesus was extolled' (Acts 19. 17). It disturbs me that we do not keep the same time as Germany. It hinders and prevents prayer together. It is the same every evening. But: 'We thank thee, O God, . . . that thy name is so near' (Ps. 75. 1).

20th June, 1939

In the morning a letter from my parents from South Germany. Nothing from Stettin. Visit Leiper. The decision has been made. I have refused. They were clearly disappointed, and rather upset. It probably means more for me than I can see at the moment. God alone knows what. It is remarkable how I am never quite clear about the motives for any of my decisions. Is that a sign of confusion, of inner dishonesty, or is it a sign that we are guided without our knowing, or is it both?

Isa 45. 19; I Peter 1. 17.

Today the reading speaks dreadfully harshly of God's incorruptible judgement. He certainly sees how much personal feeling, how much anxiety there is in today's decision, however brave it may seem. The reasons one gives for an action to others and to one's self are certainly inadequate. One can give a reason for everything. In the last resort one acts from a level which remains hidden from us. So one can only ask God to judge us and to forgive us.

Visit Dr. Bewer; very friendly reception. In the afternoon David Roberts. Long theological conversation. Criticism of the Fundamentalists, when it comes to the point he does not think that they are any more reliable than the Riverside Church people. Fosdick, the Anti-Christ in the eyes of the Broadway Presbyterian. America forty years behind Germany. Twenty years behind Scotland. It seems that Germany is still the land of spiritual discoveries.

233

Evening with Van Dusen. Write letters. Half past nine for an hour with Bewer. How good it is to speak German again. At the end of the day I can only ask God to give a merciful judgement on today and all its decisions. It is now in his hand.

21st June, 1939

Worked quietly in the morning. Very hot. In the afternoon to the Metropolitan Museum, El Greco (View of Toledo completely in green), Memling (Head of Christ) were particularly pleasing. Entertained very kindly and generously by the Bewers in the evening. I am surprised how much more freely one gets on with these people than last time. It was so good to think and speak again in German. I have never felt the resistance which the English language offers to my thoughts so strongly as here in New York. In this language I always feel dissatisfied with myself. Bewer's verdict on America was important to me – and his war experiences. They can give themselves over unrestrainedly to hate, perhaps immaturely. Of course I still keep having second thoughts about my decision. One could have also given quite different reasons: first, I am here (and perhaps the very misunderstanding was a guidance); they say that it was like the answer to a prayer when my coming was announced; they would like to have *me*; they cannot understand why I refuse; it upsets all their plans for the future; I have no news from home and perhaps everything is going well without me, etc. Or one could ask: have I simply acted out of a longing for Germany and the work there? And is this almost incomprehensible and hitherto almost completely unknown homesickness an accompanying sign from above to make refusal easier for me? Or, is it not irresponsible towards so many other men simply to say *no* to one's own future and that of many others? Will I regret it? I may not. Despite everything there is first of all the promise, then the joy of working at home and finally the other, that I am trying to suppress. The reading is again so harsh: 'He will sit as a refiner of gold and silver' (Mal. 3.

3). And it is necessary. I don't know where I am. But he knows; and in the end all doings and actions will be pure and clear.

22nd June, 1939

No news from over there. Invitation to Boericke's. I am going next week. Worked and wrote in the morning. I am most sorry about my decision for Sabine. Read in the afternoon. Niebuhr, an interpretation of Christian ethics. The questioning is still completely between orthodox and liberal criticism, but there is no really new beginning. 'Myth' instead of Word of God. Evening in the news-reel theatre, nothing special. The evening papers bring very excited news about Japan. Bewer calms me down. It is unbearable over here for a German; one is simply torn in two. Whereas a catastrophe here is quite inconceivable, unless it is ordained. But even to be responsible, to have to reproach oneself, for having come out unnecessarily, is certainly crushing. But we cannot part ourselves from our destiny, much less here, outside; here everything lies solely on one's own shoulders, and one has no voice and no rights in a foreign land. Besides, the storm will also soon break here, too. It is already bubbling fiercely under the surface. And woe betide those who are aliens here. It is strange how strongly I have been moved by these particular thoughts in the last few days and how all thoughts about the *Una Sancta* make slow progress. A tremendous amount has already been overwhelmed. I have been writing in bed since yesterday evening. A good ending. All that remains now is the readings and intercessions. In the morning a discussion with Bewer and Van Dusen about the future. I want to go back in August. They urge me to stay longer. But if nothing happens in the meantime I shall stick by 12th August. I shall then stay with Sabine. Lunch with David Roberts and his wife; very nice. We spoke about the Negro question. Nothing seems to have altered, at best the anti-lynching bill. He thinks that there is considerable danger of revolution in the south. I didn't know before that the Negroes are prevented from exercising their proper voting rights. The great Negro churches are not included in the Methodist Union (May 1939). He could not mention any new literature. Strong increase in anti-Semitism. Mountain resort: '1000 feet – too high for Jews'. – Notice: 'Gentiles preferred'.

Visited Colvin in the afternoon. Home. Read. Sat by the Hudson and thought of Sigurdshof. Why don't I hear anything? – Read Niebuhr to the end. The account of the impossibility of applying so-called Christian principles to life, politics, etc., is still the best. Criticism of Liberalism. Little new positive material . . . (Contrast between the absolute ideal and the relative-pragmatic good. Both necessary). No thinking in the light of the Bible here . . . His article about 'as deceivers yet true' is pure modernism.

They have just finished a conference on hymn-book revision below. They drag the chorales dreadfully, and use too much pedal. The clavichord is better. Readings and intercessions.

24th June, 1939

Post at last. That is a great relief. But once again it is quite clear that I must go back to work. I have done quite a lot today. W. A. Brown, 'State and Church', etc. Rodewell held me up too long in the morning. I now often wonder whether it is true that America is the country without a reformation. If reformation means the God-given knowledge of the failure of all ways of building up a kingdom of God on earth, then it is probably true. But is it not also true of England? The voice of Lutheranism is there in America, but it is one among others: it has never been able to confront the other denominations. There hardly ever seem to be 'encounters' in this great country, in which the one can always avoid the other. But where there is no encounter, where liberty is the only unifying factor, one naturally knows nothing of the community which is created through encounter. The whole life together is completely different as a result. Community in our sense, whether cultural or ecclesiastical, cannot develop there. Is that true? – Wrote cards in the evening. Felix Gilbert called. – The newspapers are grim again today. Readings: 'The one who believes does not flee' (Isa. 28. 16). I'm thinking of work at home. Tomorrow is Sunday. I wonder if I shall hear a *sermon?*

Sunday, 25th June, 1939

Service in the Lutheran Church. Church on Central Park, Dr. Scherer. Sermon on Luke 15, on the overcoming of fear. Very forced application of the text. Otherwise lively and original, but too much analysis and too little Gospel. It came home when he said of the life of the Christian that it is like the daily joy of the person who is on the way home. Again no real exposition of the text. It is very poor. Lunch with the Bewers. Conversation about the newspapers here, then about the strange silence of the American public over the suffering of Christians in Russia, about their alienation from the Bible, about the bad Sunday Schools. Afternoon and evening with Gilbert. Very complimentary to Roosevelt. He explained a great deal to me. Today is the anniversary of the Augsburg Confession. It makes me think of the brethren at home. Rom. 1. 16.

26th June, 1939

Letter from parents in Switzerland. Work all day in the library. W. A. Brown finished. Denominational methods of clergy training and ordination. It is very difficult to get a uniform picture. Tillich's formula 'theological-democratic' over against 'autocratic-sacramental' is too formal, too sociological. In theory it is connected with the lack of a reformation. The Word of God has never wholly struck and wholly freed these people. Hence too the predilection for catholicising concepts of humanity. (J. Maritain: *True Humanism.*) Today, by chance, I read II Tim. 4. 21, 'Do your best to come before winter' – Paul's request to Timothy. Timothy is to share the suffering of the Apostle and not to be ashamed. 'Do your best to come before winter' – otherwise it might be too late. That has been in my ears all

237

day. We are just like soldiers who come away from the field on leave and despite everything that they expected are forced back there again. We cannot get away from it. Not as though we were necessary, as though we were needed (by God?!), but simply because our life is there and because we leave our life behind, we destroy it, if we are not back there. There is nothing pious about it, but something almost vital. But God acts not only through pious emotions, but also through these vital ones. 'Do your best to come before winter' – It is not a misuse of Scripture if I take that to be said to *me*. If God gives me grace to do it.

27th June, 1939

Letter from my parents. Great joy, quite surprising. Work lunchtime and afternoon in the library. Tillich, Niebuhr. In the evening a visit from Professor Richardson, long conversation. He is an Englishman. One seems to stand nearer to him than to the Americans. I wonder if the Americans do not understand us at all because they are people who left Europe so as to be able to live out their faith for themselves in freedom? i.e. because they did not stand fast by the last decision in the question of belief? I feel that they would understand the fugitive better than the one who stays. Hence the American tolerance, or rather, indifference in dogmatic questions. A warlike encounter is excluded, but so too is the true passionate longing for unity in faith.

28th June, 1939

Y.M.C.A. Headquarters in the morning. The chapel is the finest room in the whole building. Roman Missal in it, among other things. Otherwise the usual picture. Work in the library for the afternoon. Supper with Professor Richardson. Then read again for a long time. 'Kingdom of God in America' – Richard Niebuhr. The newspaper reports get more and more disturbing. They distract one's thoughts. I cannot imagine that it is God's will for me to remain

238

here without anything particular to do in case of war. I must travel at the first possible opportunity.

29th June, 1939

Telegram from Karl Friedrich. Looking for somewhere to stay. Work until noon. Broken engagement in the afternoon. In the evening a good, friendly talk with Roberts, who is going on holiday tomorrow. I gave him two of my books. He promised to send me books if I write to him. The news today is so bad that I am determined to go back with Karl Friedrich. We will discuss it tomorrow. Roberts spoke very critically about the church in America. The need comes from inside. Complete indifference towards its message continually dissolves the church. 'Keep away from politics' – says that the church should limit itself to its 'religious task', in which no one is interested. I find it more and more difficult to understand how the principle of a separation of church and state fits in with the practice of the social, economic, organisational and political activity of the church. In any case, the separation of church and state does not result in the church continuing to apply itself to its own task; it is no guarantee against secularisation. Nowhere is the church more secularised than where it is separated in principle as it is here. This very separation can create an opposition, so that the church engages much more strongly in political and secular things. That is probably important for our decisions over there.

30th June, 1939

Letter from Fritz. Thoughtful and friendly as ever. Unfortunately nothing else. Telegram from Karl Friedrich, who is coming from Chicago. There is much to discuss. He has been offered an excellent professorship there; it means a decision once for all. Then my questions. As in the present situation I would in any case have gone in four weeks at the latest, with things as they are I have decided to go on the eighth with Karl Friedrich. If war breaks out I do not want to

239

be here, and it is impossible to get any objective news about the situation. That was a great decision. In the morning another letter from Paul, who was so optimistic about my staying here. Afternoon and evening the World Exhibition, the technical things. Did not write in the evening for the first time.

1st July, 1939

Went round in the morning. Karl Friedrich at mid-day. Wrote a bit in the afternoon. Then with K.F. into town, bought presents, Music Hall, cinema, the largest. Dreadful. Gaudy, ostentatious, vulgar colours, music and flesh. One can only find this sort of fantasy in a big city. K.F. disagrees. Home in good time in the evening. I could not get away all day from thinking about the situation in Germany and in the church. The readings are again very good. Job 41. 11, 'God says, Who has given to me, that I should repay him? Whatever is under the whole heaven is mine.' Rom. 11. 36: 'By him and through him and to him are all things. To him be glory for ever. Amen.' The earth, nations, Germany, and above all, the church, cannot fall from his hand. It was dreadfully hard for me to think and to pray 'Thy will be done' in view of the present situation. But it must be. Tomorrow is Sunday. May God make his Word find a hearing in all the world.

Sunday, 2nd July, 1939

Church, Park Avenue. Rev. Gorkmann (Radio preacher) on 'Today is ours', no text, no echo of the Christian proclamation. Rather a disappointment. The collects are always good between the prayer and the singing. Lunch with Karl Friedrich, then work in the afternoon, i.e. wrote something about America, *tried* to write. All day in the seminary with Karl Friedrich; discussed his plans in detail. The Americans speak so much about freedom in their sermons. Freedom as a possession is a doubtful thing for a church; freedom must be won under the compulsion of a necessity. Freedom for the church comes from the necessity of the Word of God. Otherwise it becomes arbitrariness and ends in a great many new ties. Whether the church in America is really 'free', I doubt. They are lonely Sundays over here. Only the Word makes a true community. I need some good communal prayers in my own language. The news is not good. Will we arrive in time? Reading: Isa. 35. 10! Intercessions.

3rd July, 1939

Lectures by Coffin, Richard Niebuhr, Harris. Everything strengthens me in the view that theologically the people here are where we were fifteen years ago. Work at home in the afternoon. A long conversation in the evening with a student. Gill. A full day. I have put the first general ideas for an article down on paper. But I had to be able to write it all at once. Morning prayers by Coffin were very poor. I must take care not to be remiss with Bible reading and prayer. Letter from Paul Lehmann.

4th July, 1939

Coffin in the morning; then a visit to Richard Niebuhr. Lunch with Karl Friedrich in the Empire State building. Cinema. Invitation to Niebuhrs in the evening. Very long, good conversation.[1] The American separation of church and state has the significance of 'limitation of power' in relationship to the government, not the reformation doctrine of offices. I deduced that. Niebuhr thinks that Roger Williams imagines God to work only in the spiritual sphere and that his complete indifference to the state is to be explained by that. The separation of church and state in America is no straightforward phenomenon. Intercessions, readings.

5th July, 1939

The nearer my departure comes the fuller the days become. Morning prayers by Professor Smart. Van Dusen on Descartes . . . Work in

[1] cf. Appendix 'An Imaginary Conversation', pp. 265–80.

the library. Horton, Keller. Continue in the afternoon. Conversation
at lunch with two students from the Southern States on the Negro
problem. Reception in the common room in the evening. It would
be good to stay another four weeks. But the price is too high. Letter
from Eberhard, great joy. Good ideas about John 2. Still no answer
to my decision. The readings call for thankfulness.

6th July, 1939

I'm writing on the ship. The last two days were so full that I did not
get to writing . . .   G.S. I pp. 296–314

CORRESPONDENCE

*In the letters, Bonhoeffer expressed himself more fully, although they do
not show the extent of his struggle. Both letters and diary are needed to see
the whole picture. On 15th June, a letter in English to Dr. Leiper shows the
situation as he saw it then.*

'Coombe-Pine', Lakeville, 15.6.1939

BONHOEFFER TO LEIPER: I wish to thank you very much indeed
for the reception you gave me on my arrival in New York. I felt
quite at home when Mr. Macy gave me your kind letter and when
I met you the next morning. It is a great thing to have good friends
and fellow-Christians abroad.

These beautiful days at Dr. Coffin's country home are giving me
some time to think about my future and I am sure you will understand that I should like to put the situation before you as I see it, and
ask your advice. Before I left Germany I had long talks with my
brethren from the Brethren Council and pledged myself to return
to Germany after about a year's time to take up the training work in
the Confessing Church again, unless some unforeseen development
would change the whole situation. At first they were very reluctant
to let me go at all, since they are in need of teachers. It was only
when I expressed my hopes that I could be of some use to them by

establishing contacts with American theologians and churchmen through lectures or meetings, that they gave me leave. So from the point of view of the Confessing Church my trip to America was meant to be an ecumenical link between our isolated church in Germany and our friends over here. We all felt that to be very essential from many points of view. My personal question and difficulty with regard to military service, etc., came in only as a second consideration. Of course, my colleagues were glad, that I would be able to postpone my decision for at least one year. Now, I am sure, all that could not be made quite clear in correspondence before I left Germany. But before we are going to work out my programme for the immediate future, however long it might be, I feel strongly, that everything ought to be quite clear between us. I deeply appreciate, and so did my friends, your readiness to invite me to come to this country and I am most happy indeed to be here again and to meet old friends. There are, however, a few questions which we have to clear up before I start my work over here, and I wish you would help me to do the right thing. The post which you are kindly intending to confer upon me attracts me from every point of view. I feel strongly the necessity of that spiritual help for our refugees. When I was pastor in London I spent most of my time with these people and I felt it was a great privilege to do so. At the same time that post would offer me an unusual opportunity for getting acquainted with the life of the church in this country, which has been one of my greatest hopes for my stay over here. The only thing that makes me hesitate at the present moment of decision is the question of loyalty to my people at home. All of us, of course, were well aware of the fact that it means running a risk for a confessing pastor to go to America with the intention to go back to Germany, and we all agreed that I should take that risk and pay the price for it, if necessary, if it is of a true value to the Church of Christ there and here. But, of course, I must not for the sake of loyalty to the Confessing Church accept a post which on principle would make my return to Germany impossible. Now, my question is whether that would not be the case with any post that is officially concerned with refugee work? As a matter of fact, I am afraid, it would be so. Now, if that is true, what can we do about it? Is there a possibility of giving that post a somewhat larger scope? I have no particular idea, but if, for instance, it were possible to interpret that post as a sort of invitation, as a 'guest post' from the Federation of Churches so as to enable me to get acquainted with the church activities in New York and to cooperate in some respect (whereby, of course, some of that pastoral work of which you have been thinking might be conferred upon me on the respective occasions), I think, that would change the matter a good deal. But, of course, I have no idea under what heading such a thing could be done. This is the first point, which I should very much like to have your advice on.

Secondly, when Reinhold Niebuhr wrote to me first in February he was hoping to provide a few lectureships for me all over the country, so as to give me an opportunity of seeing a good deal of the theological schools and of getting in contact with the professors of Theology. That, of course, would be very much in the line of my work in Germany and I should be greatly interested to do that sort of work. Now, do you suppose, that the post in New York would leave the necessary time to do some investigation and some visiting of that sort?

Finally, let me add a very personal remark. My best friend in Germany, a young confessing pastor, who has been working with me for many years, will be in the same conflict with regard to military service, etc., at the latest by next spring, possibly in the fall of this year. I feel it would be an utmost disloyalty to leave him alone in Germany when the conflict comes up for him. I should either have to go back to stand by him and to act with him or to get him out and to share my living with him, whatever it be, though I do not know if he would be willing to leave Germany. That is a last personal, but not only personal reason, why I feel bound to keep my way back open. I am sure, you will appreciate that this is a duty of *Bruderschaft* which in these times one simply has to fulfil.

Now I have put my case before you. I know, I am causing you a lot of trouble with all that. But you know us Germans and that we are sometimes a little complicated, and more than that, you know the Confessing Church and its needs. I need not assure you again how grateful I am for all that you have been doing for our cause and for me personally. It is just therefore that I feel you must know my whole case before you go on with me. If you should think it impossible to find the right post for me, after you have heard all that, please feel entirely free to tell me and then we should try to make the best of the next few months and I should return to Germany, certainly very grateful for all the friendship I have experienced over here again, in the later part of the fall. My friends at home would only be too glad, if I came back a little earlier than they expected. But if you would see a way through all these difficulties, then I shall stay here with great pleasure, interest and gratefulness.

I am going to Eaglesmere for Saturday. I am looking forward to seeing you next week. The 'Prophet's Chamber' at Union is lovely and I am enjoying Union a lot.

With many thanks for everything.   G.S. I pp. 316–19

A letter from Germany increased his uneasiness and he wrote a postscript a few days later.

19th June, 1939

BONHOEFFER TO LEIPER: I have just received a letter from Dr. Freudenberg asking me urgently not to take over the refugee post if I wish to go back to Germany. He also calls my attention to the fact that there are many of our Confessing pastors who will never be able to return to Germany and from whom, therefore, I should not take away the chance of this post. I hope you will be able to

245

spare an hour of your time tomorrow for me. We must get clear about it . . . I hope you have got my last letter.   G.S. I p. 319

The decisive letter, however, was written to Reinhold Niebuhr at the beginning of July and describes vividly the taking of the decision to return home.

July 1939

BONHOEFFER TO NIEBUHR: . . . Sitting here in Dr. Coffin's garden I have had the time to think and to pray about my situation and that of my nation and to have God's will for me clarified. I have come to the conclusion that I have made a mistake in coming to America. I must live through this difficult period of our national history with the Christian people of Germany. I will have no right to participate in the reconstruction of Christian life in Germany after the war if I do not share the trials of this time with my people. My brethren in the Confessing Synod wanted me to go. They may have been right in urging me to do so; but I was wrong in going. Such a decision each man must make for himself. Christians in Germany will face the terrible alternative of either willing the defeat of their nation in order that Christian civilisation may survive, or willing the victory of their nation and thereby destroying our civilisation. I know which of these alternatives I must choose; but I cannot make that choice in security . . .   G.S. I p. 320

A DIARY FRAGMENT

Bonhoeffer left New York on 7th July. His days on board ship were peaceful. The tension was over as this fragment of a diary shows:

6th July, 1939

In the morning down town to settle the travel arrangements. Stock Exchange on the way back. Shopping. I met Paul Lehmann in my room about half past two. He had come from Columbus, Ohio, to see me again. Great delight. From now on the rest of the time with him. Prepared a lecture.

7th July, 1939

Last day. Paul tried to keep me back. It's no good. Van Dusen lecture. Pack. With Hans Wedell before lunch. Theological conversation with Paul. Farewell in the seminary. Supper with Van Dusen. Go to the ship with Paul. Farewell half past eleven, sail at half past twelve. Manhattan by night; the moon over the skyscrapers. It is very hot. The visit is at an end. I am glad to have been over and glad that I am on the way home. Perhaps I have learnt more in this month than in a whole year nine years ago; at least I have acquired some important insight for all future decisions. Probably this visit will have a great effect on me.

8th July, 1939

On the ship. It is quiet and hot. The sea journey has lost the charm of novelty. Read a great deal, a book on America (which was very bad; the style so bad that a great deal was obscure) – Practical Religion – good articles.

9th July, 1939

English service, which was well attended, but probably as a change from the monotonous life on board, like the cinema, etc. Text: 'There will be no more sea' (Rev. 21. 1). Sermon sentimental and wordy. Conversation with Karl Friedrich about theological matters. Read a great deal. The days are noticeably shorter by the loss of an hour. Since I have been on the ship my inner uncertainty about the future has ceased. I can think of my shortened time in America without reproaches. Reading: 'It is good for me that I was afflicted, that I might learn thy statutes' (Psa. 119. 71). One of my favourite verses from my favourite psalm.　　　G.S. I pp. 314–15

247

Bonhoeffer spent a few days in London on the way back and failed to contact the Bishop of Chichester to whom he wished to give an explanation of his decision to return. Instead, he wrote to him and posted the letter in London.

London, S.E.23, 22nd July, 1939

BONHOEFFER TO CHICHESTER: When you were in London on Thursday I asked Hildebrandt to tell you that I had already come back from U.S.A. and that I am on my way to Germany. Unfortunately, he forgot to tell you. Now I can only write a few words of explanation and to say 'goodbye' to you. I shall leave on Tuesday morning. On my arrival in New York Dr. Leiper very kindly offered me the post of a refugee pastor (I mean a pastor for the refugees) in New York. This post was to be connected with lectures in various places. Of course, I was rather surprised about this offer and told Dr. Leiper, that I had promised to the Confessing Church to come back at the latest after a year unless the political circumstances would make that impossible. So it was just a question of loyalty whether I could accept a post which by itself would make my return doubtful or even impossible. I discussed the problem with my friends very thoroughly and decided to decline the offer for three reasons: I was bound to my promise to go back next year; there were many non-Aryan brethren who are much more entitled to such a post; I had got my leave of absence for another purpose.

It was a difficult decision, but I am still convinced, I was not allowed to decide otherwise. That meant my early return to Germany. Kindly enough, I was invited by Dr. Coffin and Van Dusen to stay at Union Seminary as long as I wanted. But when news about Danzig reached me I felt compelled to go back as soon as possible and to make my decisions in Germany. I do not regret my trip to U.S.A., though, of course, it had been undertaken under different presuppositions. I have seen and learned much in the few weeks over there and I am looking forward to my work in Germany again. What

248

sort of personal decisions will be asked from me I do not know. But nobody knows that now.

My passport expires next spring; it is therefore uncertain when I shall be in this country again. Let me thank you today for all help and friendship and real understanding in the past and in the future. We shall never forget you during the coming events. I thank you for what you have done for my brother-in-law and his family. It has meant everything to them. Will you allow me to leave them in this country with the confidence that they may approach you whenever they need advice and help? Of course, their future is unsettled, too, and it will require much patience and much energy before they can start afresh. Nevertheless I am confident that they finally will not suffer more than they can bear.   G.S. I. pp. 320–2

INVITATION TO EDINBURGH

Bonhoeffer was back in Berlin on 27th July. In his absence much had happened. The resistance movement had gathered strength and there was widespread unrest. The declaration by Britain that she could not entertain any further territorial demands by Hitler had brought the possibility of war nearer.

While Bonhoeffer had been in America, an invitation had arrived from John Baillie for him to give the Croall Lectures in Scotland. He was attracted to this, but felt the need to postpone.

Edinburgh, 15th June, 1939

BAILLIE TO BONHOEFFER: I am one of the trustees of the Croall Lectureship Trust, and I am writing to you to ask you whether you would be prepared to accept nomination as a lecturer during next Winter. The duties of the lecturer are simply to deliver about six lectures on a theological subject of his own choosing, but the lectures must be published afterwards in book form . . .

Some suitable dates, perhaps sometime between October of this year and March of next might be arranged between the lecturer and the trustees ... I shall write no more at present, but shall await an answer from you. I was most interested in all Professor Niebuhr had to tell me about you. My wife and Jan send you their warmest greetings, and so do I.

London, 22nd July, 1939

BONHOEFFER TO BAILLIE: I have just returned from America and received a letter from Germany with some indication of an invitation from you to Edinburgh for the purpose of lectures there next spring. Thank you very much indeed for this invitation. I will come with the greatest pleasure, if I get out of Germany by that time ...

Berlin, 24th August, 1939

BONHOEFFER TO BAILLIE: ... I must tell you that it will be very difficult for me to get out in October and I should like to ask you if any time after 1st or 15th December would be acceptable for the committee. I am thinking of the following topic: 'the death in the Christian message' ...   G.S. II pp. 361–2

The war made this impossible. It appears that Bonhoeffer later decided that he would do the Croall Lectures on the meaning of death, but they were never delivered.[1] He was right to say that October would be difficult for him to get out. On the day he wrote, 24th August, Ribbentrop was signing the German–Soviet Pact, and a week later Hitler sent his armies into Poland. The war had started.

THE FIRST CIRCULAR LETTER OF THE WAR

Bonhoeffer took up his work of caring for the younger theologians and his first circular of the war shows how quickly he was back at work. The date is 20th September, 1939:

[1] The substance of these lectures was eventually contained in *Ethics*, SCM Press, 1955; Fontana Library, 1964.

BONHOEFFER TO THE BRETHREN: In answer to an official question, I have received the news, which I pass on to you today, that our dear brother Theodor Maass was killed in Poland on 3rd September. You will be as stunned by this news as I was. But I beg you, let us thank God in remembrance of him. He was a good brother, a quiet, faithful pastor of the Confessing Church, a man who lived from word and sacrament, whom God has also thought worthy to suffer for the Gospel. I am sure that he was prepared to go. Where God tears great gaps we should not try to fill them with human words. They should remain open. Our only comfort is the God of the resurrection, the Father of our Lord Jesus Christ, who also was and is his God. In him we know our brothers and in him is the abiding fellowship of those who have overcome and those who still await their hour. God be praised for our dead brother and be merciful to us all at our end. The parents of brother Maass live at Stralsund – Pastor Maass, Ketelhotstrasse, 8.

I know that the following brethren are now with the army: Maechler, Dobrick, v.d. Marwitz, Mickley, Wolfgang Schmidt, Gerhard Krause, Block, Martin Schaaff, Berg, Buchmann, Schrader, Pompe, Lynker, August, Winkelmann, Sander. Despite inquiries, I still have no army post office numbers from brothers Corbach, Seydel, Harhausen, Giese, Nimz, Hofmann, Büchsel, Schröter, Winfried Krause. Others are likely to be called up at any moment. Please let me know as soon as anyone is called up, or if there is someone not on the list whom I ought to know about. Let me know all the army post office numbers that you have. And take time to write to the brethren out there as often as possible. And above all, we must not neglect the greatest service that is left to us, our faithful daily intercession. There is so much that we must ask for our brethren with the army, but first and last always this, that at all times they may show themselves to be Christians, that they may do a real service to many of their comrades, and that Jesus Christ may be their sole comfort both in life and death.

Many of us have been inwardly disquieted during the past few weeks. We know that our brethren are out there in all sorts of battles and dangers, we hear of the death of a brother, and we feel an urge, 'I too must be where my brethren are, I don't want anything more than they have'. This often weighs us down completely, and then everything that we do seems so superfluous. Indeed, even the questions about the life of our church, for which we have fought so far, sometimes seem incidental in the light of events in the outside world. We think that once again everything ought to be completely different, that we should leave the whole past behind us and begin all over again. Who can't understand that? But, dear brethren, those of you who have not yet been called up, it is all-important that we do not throw away the grace that God has so far given to us, that we do not despise our office, but learn to love and honour it highly at this very time. We have been called to be preachers of the Gospel and shepherds of the community, and as long as we fulfil this task, God will ask us only one thing, whether faithful service to his community has suffered damage, if only for a moment, through our fault, whether we have despised his community and the brethren whom he has given to us, if only for a single moment.

We may still preach, and so we should do, as before, with good, free consciences. And we should be faithful pastors who do not deny their church even in times of need. We know that God requires this service of us today, and this is the greatest possible service that we can render to men. We do not ask what we may feel like today or tomorrow, but what our task is. So let us not bicker and do each other harm, but be glad, and serve.

The texts for 1st September were surprising and promising enough: 'Seek the Lord while he may be found, call upon him while he is near' (Isa. 55. 6), 'Behold, now is the acceptable time; behold, now is the day of salvation' (II Cor. 6. 2). What does that mean, but that God's hour has struck, it is high time for repentance and prayer, the day of glad tidings has dawned, the harvest of the Word of God will be greater than the harvest of death, victory belongs not to the world but to God? If we really believe that, we and our people will be helped.

We are preachers of justification by grace alone. What must that mean today? It means quite simply that we should no longer equate human ways and aims with divine ways and aims. God is beyond all human plans and actions. Everything must be judged by him. Anyone who evades this judgement of God must die, anyone who subjects himself to it will live; for to be judged by God is grace that leads to life. He judges in order to have mercy, he humbles in order to exalt. Only the humble will succeed. God does not confirm human action, but cuts across it, and thereby draws our gaze above, to his grace. In cutting across our ways, God comes to us and says his gracious 'Yes' to us, but only through the cross of Jesus Christ. He has placed this cross upon the earth. Under the cross he returns us to the earth, and its work and toil, but in so doing he binds us anew to the earth and to the men who live, act, fight and suffer upon it. 'You then, my son, be strong in the grace that is in Christ Jesus' (II Tim. 2. 1), 'Be strong, and show yourself a man, and keep the charge of the Lord your God' (I Kings 2. 2 f.).

I don't know whether we shall have as troublesome a time now with the question of the righteousness of God as there was in the last war. It almost seems to me as though there had been a change here. Christians today probably know more about the biblical verdict upon the world and history, so they will perhaps be confirmed in their faith, rather than sorely tried, by present events. The non-Christians have already finished too completely with the question of the righteousness of a personal God to be overcome with it. Nevertheless, under the pressure of events the question cannot be left completely out of account, on either side, and we shall often have to listen, like the writer of the 42nd Psalm, to the complaint, 'Where is now thy God?' Is it true that God is silent? It is only true for the one whose God is the God of his own ideals and thoughts.

He will have to be given the biblical message of the power and fearfulness of the Creator and Lord of the whole world. 'Who has commanded and it came to pass, unless the Lord has ordained it? Is it not from the mouth of the Most High that good and evil come?' (Lam. 3. 37 f.). 'I am the Lord and there is none other, I form light and create darkness, I make weal and create woe.' (Isa. 45. 6 f.). 'Does evil befall a city, unless the Lord has done it?' (Amos 3. 6). This God, who makes the nations drink from the cup of his wrath and throws them into confusion (Jer. 25. 15 ff.) is the father of our Lord Jesus Christ, whose counsel is wonderful and who will carry it out gloriously to the end (Isa. 28. 29). Is God silent? No, he speaks the silent language of his fearful power and glory, so that we become small and humble and worship him alone. And in pure grace he speaks the clearly perceptible language of his mercy and loving kindness to the children of men through the mouth of Jesus Christ, in whom we have the omnipotent God for our own father. 'Holy, holy, holy is the Lord of hosts; the whole earth is full of his glory' (Isa. 6. 3).

So our hearts and our eyes cannot be caught and dismayed by daily events, however closely we follow them. Above them, we seek and find God the Lord, and in reverence look upon his works. We seek and find our Lord Jesus Christ, and firmly believe in his victory and in the glory of his community. We seek and find God the Holy Spirit, who gives his word power over us, greater power than the world can ever gain over us. And so we pray that the work of the triune God will soon be consummated.

Death has again come among us, and we must think about it, whether we want to or not. Two things have become important to me recently: death is outside us, and it is in us. Death from outside is the fearful foe which comes to us when it will. It is the man with the scythe, under whose stroke the blossoms fall. It guides the bullet that goes home. We can do nothing against it, 'it has power from the supreme God'. It is the death of the whole human race, God's wrath and the end of all life. But the other is death in us, it is our own death. That too has been in us since the fall of Adam. But it belongs to us. We die daily to it in Jesus Christ or we deny him. This death in us has something to do with love towards Christ and towards men. We die to it when we love Christ and the brethren from the bottom of our hearts, for love is total surrender to what a man loves. This death is grace and the consummation of love. It should be our prayer that we die this death, that it be sent to us, that death only comes to us from outside when we have been made ready for it by this our own death. For our death is really only the way to the perfect love of God.

When fighting and death exercise their wild dominion around us, then we are called to bear witness to God's love and God's peace not only by word and thought, but also by our deeds. Read James 4. 1 ff.! We should daily ask ourselves where we can bear witness in what we do to the kingdom in which love and peace prevail. The great peace for which we long can only grow again from peace between twos and threes. Let us put an end to all hate, mistrust, envy, disquiet, wherever we can. 'Blessed are the peacemakers, for they shall be called the children of God.'

I have been back from my travels for some weeks. Fritz got married the day before yesterday. Work in the summer was very enjoyable. I would very much like to send you a report of my travels, but it is a long story, and I don't know how I could tell it to you. It all seems a long time ago now.

I am thinking of you and your work in my prayers. God bless and keep you, your homes and your churches. May he grant us all his peace.   G.S. II pp. 553–8

APPENDICES

INDEX

Appendix 1

15th November, 1935

As I got out of a farewell speech on your departure, thereby, I am sure, pleasing you as much as I pleased myself, I will now at a rather greater distance write something of what I would have said. Summer 1935 has been for me, I believe, the busiest time of my whole life, both personally and professionally. In both respects I have learnt more than ever before by living and working with you, despite Br. Maechler's complaint that I did not always work as hard as he would have wished from his superior! Br. Schönherr has told you that all together we have learnt afresh new and important things. So I want to thank you for the past semester. You have made my work easy for me.

In the meantime, the picture here has altered, but the 'remnant' remaining reminds me of you all every day, and in the first few days I kept being surprised that new faces were to be seen alongside the familiar ones that remained. But, gradually the new ones are also becoming familiar, intimate and good brethren. The old brigade is helping me a great deal with the work, and while last semester I had to begin all by myself, this time six brethren are helping me.

We are thinking of you a great deal during these weeks and have firm confidence that you will stay with our cause and on the road which we have recognised to be the right one. Of course this is harder for you than it is for us. But with the resources given to us, we are ready to help you where you need us. I would be glad to visit one or other of you. Write if you want me to. But, in any case, be sure that our house here is wide open to you whenever you come. And you will find here your old faithful brethren.

DIETRICH BONHOEFFER

We are writing to you to let you know that you will not be alone in the coming days. After the events of the last few days, we must now in all seriousness expect a prohibition of the Confessing Church – put out perhaps in the disguised form of a prohibition of our church government. Our church government now as ever stands firmly by Barmen and Dahlem.[1] We would say this to you on the matter:

1. Under no circumstances let yourselves be misled by assertions that we are a 'movement' and not a church. This is to abandon everything that was said at Barmen and Dahlem and to stand on a level with the German Christian movement. We are no movement, but the Church of Jesus Christ.

2. A prohibition of our church government would be a prohibition of the Confessing Church.

3. Even a prohibited church government remains irrefutably our church government, the only government to which we must appeal at any time, whose directions alone are binding on us.

4. The signing of any reciprocal agreement is forbidden.

5. No order which is contrary to that of our church government may be obeyed without the express direction of the church government.

6. In this respect you are responsible for brothers near to you. Keep with them!

7. We need not tell you that we should be glad to welcome any who want to join our side.

Dear brethren, we can only prepare ourselves for the hours which lie ahead by strong and unwearying prayer and by wakefulness in everything. We shall now see whether our prayer and our life has been up till now a preparation for these hours of confession. If we are steadfast in prayer, we may confidently trust that the Holy Spirit will give us the right word at the right time and that we will be found faithful. It is a privilege to be allowed to stand alongside our brothers, but, near or far, each day we are bound together by the prayer that on the day of Jesus Christ we shall stand before him united in joy. Here then each stands or falls by his Lord. Christ is visiting us, that is Advent – 'Blessed are those servants whom the Lord, when he comes, finds watching.'

THE BRETHREN AT FINKENWALDE

[1] See notes, page 38.

14th December, 1935

We hope that all of you have now received our second letter. To many its contents will have been obvious, but it is good to hear someone else repeat the word we know to be true and at the same time to be extremely dangerous. The situation, as we must now see it, seems to justify this further letter with all its explicit and implicit consequences. The greatest trial in the immediate future will in all probability be that of loneliness. Because the circular letters of the Council of Brethren have been prohibited, very little news now reaches the individual, and then with all the uncertainty of oral tradition. But this trial has become far more serious for us all as a result of the attitude of the Lutherans, beginning with Küssner's letter and going on to Marahrens' letter to the committee. For them, so proud that their confession remains intact, the cause of the Confessing Church is suddenly just a 'concern'. The provisional government of the church (VKL) wishes that it had never taken over governmental functions and stands firmly behind Zöllner. Now the provisional government has really gone at last, and a government has been formed which is more faithful to the confession. Today we have a circular letter to that effect from Niemöller and his church. So the damaged areas of the church are isolated, and in view of article XXVIII/CA it could even be that we are the ones with an intact confession. . . . The necessary consequences now make themselves quite clear: the whole apparatus of the press and everything that shapes public opinion will now attack the sole remaining 'disturber of the peace', the Confessing Church of the Old Prussian Union. Jacobi, in fact, is already feeling it. Who knows how our congregations will fare? But the issues at stake are whether we confess or deny and the salvation of the soul and on these matters we must stand, even if we are by ourselves. It is the *status confessionis*, indeed the confession of the freedom of the church, and there can be neither permanent nor temporary solutions unless they accord with the complete truth. . . .

We have been equipping ourselves long enough. Now the long time of waiting is to be justified with particularly joyful service. And we have the means of standing in this struggle. Remember once again your meditation time, the time for which we simply must make room. . . . We can only overcome our solitude in prayer and meditation, by the nearness of our Lord, who has promised to be near to us in prayer and in the Word. We must believe that and really try to live by it, resting ourselves on his promises. And because we now know this fellowship in Christ and want to live by it, especially in these times of emergency, let us take our promise to visit the brothers quite seriously. Today all the responsibility is with those who are by themselves.

Above all, remind yourselves that we are with you every evening in our prayers. . . .

ALBRECHT SCHÖNHERR

15th January, 1936

May we say a few more words about the situation? We have already reported the essentials, as we see them, in our previous letter, and we have really no reason to alter anything that was said there. But we would like today to give you a few thoughts of a more practical nature, with which our position can be made clear even to a non-theologian. That is still our task now, not to let ourselves be driven along, but to stand in opposition and to attempt to hold back the others. Basically our situation is similar to that obtaining in the summer of 1933. Many people have gone over to the German Christians in the good faith that by their intervention they could snatch the tiller round and steer a good course. But they have failed, because the course which a church is following depends not on the intervention of any personality in the church, however prominent, but on the truth of the cause.

If the root is rotten, even the sound twig grafted on will not help. The cause has no truth because the true *vocatio* is missing. Only the *rite vocatio* has the promise, and that is decisive, because the work of the church can never be founded on the efforts of individuals, only upon the promise of the Lord. Because the *vocatio* is lacking, nothing good can be expected from the start, and even if 'success' should be achieved, it could only be the success of Satan. The Councils of Brethren of the Synods of the Confessing Church are alone *rite vocati*. Even though they are appointed under an emergency law, the word 'emergency' is only an indication of the circumstances, not of the status, of this law. Even a law born of emergency is a valid law. We have therefore submitted ourselves to our Councils of Brethren as our regular church authority. We are no vagabonds who belong today to this regiment, tomorrow to another. We have no reason to break with one church government because another church government is offered us from outside. The only reason for this would be a violation of the confession and we will hardly be able to convict our church government of that. So why change the church government? Particularly when we have every reason to fear the formation of a new National Church. For the state does not usually give up what it has in its hands, and it has in its hands the administration of finance and, with the committees, spiritual direction – that is particularly so with a state like this one which understands itself to be total; its actions with the church must lead us from the start to expect an extension of its authority. Then the National Church also brings with it the power to silence heresy, for the sake of political peace. If the church surrenders the '*recte docere*' (CA 7) it is no longer a true church. We must avoid seeing the church as another historical form which has its reality in the mere fact of its existence. The church has its reality in that it abides in the truth. If it falls from the truth, though only for a moment, it is no longer a church but some religious association, which does not have the promise. If we give up the truth or put it in the background even just for the time being, we thereby surrender the promises of God. One more word about 'legal aid'. In January 1935, the VKL asked the state to recognise a committee for the purification of the church, to be nominated by the church. So there was never any question of intervention in the church. We never appealed, we merely asked for recognition.

Perhaps we have been able to help you a little with these remarks and you in turn will be able to help other brethren.

Here in Pomerania we discussed these questions last Friday in Stettin. There were about two hundred clergy there, of whom about three quarters wanted to recognise the Council of Brethren as the church authority for the future. Greifswald was among the dissident quarter. Br. Bonhoeffer and Br. Onnasch spoke, both, I believe, very forcefully. There were some welcome voices among the other brethren too. Last Sunday we had our first Confessing Service here, with forty-six people. Br. Bonhoeffer preached about the building of the wall (Nehemiah), attaching a reading of the pulpit proclamation. The people were very much in favour, and some new people even attached themselves to the Confessing Church. Accordingly we had a meeting and formed a Council of Brethren. We must also give you some sad news; Br. W. has left us and submitted to the committees. . . .

. . . The community also spent Christmas Eve here; it was a wonderful experience, not the least being the generous food parcels!

ALBRECHT SCHÖNHERR

263

17th February, 1936

We have started something else; some intensive parish work. We have been working regularly in the individual Confessing congregations in Stettin ever since the beginning of the semester. The work brings great joy, because one is continually surprised what a firm grip of the church situation there is among the non-theologians. Sometimes when one comes from meetings of pastors one is shattered at how little the theologians want to see what is really at stake. This work has been further deepened to a regular friendship between our seminary and the Stettin congregations. It was pioneered in discussions with the leaders of the Confessing congregation, and was openly announced last Sunday in a visit of 120 to 130 members of the Confessing Church from Stettin. The guests had been invited for 4.30, but the crowds were already streaming in at coffee time. . . . Then – not without ulterior motives – we took them round the house in small groups until the bell went for the service. Br. Rott preached and the brothers sang. . . .

A wonderful experience for everyone who shared in it . . . was a trip to Greifswald by Br. Bonhoeffer and four other brethren. The students had invited him for a lecture and to preach. All went off most satisfactorily; five hundred people went to the afternoon service in St Mary's church!

Br. Lekszas . . . has now already gathered a group of members of the Confessing Church in other faculties. He has further succeeded in seeing that the students do not automatically join in the Greifswald committee course. . . .

ALBRECHT SCHÖNHERR

G.S. II pp. 458–60, 461–6

Appendix II

AN IMAGINARY CONVERSATION

This began in the room of P. H. Newby, the novelist and Controller of the BBC's Third Programme. We had called in Terence Tiller to help us decide the best way to celebrate the 20th anniversary of Bonhoeffer's death in a way worthy of the Third Programme. That anniversary coincided with the publication of the first volume of Bonhoeffer's papers, 'No Rusty Swords', which I had edited, and for this reason I was consulted about the programme. Terence Tiller had long experience of the 'dramatic documentary', especially on the Third Programme, and in particular in the form, which he had developed over the years, of the 'imaginary conversation'. This form recaptured the probable text of conversations between famous people who had met or who could have met. It was inevitable that sooner or later our minds would be given to the consideration of a possible 'imaginary conversation' including Bonhoeffer. It was left to me to suggest a conversationalist worthy of the man, and a real or possible occasion of meeting. There were many possibilities. He could have met the Mahatma Ghandi, whom he planned to visit; he could have met Pierre Teilhard de Chardin, whose books were not published during Bonhoeffer's lifetime although they were written and the two men had a great deal in common. There was a bewildering choice. At last, I settled upon an evening in New York in July 1939, which Bonhoeffer spent with Richard Niebuhr. It was just after he had decided to return to Germany and both men were primarily interested in how ethical judgements are made. It was almost certain that they discussed 'Ethics', particularly in relation to Bonhoeffer's recent decision. I assumed they did. The more I thought about it and the more I worked on the 1939 material, the better the idea seemed to me. Both men had left papers on 'Ethics', intended for publication but not ready for the publishers.[1] These papers had subsequently been written up and published. The 'imaginary conversation' could therefore be based upon a considerable amount of available

[1] Dietrich Bonhoeffer, *Ethics*, SCM Press and Fontana; Richard Niebuhr, *The Responsible Self*, Harper & Row.

material. On Bonhoeffer's side, I had the diaries of the period and his letters, most of which appear in this volume and in his 'Ethics'; on Niebuhr's side, I had 'The Responsible Self'. With this material and strictly observing the rules, I wrote up a possible conversation which included only ideas and possible phrases used by the two men. The first draft of this conversation was sent to Terence Tiller, who rewrote it for radio. He extended it, and part of the last page is his work. We finally worked through it with the two actors who co-operated sympathetically.[1] The programme was broadcast in September 1965, the year of the 20th anniversary, and twice repeated. As this book ends with the return of Bonhoeffer to Germany and the outbreak of war, it seemed appropriate to put the text of this 'dramatic documentary' at the close of this part of his works. It vividly illustrates, and I believe authentically, 'the way to freedom' which Bonhoeffer trod.

In July 1939 Dietrich Bonhoeffer was in New York and had decided to return to Germany after a very short visit, for reasons that are evident in his letters and diaries.[1] During his short visit, he discussed this momentous decision with many people, but we do not have a full record of the arguments he used. There was one person he met and talked with who would have been particularly interested in the reasons for his decision. This was Richard Niebuhr, brother of Reinhold, who had a special concern for 'Ethics' on which he lectured at Yale. Richard Niebuhr's attitude to ethics resembles that of Dietrich Bonhoeffer at many points, although fundamentally it is different. This makes a good basis for a discussion, which surely took place when these two men met. Both held back from committing their thoughts on ethics to a book until it was too late to publish. Both 'Ethics' by Dietrich Bonhoeffer and 'The Responsible Self' by Richard Niebuhr were published from unfinished manuscripts, posthumously. From these two books and from Bonhoeffer's letters and papers, an attempt has here been made to reconstruct a possible conversation between these two theologians, early in July 1939, when Bonhoeffer had already written to Reinhold Niebuhr of his decision to return. Dietrich Bonhoeffer and Richard Niebuhr spent the evening of 4th July together in New York.

NIEBUHR: You have decided to return to Germany?

BONHOEFFER: I have. But, as you may imagine, not without great searching of heart – and some misgiving.

NIEBUHR: Of course, I can have no doubt of that. But the decision

---

[1] Hugh Burden and Duncan Carse.

[2] See pages 221 ff.

surprises and disappoints many of us. You have criticised American preaching considerably, and I think justly. But how is it going to be put right if people like you, who can see the weakness of our situation, do not stay to put it right?

BONHOEFFER: With these hands – this voice – alone?

NIEBUHR: Not single-handed, no; but surely you see that there is work for you to do here?

BONHOEFFER: And not in Germany?

NIEBUHR: In Germany on the other hand, you are simply walking into trouble. You have said many times yourself in conversation and in lectures that you are bound hand and foot in Germany. Is it really responsible of you to go back to a country for purely emotional reasons?

BONHOEFFER: Believe me, my thought has gone deeper than that!

NIEBUHR: What practical reasons can you have? Your seminary has been closed and you dare not re-open. You cannot teach in Berlin. Your preaching is restricted, and publication is out of the question. You are a marked man; and we all know that so long as the Nazis are in power, there is a real danger of your arrest and execution.

BONHOEFFER: There is also hope of doing battle for the soul of Germany.

NIEBUHR: This battle for the soul of Germany can surely be fought better from the vantage point of America. It looks as though there will be war, but America is unlikely to be involved despite her sympathy with Poland and her natural alliance with France and Britain. Here you will not be among enemies of your country, only critics; and you are one of them yourself. Here is the best possible place for you to make your contribution to the struggle with effect and with safety.

BONHOEFFER: Safety! Can any virtue operate in the mere seeking of safety?

NIEBUHR: It is not the coward's way I am advocating, but the sensible way. Mock heroics have no part in a struggle as serious as this. God in Christ is doing something with the world and our part is to fit into what he is doing. Is your decision to return to Germany any more than an obedience to an unwritten law of behaviour, doing with courage what your class expects of you? Should you not consider what God is doing with Germany and ask yourself where your action fits into this?

BONHOEFFER (*a little bitterly*): Am I, then, to take more time – more safe time – to 'consider', while others act?

NIEBUHR: Forgive me if I have been too frank. I am deeply concerned as we all are that you should not throw your life away. When my brother arranged the invitation for you over here, he believed that he was preserving you for a greater struggle, which would mean the eventual rebuilding of Germany, and at the same time enabling you to make that contribution to theology which we believe you can. We haven't so many theologians that we can afford to throw one away!

BONHOEFFER: I am glad you are frank; and I want you to know how much I appreciate the concern of my American friends for my welfare. And I am honoured that you think me able to help repair the torn fabric of American theology. Like you I deplore it! A few days ago, I listened to a sermon in Riverside Church about 'getting an horizon'. The image of God as man's 'necessary' horizon was blasphemous!

NIEBUHR: But well-intentioned, surely? Naïve, no doubt, but —

BONHOEFFER: Blasphemous! This sort of idolatrous religion stirs up the flesh, which is usually kept in subjection by the Word of God! Such sermons make for libertinism, egotism; it seemed to me that the preacher had failed to recognise that you can get on quite well without religion, even better! Perhaps you Americans are more religious than we are. But if that kind of sermon goes on you are certainly not more Christian! One day the storm will blow with full force on that kind of religious hand-out.

NIEBUHR: Even so, from the human point of view ...

BONHOEFFER: Oh, from the human point of view, no doubt the thing is attractive. But I prefer simple rustic preaching. You're quite right that there is work for a theologian here, but surely only an American can remove all this rubbish. You and your brother are the people to do it, not me. If I were to stay in America it would not be to improve your theology. It would be to minister to my fellow countrymen over here and to keep you and them informed about the progress of the struggle against the Nazi perversion of the Christian faith.

NIEBUHR: Surely even that would be valuable – could you not do at least that?

BONHOEFFER: I was able to do it in England a few years ago, when I ministered to the German-speaking congregation in London. I could do it again, but there are others to do it; and I have already been urged by my colleagues in Germany to keep such a post open for men who are in more certain danger than I am. After all, you can exaggerate the danger I am in. When I return to Germany, I return to a number of friends in high places. I shall use all the contacts I can, to work effectively.

NIEBUHR: How effectively, with your freedom of action so restricted?

BONHOEFFER (*impatiently*): Of course I could be more free here, and be able to write my lectures on 'Ethics'. And, like Karl Barth, it is true that I am first and foremost a theologian and want to work at my theology. In different times, it would be attractive to spend this second term in America. I am already fascinated by the changes I have seen since my last term here as a very young man. But you yourself have pointed out the problem. What is God doing with Germany and where does my decision fit into that plan? If I face that decision on a short-term basis, then I can say that it is more reasonable to ask how I can best serve the purposes of God in his dealings with my country; and I might well decide to stay here. But, the issues are changing daily. I shall have no right to participate in the reconstruction of Christian life in Germany after the war, if I do not share the trials of this time with my people.

NIEBUHR: 'After the war' –? You feel that this is an inevitable complication?

BONHOEFFER: Surely the news from Danzig makes it evident to us all that Germany will soon be at war with France and with Britain? It will not be long before a world war comparable with the terrible 1914 war is upon us. Then it was an old-fashioned struggle for power, and the guilt was evenly balanced on both sides. You know that I have never subscribed to the view that the sole guilt for that war rested with Germany. On this point, I agree with Adolf Hitler! The Versailles Treaty was unjust. But this war will be different, Christians in Germany will face the terrible alternatives of either willing the defeat of their nation that Christian civilisation may survive or willing the victory of their nation and thereby destroying our civilisation. I know which of these alternatives I must choose, but I cannot make that choice in security.

NIEBUHR: I can understand that. It is really the same thing as saying that you cannot take part in the rebuilding of Germany, once the war is over, unless you have felt the pressure of events in Germany during the war. We both see the importance of involvement. But must you make the decision now, and is it so important that you return at once to Germany?

BONHOEFFER: I think it is. For a long time now, I have been trying to think through the concept of man in his fullness. Like you, I am convinced that what God is doing with us is making us into men. The purpose of God is that we should be human.

NIEBUHR: Yes.

BONHOEFFER: It seems equally clear from the New Testament that being human means being free.

NIEBUHR: I agree.

BONHOEFFER: We might therefore be said to be progressing towards freedom. Perhaps full freedom cannot be reached until we embrace death, but meanwhile there are stages. Discipline is the first stage a young man learns. That is obvious – freedom requires a certain control of our powers – our unruly members! But the next obstacle to be overcome is – indecision. I am sure that the second stage to freedom is action.

NIEBUHR: Even if the action itself is ill-judged?

BONHOEFFER: Conceivably. My decision to come to America was a blow struck for freedom – even though I am now convinced that it was wrong. Your advice to wait is one I cannot take. I must decide and act now, in the light of the events as I know them. Waiting is curtailing my freedom too much. I cannot live with this awful decision hanging over me. I must decide – even if I take the wrong decision. A man can live with his mistakes. He cannot remain free if he has to live with his indecisions. There are enough facts before us today to decide – therefore we must decide.

NIEBUHR: You have the impatience of a young man still. But I agree with you about the slavery of indecision. Can we look at this problem as a problem in ethics?

BONHOEFFER: It is precisely that.

NIEBUHR: Well, you know how I dislike ethical systems, and have delayed writing on my own subject simply because I fear that an ethical system written down is in danger of becoming fossilised.

BONHOEFFER: Is that not my own point? Ethics is a living response, an active response, to the situation.

NIEBUHR: Well, now: you appear to have made three points that will help one come to ethical decisions. The first two, I accept: there is no interest in theoretical ethics for our age; and concrete ethical problems rather than principles are the stuff of ethics. The third worries me because it seems irresponsible, although it is largely true: you say that a decision must be made, even if it is the wrong one. Of course, it depends upon how soon you make the decision.

BONHOEFFER: So I maintain.

NIEBUHR: I take it that you mean, when all the facts are known and there seems little chance of new light coming, we should not wait around in indecision, but act?

BONHOEFFER: Yes. But I would go farther. The rightness of the action is not the all-important thing. Luther maintained – and, I believe, rightly – that what is worse than a good man doing wrong is a bad man doing right! Far worse than doing evil is being evil.

NIEBUHR: Dangerous doctrine, particularly for a shallow man. But I think we know what Luther meant, and will not interpret this in the light of irresponsible action. This does not mean that it is of little consequence what we do, but rather that what we are is more important. I imagine, however, that neither of us would use that argument to excuse our wrong doing nor to avoid hard thinking about the decision to be taken. It is, however, in the long run a safe-guard to know that God will forgive and understand if after careful consideration our fallible nature leads us to the wrong decision. No decision can ultimately destroy us. But how do we arrive at as clear a mind as possible about the rightness of an action? I take it that both of us agree that there is no Christian law – you have said as much in your study of 'The Sermon on the Mount' – *The Cost of Discipleship* – a very helpful book, by the way.

BONHOEFFER: I am glad you find it so. Well, yes: here we are at one – if I have understood your own books right. I cannot believe that the Sermon on the Mount was intended to be the Christian version of the Law. Ethics is a matter of blood and soil, the Nazis are right about that; but it is also a matter of him who made both blood and soil. The trouble arises from this duality. There can be ethics only in the framework of history, in the concrete situation. The concrete need lays its claim upon me and I must respond.

NIEBUHR: But, surely, how you respond is the question?

BONHOEFFER: Indeed yes. At one time, I was convinced that the rich heritage of Christian experience through the ages could help me more than I am now prepared to admit. Nazism has shown me the depths of the demonic, as I do not believe we have seen it since the Middle Ages.

NIEBUHR: If even then.

BONHOEFFER: If even then. Well, in the face of this clear revelation of the demonic, I am far less inclined than I was to believe that reason is our guide. In fact it seems to me that the ethics of yesterday are no longer effective for the greater powers of evil we face today. Our fathers fashioned weapons to combat evil. These weapons were honourable in their day, but they should now be in the museum. We must fashion our own weapons.

NIEBUHR: That sounds right; but I should be happier if you were to develop it a little.

BONHOEFFER: Very well. I have often been distressed, particularly over here in America, to note the failure of reasonable people to perceive either the depths of evil or the depths of the holy. With the best of intentions they believe that a little reason will suffice to clamp together the parting timbers of the building. In their desire to see justice done to both sides they are crushed between the two clashing forces, and end by achieving nothing. If you attempt this reasonable impartiality with the kind of forces we have been dealing with in Germany, you will soon be forced to retire from the scene, bitterly disappointed at the unreasonableness of the world.

NIEBUHR: If you put it in such extreme terms –

BONHOEFFER: Extreme? Some of those who want me to stay in America are unconsciously already doing what I have described. In my country, the reasonable people have fallen to the even greater danger of yielding unresistingly to the stronger party. Reason, Conscience, Duty, Freedom, Virtue. These concepts of yesterday were honourable in their time, but they are useless to meet the demonic forces of today. We need stronger weapons.

NIEBUHR: Your rhetoric is convincing, but I think stronger on the negative than on the positive side. I agree with your insistence that the older forms of ethics are inadequate. You seem to find certain concepts too weak – reason, conscience, duty and so on. I am inclined to think that what is at fault is rather our view of man himself.

BONHOEFFER: In what sense?

NIEBUHR: We have thought of man under two images – man the maker and man the citizen. I am sure that these images are now inadequate. I think it is these images rather than the inadequacy of reason that you should be attacking. These images have led to a superficial use of reason. Clearly, a little reason cannot hold together the parting timbers of a decaying society, but we know a great deal more about man and the way in which his reason functions than we used to.

BONHOEFFER: But that does not make any more valid this constant appeal to reason.

NIEBUHR: If you mean that the attitude to ethical problems needs to be more serious than just the call to be reasonable, I naturally agree with you. But that does not exhaust the use of reason. Reason is a tool used also in the field of psychology to discover man's darker interior. I think this helps us to see the depths of evil in man and to unmask his apparently most honourable dealings. Discoveries in the unconscious support your view that 'being evil is far worse than doing evil.'

BONHOEFFER: In no country is greater faith placed in psychological studies, than in America. Yet it is precisely in this country that both you and I find true insight lacking. Are you not merely substituting – trying to substitute – one system for another?

NIEBUHR: Although I have as little liking for systems of ethics as you have, I am sure we need a framework to our thinking. Let me now develop mine: In all ethical decisions, the only absolute is God, revealed to be both power and goodness. With this background I would propound three consequent motifs in my ethics – the whole person is involved in a moral decision; moral action is response in the light of the total context; and moral decision is the result of experience – always in flux. As you know, I have always believed that the most helpful concept in ethics is that of 'response'. It is surprising how recently the word 'responsible' has entered the field; yet, it now dominates the field. We talk of a responsible action when we mean the right action in the circumstances. I would prefer to keep the root meaning of the word – response. Hence, against the background of the power and goodness of God, which assumes a meaningful activity in history even if it does not require a reasonable world, I am saying that the response of man in moral decision must be with his whole person. Not only his reason, nor only his emotion. It must also be in the light of the total context, not only the immediate aspect of it, and based upon the accumulated experience of former decisions.

BONHOEFFER: We are not greatly at issue here, provided that the man's response is in the form of action.

NIEBUHR: But should not your decision to return to Germany be tested against these principles? I am bound to suspect that you are acting with undue haste. Have you sufficiently examined your motives to see whether in this moral decision you are responding with your whole self? You are an eminent theologian and have already contributed much to our thinking, but you have much more to contribute. If you return to Germany, there is little chance that we shall hear more from you until the war is over. By then, you may well be dead.

BONHOEFFER: We have already dismissed that argument.

NIEBUHR: In one sense, yes. But does God not have a purpose for theologians like you? Is it not possible that all your elaborate training in Germany, in the U.S.A., and in England has prepared you to be the very man who can reconcile the theologies of America and Europe, and do more for the unity of the church than any man living? You should respond, not only as a German, but also as a theologian of the universal church.

BONHOEFFER: That is to say, with my 'whole person'?

NIEBUHR: Exactly. And, if with the whole person, also with a due consideration of the total context. You are responding to the context of the German churches and their struggle against Nazism. I do not deny the importance of this. But it is not the total context of your life nor of this decision. You have taken a prominent part in the development of the ecumenical movement, and these coming war years may be crucial for its further development. It is unlikely that our plan to form the World Council of Churches in Holland in two years' time will now materialise; but if it is to be formed after the war is over, we shall need there men like you, particularly if in the intervening years you have acquainted yourself sympathetically with the American churches and helped to bring them to a more serious consideration of the issues of union.

BONHOEFFER: But I have already said that I can do nothing for the American churches, in the sense that you wish me to. As for the rest of the task . . .

NIEBUHR: Your unique suitability for this task is part of the total context.

BONHOEFFER: I cannot believe myself so 'uniquely suited'.

NIEBUHR: Then at least add my belief to the total context, and finally you must look more seriously at your experience of the past few years. What you gained from a year or more in England enabled you the better to lead your seminary of the resistance at Finkenwalde. In assessing the value of staying on in America, you should take into account the value of your stay in Britain at an equally critical period of your history. Karl Barth was critical of your action then in a way that suggests your own attitude today. Experience should guide you more than it appears to be doing. All this, I say, should be recollected in the light of the accepted background of the power and the goodness of God.

(*Slight pause.*)

BONHOEFFER: I think I would have accepted your reasoning more completely a few years ago than I do now. There was a time when I saw it as my duty to assert that I was a member of the universal church. I rejected the idea of a German ethic, and my battle against the German Christians has shown how firmly I resist their sort of nationalism. But there is a second stage in my thinking at this time; and you have ignored it.

NIEBUHR: Not intentionally.

BONHOEFFER: No; but its rejection is implicit in your repeatedly stressing universality. Although a Christian is a citizen of another world and a member of an international society, he must not evade his national responsibilities by escaping into internationalism. I am a German and I must share the sorrows and sins of my people. You accuse me of responding too much as a German, but that is what I am. My whole person is German. Socrates drank hemlock rather than cease to be an Athenian. This was not mere patriotism, but a recognition that he was involved in the guilt of Athens as well as its glory. I am a German and cannot opt out of the responsibility that entails. You claim that we must discover what God is doing and then how we fit into it. The context is all important here. God is doing quite a lot of things into which we cannot fit! The question really becomes, not so much what God is doing, but what is God doing with me in my total context?

NIEBUHR: You yourself are compelled to use the phrase!

BONHOEFFER: Yes, yes; but you must understand how I see my context, and my goal. As I see it, my goal is to help rebuild the spiritual wastes of Germany. For this reason, I took a leading part in the Confessing Church in its resistance to the German Christians because with the support of the Nazis they were perverting the theology of the church. My part was theological. I led the seminary at Finkenwalde to train men to think clearly in the days of confusion. I played my part in the writing of the Barmen Declaration, which gave a theological sheet anchor to the resistance, because I believed our struggle was not political but theological. My time in England was spent in trying to persuade the ecumenical movement that the Confessing Church was the true church in Germany and that the German Christians were no church. It seemed to me then and it does still that the issues we are facing in Germany are for the whole church and not only for Germany. These issues are far more serious than you seem to realise. You are worried about my personal survival but far more is at stake than this. It is not even limited to the survival of the Christian church in Germany. Our struggle is for the survival of man as man. I am more concerned with this than I am with the survival of the Christian church in Germany or anywhere. But the key to the future of the church lies in what is happening in Germany now. And so both as a German and as a member of the universal church, I have to return. As a German and a Christian, I have to choose between the two dreadful alternatives which I have already mentioned.

NIEBUHR: To will either the defeat of Germany, or the death of our civilisation . . .

BONHOEFFER: Exactly so. And I repeat that I know I shall choose to will the defeat of my country. That is no easy choice for a German, and I cannot make it in the security of the U.S.A. I know that the decision to return may involve my death. Even if it does, I shall have played my part, if only by my death, in helping to rebuild those spiritual wastes. But I am not going back in order to die. I shall do everything I can to avoid dying! I intend to live and to be there at the end of the war to participate in the rebuilding. I cannot do that if I have been in hiding during the crucial war years.

NIEBUHR: Yes, you made that plain, quite early in our conversation. You would not be free, you said, except in action. But must action imply inevitable suffering, and probable death?

BONHOEFFER: I have already said something about the first two steps on the way to freedom. Discipline and Action are to me obvious. And – yes – I have a feeling that the next two are Suffering and Death. You yourself said in one of your lectures 'it is in the response to suffering that men define themselves'. That is what I mean by the next stage in freedom.

NIEBUHR: We are nearer than we think in our attitude to moral decision, but I am still not convinced that you are taking the proper step. The final question in ethics is not 'What shall I do?' nor 'What is my goal?' Surely it is, 'To whom or what am I responsible, and in what community or interaction am I myself?' I ask only that you carefully look at the four responses you must make: you respond to interpreted action, have you rightly interpreted the pressure of your colleagues in Germany for you to return? You respond in accordance with that interpretation, have you taken the right decision even on the basis of your own interpretation? You respond in anticipation of the effect of this decision, have you like a good chess player, sufficiently considered the effect of this decision? You respond in the context of social solidarity, have you not acted alone?

BONHOEFFER: Which of your many questions do you really want me to answer? As you yourself hint, they all depend ultimately upon the first, longest, and most fundamental, and may in a sense be answered, be all answered at once, by answering that.

NIEBUHR: Precisely. This is why I demonstrated its complexity.

BONHOEFFER: In the last resort, 'to whom am I responsible' admits of only one answer, which both of us would give. But I am more concerned with the *structure* of responsibility, the way in which it *works*.

NIEBUHR: Naturally you would be, as a believer in *action*.

BONHOEFFER: Yes, but not irresponsible action. It is because I believe that man is always a deputy – a father acting for his children as a father; a member of a nation or a class acting for his nation or class as a member; a lover acting for his beloved as a lover – man always acts in relation to others, even as a sinner! Man cannot live as if he were isolated. As a man he needs to be both at one with himself and in relation to other men. His deputyship requires that he completely surrender his own life to the other man or men whom he represents. My responsibility is to my fellow-Germans, whatever the nature of their pressure upon me to return. My deputyship requires that I look not only at the motive, but also at the outcome. Does this not answer two of your questions at once?

NIEBUHR: Only one: your actual return may still not be the right decision.

BONHOEFFER: 'Right'? When and where 'right'? When one accepts responsibility, one does not establish one's line of conduct, in advance, by a principle that must be absolutely valid. The decision is made only within a concrete, present, situation. One does not envisage an 'absolute good', an absolute rightness; one merely prefers the relatively better to the relatively worse. One looks for what is needful *here and now*, in accordance with reality.

NIEBUHR: Yes, if by 'in accordance with reality' you mean 'in accordance with Christ'.

BONHOEFFER: In accordance with reality is the only way we can understand what 'in accordance with Christ' means. You are not I know trying to suggest a return to the old 'imitation of Christ'. We must act in accordance with reality because that is how we discover what accordance with Christ means. I do not of course mean that one may therefore smugly abandon the world to its fate. But the assured rightness that you require in me, must in a sense be empirical. That, in fact, also answers the third of your questions . . .

NIEBUHR: Whether you have adequately considered the *effects* of your decision . . .

BONHOEFFER: You see, of course the most earnest thought must be given to the consequences of one's action, so as to do what is necessary at a given and actual time and place. But the man of responsible action does not claim to know, for certain, the ultimate rightness of his act. The act is delivered up to God at the moment of its performance.

NIEBUHR: Nevertheless, you act *alone* in that moment – *and* in the decision that leads to it. Is there not arrogance here?

BONHOEFFER: Ultimate ignorance of one's own good or evil (present or future), reliance therefore upon grace, is essential to responsible action. Precisely when it is *not* performed in arrogance or certainty, but is done humbly, the action can be sustained.

NIEBUHR: We have already spoken of one probable consequence of your return to Germany. You will certainly come into conflict with the Nazi state – even if you are not discovered to be so, you will be so in conscience. This will probably result in your death . . .

BONHOEFFER: There is no need to return to this question.

NIEBUHR: I return to it in a new light. As you have said, you are a German: you feel that your duty is towards Germans, even though your wider duty may result in the overthrow of Germany.

BONHOEFFER: Yes. Exactly.

NIEBUHR: Now, I have understood much of your struggle in that last decision; but surely the decision itself involves further conflict? Not only are you setting yourself up as a potential destroyer of your country's laws – even of its existence – you are also *inviting* your own death.

BONHOEFFER: Sooner or later, in any man's life, observance of the laws of a state – or observance of any such formal 'duty' will conflict with the necessities in men's lives. You challenged me, earlier, with acting alone: well, these extraordinary necessities appeal to the freedom of the responsible man, who has now no protection from formal law; he *must* take his decision as a free venture.

NIEBUHR: Even if he is aware of involving himself in what is normally a guilty action?

BONHOEFFER: Responsibility includes the readiness to accept guilt as well as freedom. Only in this way can a man remain attached to the ultimate reality of human existence – that is, to Christ.

NIEBUHR: But surely, action against the dictates of one's conscience is precisely analogous to *physical* suicide?

BONHOEFFER: Most certainly – all Christian ethics are agreed on that. *But*: conscience is a call to man's unity within himself.

NIEBUHR: Yes, very well, I freely grant you that it originates in a man's own ego – compels him by a law of his own finding. But if the point of a man's inner unity is Christ. That is if he has allowed Christ to mould his life from within – what Paul means by 'transformed by the renewal of your minds', in Romans 12 – according to its own proper form; that would be according to the mind of Christ. Then his individual conscience is safe – one might say, Christ *is* his conscience.

BONHOEFFER: We have returned, you see – haven't we? – to my concept of freedom. I do not admit that in returning to Germany, in endangering both legality and even survival, I am *necessarily* taking guilt upon myself. But suppose I were: when a man takes guilt upon himself, in responsibility, he does it in the knowledge that liberty is *forced* upon him. He does it, of course, not in the insolence of his own power, but in utter dependence upon grace – costly grace. The responsible man acts in the freedom of his own self – we have discussed what this freedom means – without the support of men or principles. Nothing can answer for him, or exonerate him if necessary, except his own deed and his own self. Before himself he is acquitted by his conscience; before God, he hopes only for mercy and forgiveness.

Index of Scriptural References

Exod. 17:11	162	
Lev. 10:1ff	187	
Num. 12:1	187	
16:11	187	
32:5–6, 16–23	183	
Deut. 6:6	217	
30:11f	193	
Joshua 1:8	193	
22:3–4	183	
I Sam. 15:16	188	
I Kings 2:2	253	
12:25–33	189	
Job 41:11	240	
Ps. 13:5	229	
28:7	216	
42	253	
44:22	216	
74	201	
75:1	233	
119:45	67	
119:71	247	
119:105	231	
119:147f	58	
119:164	58	
Isa. 6:3	254	
21:11f	67	
28:29	254	
35:10	241	
41:9	215	
45:7	254	
45:19	233	
55:6	252	
Jer. 3:15	188, 193	
23:21	186	
25:15ff	254	
Lam. 3:26	228	
3:37f	254	
Ezek. 33:2ff	184	

Amos 3:7	254	
8:11	187	
Haggai 1:2–4	169	
Zech. 2:12	201	
7:9	215	
Mal. 3:3	234f	
Matt. 5:7	215	
6:24	190	
6:32	193	
7:6	151	
9:38	186	
10:6	187	
10:13f	62	
10:32	181	
12:30	93, 100	
13:8	231	
16:19	149	
18:15f	156	
18:17, 18	156	
18:18	149, 150	
24:13	200	
26:45b–50	137	
28:21	187	
Mark 7:37	122	
9:40	93, 100	
Luke 8:15	200	
12:32	193	
14:28ff	191	
15	237	
John 2	242	
3:21	176	
5:14	106	
7:17	177	
12:26	215	
17	181	
20:23	149	
Acts 1	45	
1:23	185	

Acts	2	45
	2:37	46
	2:38*f*	49
	2:38	152
	2:42–7	47, 48, 49
	4:32*ff*	48
	5	157
	6:4	57
	6:5	160, 185
	8:8, 35	152
	13:2	160
	13:3	185
	15:40	217
	16:6	187
	19:13	187
	19:17	233
	20:28	159, 160
	21:20	183
Rom.	1:16	237
	1:36	240
	6:2	152
	9:3	158
	9:4*f*	201
	10:15	186
	11:11–15	201
	12:1*ff*	152
	12:16	182
	14:23	176
	15:5	182, 199
	16:17	155
I Cor.	1:2	180
	1:6*ff*	200
	1:10	182
	1:11*f*	159
	5:2	160
	5:5	156, 157
	5:11	155
	6:1	184
	10:16	153
	11	184
	11:24	153
	11:29	153
	12:1*ff*	152
	12:25	181
	12:28	160, 185
	13:12	216

I Cor.	14:26	160
	14:34	184
	16–22	158
II Cor.	1:1	180
	2:6*ff*	156
	5:17	47
	6:2	252
	6:14*ff*	190
	10:6	184
	13:10	184
	13:11	182
Gal.	1:3*ff*	190
	1:8	158
	1:9	159
	3:27*f*	152
	6:15	47
Eph.	2:15	47
	4:5	181
	4:11	160, 185
	4:15	178
Col.	2:18	198
	3:9	47
	3:16	154
I Thess.	5:11, 14	154
	5:14	155
II Thess.	3:6	155
	3:14	155, 156
	3:15	155
I Tim.	1:3	159
	1:20	156, 157
	3:2	158
	3:2*ff*	184, 188
	3:10	188
	3:15	154
	4:13, 16	159
	5:20	156
	5:21	156
	5:22	157, 158, 188
	5:23	160
	5:24	154
	6:4*f*	159
	6:5	155
	6:5, 20	159
II Tim.		183
	2:1	253
	2:2	158, 188

II Tim. 2:12	200	
2:14	159	
2:15	159	
2:17	157	
2:21	157	
2:24	158	
2:25f	155	
2:26	159	
3:5	155	
3:6f	159, 189	
3:7f	159	
3:10	159	
3:14	159	
4	237	
4:2	154	
4:15	157	
Titus 1:5	160	
1:9	158, 159	
1:10	159	
2:10	155	
3:8	159	

Titus 3:10	189	
3:11	156	
Heb. 12:2	200	
13:13–14	68	
James 1:12	193	
3:1	188	
4:1ff	255	
5:16	150	
I Peter 1:17	233	
2:18	184	
1:6	200	
II John 8	195	
9	189	
10	157, 159	
12	194	
III John 2	195	
Rev. 1:9	200	
2:6	159	
2:15	159	
3:11	230	
21:1	247	

Index of Personal Names

Albertz, Supt., 38

Asmussen, 72, 104

Baillie, Prof. John, letter from 249; letters to, 250

Barth, Karl, 16, 25, 43, 102, 104f, 198, 269, 275; letters from, 119ff; letters to, 115; Dogmatics, 122

Beck, General Ludwig, 194, 198

Bell, Rt. Rev. G. K. A., 134f; letters to, 203f, 210, 248

Berg, Br., 64, 251

Bernadotte, Prince Oscar, 52

Bethge, Eberhard, 65, 115, 242; letters from, 56, 72; letters to, 73f, 213, 214

Bewer, Dr. Julius, 233ff, 237

Boerickes, 235

Böhm, Dr. Hans, 209f

Bonhoeffer, Karl Friedrich (brother of Dietrich), 239ff, 247

Brandenburg, Br. Willi, 56, 66; letter from, 67f

Breit, Thomas, quoted, 104

Brown, W. A., 236f

Brunner, Emil, 120

Burlingham, R. E., 132

Büsing, Wolfgang, 41

Camus, Albert, 19

Canaris, Admiral W., 194

Cavert, Dr. Samuel McCrea, 212, 219; letters to, 220f
Chamberlain, Neville, 198
Chichester, Bishop of, *see* Bell
Coffin, Dr. Henry, 211, 221, 227, 241f, 246, 248
Colvin, H., 236
Craske, Bishop F.W. T., 132

Dibelius, Martin, 43, 72

Eger, Herr, 107
Eidem, Dr. Erling, 51ff, 56
Elliot, Roland, 210f
Espy, Dr. R. H. Edwin, 132f, 136f
Eugene, Prince (of Sweden), 52

Fenn, Eric, 132
Ferber, Fräulein Dr., 217
Fosdick, Prof. H. E., 233
Freudenberg, Dr., 245

Gandhi, M. K., 119, 265
Gellert, 72
Gerhardt, Paul, 72f
Gerstenmaier, Dr. Eugen, 208f
Geyer, 100
Giese, Br. Kurt, 162, 251
Gilbert, Felix, 237
Gill, Theodore, 241
Gollwitzer, Helmut, 15, 22ff, 107; quoted, 96ff
Gorkmann, Rev., 240
Gramlow, Supt., 63
Grunow, Br. R., 63f
Guillon, 132

Harhausen, Christoph, 41, 63f, 251
Harnack, Adolf von, 73, 217
Harris, 241
Heckel, Bishop Theodor, 52ff
Henriod, H. L., 16, 132; letters from, 135f; letter to, 134
Hessen, Philip von, 103
Himmler, Heinrich, 137, 163

Hitler, Adolf, 15, 17, 72, 115, 198, 203, 249f, 269
Hodgson, Leonard, 210; letter from 207f, letter to, 206
Hofmann, Br. Hans, 162, 251
Hromadka, Josef, 198
Hunter, Archdeacon, 132

Iwand, Prof., 73, 163

Jacobi, Dr. G., 64, 72f, 115, 261

Kalbfleisch, George, 226
Kanitz, Br. J., 64, 161
Kerrl, 198
Klapproth, Br. Erich, 161f
Koch, Br.Werner, 63, 131, 198, 202
Krummacher, Dr., 208f
Künneth, 107

Lehmann, Paul, 240f, 246f; letters from, 218, 222f, 224f; letters to, 218, 222, 226
Leibholz, Gerhard, 203f, 206; Sabine, 214, 235
Leiper, Henry, 227, 229, 233, 248; letters from, 211f, 219, 220f; letters to, 210f, 242
Lekszas, Horst, 264; letter from, 162
Lilje, Dr. Hanns, 136
Lohmann, Br. Gerhard, 41, 63, 198
Luther, Martin, 12, 15, 72, 81, 91, 102, 106, 199, 271; quoted, 98f, 112

Macy, Rev. Paul, 217, 242
Maechler, Br.W., 63, 251, 259
Marahrens, Bishop, 198, 261
Major, Georg, 102
Maritain, J., 237
Marwitz, Alexander v.d., 41, 64, 251
Matheson, George, 18
McComb, Dr. C., 231
Meiser, Bishop, 198
Melancthon, 103
Mickley, Br. Johannes, 162, 251

Newby, P. H., 265
Niebuhr, Reinhold, 220, 222, 225, 244, 266; letters from, 210*f*, 218*f*; letters to, 219, 224, 246
Niebuhr, Richard, 14, 235*f*, 238, 241, 265*ff*
Niemöller, Martin, 17, 72, 74, 161*ff*, 194, 231, 261; DB's letter to Mrs. Niemöller, 163*f*
Niesel, Wilhelm, 160

Oldham, Dr. J. H., 132
Onnasch, Fritz, 65, 263
Oster, General, 194

Pauck, Prof. W., 224
Press, Dr., 224
Preuss, Br. Adolf Friedrich, 57, 63

Ribbentrop, 250
Richardson, Prof. Cyril, 238
Richter, 224
Rieger, Dr., 204
Rittelmeyer, 100
Roberts, David, 233, 235, 239
Rodewell, 236
Rossi, Signorina, 132
Rothe, 44
Rott, Wilhelm, 51, 64, 119, 121, 264

Sack, 194
Sasse, Prof. Hermann, 107, 111, 118
Scherer, Dr. Paul, 224, 237
Schlatter, Adolf, 102
Schlemmer, Hans, 73
Schneckenburger, 118, 122
Schneider, Paul, 164
Schönfeld, Dr. Hans, 132, 210

Schönherr, Albrecht, 37, 41, 62*f*; circular letters from, 261*ff*
Schrader, Br. Wolfgang, 64, 162, 251
Seydel, Br. Gustav, 161, 251
Sichtig, Miss, 132
Smart, Prof., 241
Smidt, Pastor Udo, 132*f*
Söderblom, Archbishop Nathan, 52
Sparring-Petersen, Rev., 132
Strange, Dr., 132
Sutz, Erwin, 115, 119
Sweden, Archbishop of, *see* Eidem

Tatlow, Canon Tissington, 210
Temple, Archbishop William, 210
Thadden-Trieglaff, Reinhold von, 173
Tholuck, 117, 121
Tiller, Terence, 265*f*
Tillich, Dr., Paul, 220, 237*f*
Tomkins, Rev. Oliver, 209
Toureille, P. C., 132
Traub, Helmut, 213

Van Dusen, Dean Henry P., 212, 219, 221, 227, 234*f*, 241, 247*f*
Vibrans, Br. Gerhard, 62, 66
Visser 't Hooft, W. A., 204, 206
Vogel, Heinrich, 73

Wahl, Dr. H., 208*f*
Wedell, Hans, 247
Williams, Roger, 241
Wolfe-Halle, Prof., 63
Wurm, Bishop, 198

Zernoff, Dr. N., 132
Zinzendorf, 72, 193

General Index

action, 13, 15, 18, 277
American Committee for Christian German Refugees, 219f
'Anselm', 117
anti-semitism, 198, 236
Augsburg Confession, 24, 83, 89, 98, 101ff, 110, 237; Declaration, 99
Austria, 17, 194

Bad Oeynhausen, Synod of (1936), 38ff, 92, 108, 114
baptism, 80, 84, 99, 151f
Barmen, Synod of (1934), 24, 86, 102f, 114, 165, 167, 172ff, 192ff; Declaration, 15, 22f, 38, 40, 87ff, 96ff, 108ff, 122, 178ff, 260
Berlin, seminary of Confessing Church in, 131, 160
Bielefeld, 70, 130
Blöstau, 70, 130, 163
Beatitudes, 18, 19
Buchenwald, 164

Central Bureau of Interchurch Aid, 211f
Chamby, 74, 114f, 133f
Christology, 81
church discipline, 149ff
church government, 179ff, 260, 262
church union, 22, 75ff, 112, 118
communion, 85; see also eucharist
Confessing Church of the Old Prussian Union, 13ff, 22ff, 42, 61, 72, 74f, 94, 107, 121; organisation of communities, 30ff, 70f, 117; in Pomerania, 164ff; in DB's report on Finkenwalde (1936), 123f; and ecumenical movement, 129ff, 204ff; and church government, 38ff;

and nature of true church, 107ff; separation from National Church, 86ff, 97ff; attempted destruction of, 149ff; at outbreak of World War II, 250; Synods, see Bad Oeynhausen, Barmen, Dahlem; see also Finkenwalde
confession of faith, 11, 23, 31, 71, 80ff, 84, 91, 105, 120, 260ff
confession of sins, 150ff
Croall Lectures, 249f
Czechoslovakia, 198

Dahlem, Synod of (1934), 86, 92, 113f, 165, 167, 172ff, 179ff, 192ff; Declaration, 15, 22, 27ff, 87f, 96, 101, 110, 174ff, 178, 260; Christ Church, 162
Dahme, 161
death, 19ff, 250, 254f, 277, 279
Denmark, 42, 51
Die Christliche Welt, 73
discipline, 11ff, 18, 31, 57, 112, 277
Dogmatics, 122

ecumenical movement, 41f, 90, 114, 129, 147, 204ff
Eden Seminary, 225
Edinburgh, 210, 218; DB's plans to visit, 249f; Conference (1937), 208
Elberfeld, 70, 130f
England, 16, 42, 130; DB's visit to, 132, 203
eucharist, 152f
Evangelische Theologie, 75, 97

Faith and Order Movement, 17, 207f
Fanö, 90, 114
Federal Council of the Churches, 217

286

Finkenwalde, 12, 16f, 32ff, 42, 51, 61f, 68ff, 115; annual report (1936), 122ff; circular letters from, 46f, 61f, 160f, 259ff; greetings from, 33f, 54f; news letters from, 161f; year of destiny (1937), 129f, 137; destruction of Confessing Church, 147, 149, 162f, 194; seminary closed, 163, 212f
Formula of Concord, 101f, 110f
Frankfurt am Oder, 34, 57, 67
freedom, 11ff, 240, 270, 280

Geneva, 16
German Christians, 16f, 62, 66, 70f, 74f, 86ff, 96f, 100, 107, 109f, 113, 120, 147, 170, 179ff, 210, 262, 276
German Evangelical Church, 97, 101, 103f, 135, 194, 208
German-Soviet Pact, 250
Gestapo, 160
Gifford, Lectures, 210
Greek Orthodox Church, 84
Greifswald, 32, 62f, 263

Helbra, 65f
heresy, 71, 189f, 263

idealism, 42

Junge Kirche, 51f
justification, 81, 116, 120

Kelham, 11, 33, 131
Köslin, 34

leadership principle, 13, 38
Lutheran Churches, 24, 89, 99, 104ff; Lutheran Council, 66; Lutheran National Church, 66; doctrine, 75, 81, 91f; orthodoxy, 44
Lutherans, 22ff, 81ff, 91f, 103, 110f, 118, 261

materialism, 43
meditation, 31, 35, 57ff, 67f, 117, 121, 124, 261

Mirfield, 11, 13, 33, 131
mission, 126, 206; mission preaching, 151f; British missionary societies, 206
Munich, 17, 198

Nagelsbach, 100
National Church, 86f, 90, 92, 94, 97, 100, 166, 170, 174, 263; National Church Council, 114; see also German Christians
National Socialism, 13, 17; see also Nazism
Naumburg am Queiss, 70, 130
Nazism, 14ff, 72, 268, 271f, 276; Hitler Youth, 13
Neuruppin, 161f
New York, 218, 220ff, 229ff

Olympic Games (1936), 72, 74
Orthodoxy, 79, 83, 90f
Oxford Conference (1937), 17, 84, 114, 132f, 135ff, 147

Pastor of Buchenwald, 164
patience, 199ff
Pietism, 73, 79, 180; Wuppertal pietists, 120
Podejuch, 33, 125
prayer, 13, 31, 59, 61, 112
preaching, 150f, 186f

Reformation, 75ff, 82ff, 101
Reformed Churches, 22, 24, 89, 103ff, 112, 118
Reich Church, see National Church
Religious affairs, Minister for, 52ff
Religious Socialists, 120
repentance, 149f
Responsible Self, 265f
resurrection, 14, 36
Riverside Church, 230f, 233, 268
Roman Catholic Church, 44, 81, 83f, 99, 120; Roman Catholicism, 75, 79, 92, 94
Russian Christians, 205, 237

INDEX

Sachenhausen, 131
sanctification, 116, 120
Scandinavia, 130
scripture, 31, 57, 67, 120, 124*f*; as basis for Confessing Church, 173*ff*
Spain, 16
Stolp, 34
Sudetenland, 17, 198
suffering, 16, 18*f*, 181*ff*, 277
suicide, 20*f*, 279
Sweden, 42, 51, 53*ff*, 126

teaching discipline, 158*ff*
Theologische Existenz Heute, 119, 122
True Humanism, 237

Una Sancta, 235
Union Theological Seminary, 210*ff*, 219*f*, 222*f*, 226*f*, 245, 248
U.S.A., 14, 16, 22, 25; DB's last visit to, 210*ff*; negroes in, 230, 235*f*, 242; American theology, 18, 227, 230, 233, 236, 268; separation of church and state, 239, 241
Universal Council for Life and Work, 74, 132

Wedding, 16
works, DB's, *Act and Being*, 223; *Cost of Discipleship*, 12, 19, 116, 131; *Ethics*, 11, 13, 16, 19*f*, 250, 265; *Letters and Papers from Prison*, 11; *Life Together* (U.S.A. edition: *Community Life*), 12, 198, 223; *No Rusty Swords*, 13, 16, 18, 29, 114*f*, 147, 194, 265; *Sanctorum Communio* (U.S.A. edition: *The Communion of Saints*), 223; *Temptation*, 196; 'Concrete Ethics in Paul', 125; 'Confessing Church and the Ecumenical Movement', 114; 'Introduction to Daily Meditation', 12, 57*ff*; 'Discipleship of Christ', 125; 'New Life in Paul', 125; 'Power of the Keys and Church Discipline', 149*ff*; 'Protestantism without Reformation', 18; 'Question of the Boundaries of the Church and Church Union', 22, 75*ff*; 'Visible Church in the New Testament', 42*ff*, 125; 'War and Peace', 147*ff*; Judas Sermon, 17, 137*ff*
World Conference on Church, Community and State, 74
World War I, 13, 100
World War II, 250
W.S.C.F., 132, 134

Y.M.C.A., 52, 132, 135
Youth Commission, 132*ff*
Y.W.C.A., 132, 135

Zingst, 194, 196*f*
Zwinglianism, 103*f*, 111